HOW TO BE YOUR PET'S BEST FRIEND

By Michael W. Fox

Canine Behavior
Canine Pediatrics: Development, Neonatal and Congenital
    Diseases
Integrative Development of Brain and Behavior in the Dog
The Behavior of Wolves, Dogs and Related Canids
Understanding Your Dog
Understanding Your Cat
Concepts in Ethology: Animal and Human Behavior
Between Animal and Man: The Key to the Kingdom
The Dog: Its Domestication and Behavior
Understanding Your Pet: Pet Care and Humane Concerns
On the Fifth Day: Animal Rights and Human Ethics
    (edited with Richard K. Morris)
Returning to Eden: Animal Rights and Human Responsibility
One Earth, One Mind
How to Be Your Pet's Best Friend

Books for Children by Michael W. Fox

The Wolf
Vixie: The Story of a Little Fox
Sundance Coyote
Ramu and Chennai: Brothers of the Wild
Wild Dogs Three
What Is Your Dog Saying? (with Wende D. Gates)
Dr. Fox's Fables: Lessons from Nature

HOW TO BE
YOUR PET'S
BEST FRIEND

Michael W. Fox
D.Sc., Ph.D., B.Vet.Med., M.R.C.V.S.

Director, Institute for the Study of Animal Problems
The Humane Society of the U.S., Washington, D.C.

COWARD, MC CANN & GEOGHEGAN
NEW YORK

Copyright © 1981 by Michael W. Fox
All rights reserved. This book, or parts thereof, may not be reproduced in any form without permission in writing from the publisher. Published on the same day in Canada by Academic Press Canada Limited, Toronto.

Library of Congress Cataloging in Publication Data

Fox, Michael W., date.
  How to be your pet's best friend.

  Includes index.
  1. Dogs. 2. Cats. I. Title.
SF426.F69   636.7   80-24861
ISBN 0-698-11070-6

Printed in the United States of America

Acknowledgments

I must acknowledge my sincere appreciation to Ms. Sylvie Reice for her encouragement and editorial advice in writing many of the chapters in this book. Thanks also to *McCall's* magazine for permission to include much of the material from my column, "Understanding Your Pet," in this book.

Contents

Introduction

Pets today are as much a part of most people's lives as their own human kin. Keeping that in mind, I intended this book not only to deal with the principles of cat and dog care—proper nutrition and health, housing, and training—but, just as importantly, to discuss psychology and behavior—the ways pets communicate, and their social and emotional needs. Caring for the pet in your life, without a real understanding of the animal, is neither fun nor fulfilling. Keeping a pet healthy is one thing, but *understanding* it is indeed something else. Understanding leads to empathy, compassion, and more responsible ownership. The "pet" is no longer an "it," a decorative object, status symbol, or toy. It is a fellow creature who can teach us many things, not only a general reverence for life, but an appreciation of the characteristics that give it its own marvelous uniqueness.

Despite the diversity and subtlety of form and function that our various companion animals assume, we may discover a common trait: a capacity for love that grows deeper and stronger with trust and mutual understanding. It is with the goal of understanding in mind that much of the material from my *McCall's* magazine column, "Understanding Your Pet," has been assembled and updated for both people and their animal companions.

I

The Nature
of the Beasts:
Some Popular Breeds

1

Top Dogs: Be Careful of the Company You Keep

In my mail the other day was a cry for help. An elderly single lady was having problems handling her dog, which she had purchased as a puppy as a companion and protector. Unfortunately she had bought the canine equivalent of a horse—a Great Pyrenees! Knowing something about the qualities of a particular breed can help you find which one is right for you: which one fits your needs, personality, life-style, and which you could best manage, be you an experienced or inexperienced dog person, an outdoor type, or a quiet, retired urbanite.

There is an incredible variety of purebred dogs to choose from. My first piece of advice is that you *not* go to a commercial pet store and, after looking at their limited selection, buy the pup of your choice. First, consider if you really want a purebred, and why. You may be better off with a good mongrel—a "Heinz 57." Your local humane society or animal shelter should have a number of pups waiting to be adopted. In terms of all-round temperament, physical vigor, and likelihood of genetic defects, mongrels are generally preferable to purebreds.

The advantage of a good purebred is that you know what kind of temperament, special talents (such as guarding, retrieving), and mature body size and coat type you are going to get. But look out for signs of overbreeding, the "purebred-dog syndrome," a serious

You may be better off choosng a good mongrel: a "Heinz 57" *(Humane Society of the United States/Paula Wright).*

problem in the more popular breeds that have been mass-produced with little quality control. Some of these "products" have no character at all. They are just unintelligent "sweet nothings." Others are emotionally unstable—high strung, hyperactive, timid, or aggressive—and do not make reliable pets. You can best avoid these problems by locating a small breeder who takes an obvious pride in his or her dogs. Visit the kennels if possible and see one or both parents of the pups you are looking at. You can find such breeders at a dog show or in your local newspaper as well as in national dog magazines. Familiarize yourself with the various breeds by visiting dog shows and talking to their owners or handlers so you will be in a better position to find the breed that's just right for you. The following description of the more available breeds will give you a good idea as to which one you would be most comfortable with and vice versa.

We must begin by looking at the potential owner because, very often, the owner's personality, life-style, or home environment isn't compatible with certain breeds—sometimes even with any dog at all!

First, do you know how to care for and train a dog? What special diets it needs? That it should have regular checkups at the vet's? Will there be someone at home all day with the dog? If not, you may well have problems. If you are away all day and travel at lot, perhaps you shouldn't have a dog after all. Are you familiar with local ordinances pertaining to dog ownership? What of your neighbors' and your landlord's attitudes toward dogs? If you already have a dog at home who is rather possessive, or a very young child (or one on the way), a new puppy may be the last thing you want right now.

If you want a large or active dog, do you have a yard or a nearby park where you can play with, exercise, and train it? Do you want the kind of dog that needs lots of love and indulgence, or one that is more independent? If you are a sedentary type, do you know which breed might be best suited for you?

If you have a family, how do you think a new pup will fit in? Hopefully it will get the care, attention, and training it needs. Who in the house is going to be in charge? If it is to "belong" to one of the children, is the child of a responsible age or is mother going to get the brunt of caring for the pup—housebreaking it, taking it for walks, etc.? If it is a breed of dog whose long and fluffy coat will require daily attention, are you or someone in the family prepared for this, or would you prefer a dog with a coat that needs less attention? Finally, are you sure no one in the house is allergic to dogs?

Now let's talk about some of the varieties of dogs, keeping these important questions in mind. Purebred dogs are divided into the following six basic categories: terriers, hounds, sporting and non-sporting breeds, toy breeds and working breeds.

Terriers

These are mainly medium-sized to small dogs that are notoriously bold, alert, and active. Their name comes from the Latin *terra*, meaning earth, and they were originally used in hunting to chase prey (rabbits, foxes, badgers, etc.) into their holes. They became the allies of the huntsman, gamekeeper, farmer, poacher, and villager and were also, and still are, popular pets, being allowed (unlike the larger sporting and working breeds) to live in the house with the master. Many terriers carry the names of the towns or regions where they were first developed: Irish, Scottish, and Norwich terriers, for example.

These dogs are generally very good with children, always ready for fun and games. They don't always adapt well to a sedentary life. With few exceptions, their coats need only an occasional grooming. If you want a quiet, lordly, or sedate kind of dog, you don't want a terrier. But if you want a faithful and joyful companion, the terrier might be just right for you.

Wire-coated types include the wire-haired fox terrier, the Irish, Scottish, West Highland, Welsh, Lakeland Sealyham, Border, and Norwich terriers. These medium-sized dogs weigh about 20 to 25 pounds. The largest of this coat type are the Airedales, weighing about 50 pounds. The smallest are the Norwich and Border terriers and the cairns at 14 pounds and the Australian terrier at 12 pounds.

Smooth- (and short-) coated types include the smooth-coated fox terrier, and the bull terrier. The Manchester terrier is the leanest (18 pounds) and most greyhoundlike of the terriers, and there is a toy variety of this breed that weighs a mere 6 pounds. Beware of bull terriers; they can be quite pugnacious and difficult to handle with other dogs. Terriers in general can be spitfires, especially when there is a dog near their territory. Their strong territorial instinct makes them excellent house protectors since they will bark at the slightest suggestion of an intruder.

Silky- or curly-coated types (cuddly but still feisty terriers) include the Skye and Dandie Dinmont terriers. Both are short-legged characters weighing in at about 25 pounds. If you want something larger, with a curly coat, a 35- to 40-pound Kerry blue may be your breed. The Bedlington terrier is one of the most novel of dogs, looking at first glance more like a lamb than a dog. This is a tough breed in spite of its looks and was originally used in England as a ratter.

The most popular terrier from Germany is the miniature schnauzer (15 pounds), which was used on farms as a rat catcher. Like other terriers of this coat class, the schnauzer requires frequent grooming and trimming. Some people like to have a vet crop their schnauzer's ears to make them stand up (as others will do to their Dobermans and Great Danes). The American Veterinary Medical Association does not condone this practice. The operation can be extremely painful to the pup and does the animal no good. It is simply a cosmetic fad, and anyone you see who has had his dog's ears cropped is displaying ignorance, selfish vanity, and a lack of humane ethics.

Toy Breeds

There's quite a variety of "toys" to choose from. Most weigh about 6 to 8 pounds, the Chihuahua being the smallest of all breeds at 4 pounds. "Teacup" Chihuahuas may weigh less than a pound, but these are extremely rare and don't survive well.

Don't let the size of toys deceive you. They are not delicate timorous critters. Quite the contrary. In temperament they are more like miniature terriers—that means they are very active, curious, and outgoing and often get into fights with much bigger dogs. I often wonder, when I see one of these toys challenging a dog five or ten times its size, if they have any concept of how small they really are. Man has shrunk their bodies in domesticating them, but not their egos!

The toy breeds were created principally to be pets. They were first owned by the aristocracy, who could afford to keep nonworking

Look at each pup in the litter, and the mother, too, before you choose (H.S.U.S./Marilyn Breslow).

animals. Some were, and still are, miniature replicas of larger working breeds. Today they are no longer a sign of social status. They make good apartment pets and are excellent companions for sedentary people and for the elderly. Although, like all dogs, they love to run outdoors, they can let off steam and satisfy their need for activity indoors quite well.

Some refer to these dogs as lap dogs, and sometimes this is not unjustified since some owners tend to overindulge them and treat them like little spoiled brats. Like all dogs, they are responsive to training and should not be raised to be "perpetual puppies." Most of these breeds are exceptionally long-lived. All toys from a good lineage are loyal, intelligent, make good companions, and will let you know when there's someone around outdoors. Some strains are yappier and snappier than others—so bear this in mind before you get one, for neighbors and visitors may not like it. Go to a good, reliable breeder to be sure you are getting a pup from a good line. Because these breeds are small, people will often get a pair, which is a good idea if they are to be left alone for any length of time during the day.

Wiry-coated toys (which don't need much grooming) include the Brussels griffon, a perky little character, and the curious, affectionate German affenpinscher, or "monkey dog."

Long- or silky-coated toys (which require regular grooming) are very popular with those who like—and have the time—to pet and primp their pets. Some of these breeds stand close to the ground, and are not outdoor dogs since their silken tresses would soon become muddied and dirty. Those who do get outdoors often need a good trim first. In this category is the ancient Maltese terrier, a 6-pound ball of dynamite and affection that was purportedly a pet of Roman ladies. Not unlike the Maltese is the Shih-Tzu, the Chinese "lion," or temple, dog which is a very popular pet today. The "Yorkie," the silky-coated Yorkshire terrier, is the smallest of the long-haired toys, and small though it is (a mere 5 to 7 pounds), it is *all* terrier. Other breeds in this category include the silky terrier from Australia, a perky and uncommon breed, the papillon, or "butterfly" dog, from France, and the Pomeranian, a bold, miniaturized version of a Baltic sled dog. There are also three miniature spaniels—the Tibetan, Japanese, and English, or King Charles. A popular toy from

China, another lion dog, is the Pekingese, one of the most ancient of all toys. Almost unknown in this country is the bichon frisé (which means literally "curly little dear"). This was originally a popular toy of the French and Spanish aristocracies.

The most popular toy breed today is the toy poodle, which is an exact replica of the two larger kinds of poodles. Because of their popularity, look out for overbreeding and inbreeding problems such as poor temperament and genetic defects. Some people would place smaller varieties of the Sheltie in the toy category, but this breed belongs strictly to the next category.

Working Breeds

These breeds were originally developed to protect livestock, to drive cattle to market, to serve as guards on estates and game preserves, and to pull carts and sleds. Today, some make good watchdogs and guides for the blind, and some are used for police and military work. But be warned: Working dogs from good stock need to work and they don't do well cooped up indoors or in a backyard. Some of these breeds are highly trainable and if given no obedience training can become difficult to handle and a potential danger to your family and to society in general.

Sled/Draught Breeds

The Siberian husky (45 pounds) and Alaskan malamute (75 pounds) are increasing in popularity and have increasing problems since these breeds are not well adapted for a sedentary urban or suburban life. Also think twice about getting one of these breeds if you live in a hot climate. The other sled dog, the Samoyed (35 to 45 pounds), is more adaptable, having been kept more as a pet than the other two hardy breeds. All three enjoy sleeping outdoors in the coldest weather and when given a good kennel and run often do best outdoors. The Bernese mountain dog (65 pounds and up) is a large draught dog from Switzerland.

Rescuers

The Newfoundland, famed for saving lives in shipwrecks, and the Saint Bernard, the Swiss mountain rescue dog, are giant breeds

(145 to 165 pounds and up, respectively). Overbreeding has given the St. Bernard a bad reputation, and people should think twice about owning one of these giant breeds.

Guards

Faithful guardianship and an impressive physique that would intimidate any would-be intruder characterize the English mastiff (185 pounds) and the bull mastiff (110 pounds). Also included in this category are the German Rottweiler, the popular Doberman pinscher and German shepherd, and the little-known but impressive Akita from Japan. Although naturally protective, these dogs *must* be obedience-trained otherwise their potentials will go to waste and worse—they may not know when to defend you, and this could mean trouble. Never have one of these breeds attack-trained for then it will never be a reliable house dog.

Herders

Farm dogs from all over the world have become established as specific breeds. Some of them, like the collie and Shetland sheep dog, have been bred for so long now as pets that they are no longer working dogs. As such, they adapt better to a nonworking and more sedentary life than other breeds, such as the Border collie, the black-and-white wonder dog of today's shepherd.

Some of these include the beautiful Belgian sheepdog and the Tervuren (good alternatives if you want a German-shepherdlike dog that's highly trainable); the Bouvier de Flanders from Belgium, a large cattle dog; the Puli and Komondor from Hungary (which has a stringy mop of a coat); the Briard from France's farms; and the standard and giant schnauzers from rural Germany.

The Welsh corgi is popular with English royalty, and at 20 pounds and standing a mere 11 inches at the shoulder, it is the smallest working dog. Like the Australian heeler, it nips at the cattle's feet to drive them and is a hardy and courageous but sometimes headstrong little dog.

The other two breeds I wish to mention in this category are very popular today. The Old English sheepdog, the shaggy-haired drover's dog of old, is an odd animal to have as a pet. It's cuddly coat and bouncy, playful nature have contributed to its popularity, but beware of the pitfalls (of overbreeding) and think twice before getting such a popular type. Its coat needs constant attention, and while they make good family pets they need space and freedom.

The Great Dane from Germany, a boarhound, is America's most popular giant breed, measuring 32 inches and more at the shoulder. I have some reservations about someone's getting one of these as a pet. But like many Saint Bernards and collies (and Afghans and Irish setters, see below), some are just big, quiet "boneheads" lacking both character and vitality. They make nice ornaments, but if you want a good one, you will have to find a reliable noncommercial breeder.

Nonsporting Breeds

In this category is a whole smorgasbord of breeds that have endured as pets long after they ceased to be used for the specific purposes for which they were originally bred. Some of these breeds include the English and French bulldogs; the Boston terrier; the small shaggy Tibetan Lhasa apso; the schipperke, or small Belgian barge dog; the Dalmatian, or coach (or fire) dog; the chow chow from China (bred to hunt and to be eaten!); the keeshond, or Dutch barge dog (which is not unlike a Samoyed). Also in this category are the standard and miniature poodles, derived from European hunting and circus trick dogs. The poodles are the most popular today, but a little Lhasa apso or schipperke can make an interesting pet for someone who wants something small and different. Dalmations and chows can be difficult to handle and are not the kind of dog an inexperienced person should first acquire.

Hound Breeds

There are two basic types: the long-limbed coursing, or "gaze," hounds built for stamina, speed, and keen vision and the small to medium-sized tracking hounds that hunt more by scent (the "scent" hounds).

As with the working breeds that are no longer used for work, many of these hound breeds have been altered through selective breeding such that they adapt well to a passive life as a household pet. But this is not always the case, and a large gaze hound who is cooped up all day and never allowed to race may develop serious behavior problems. The smaller scent hounds can be a problem, too, since once they get the scent (in the park) they won't come back for a while and may leave you miles behind!

The largest of all breeds is the Irish deerhound (33 inches and up at the shoulder), a leaner version being the Scottish deerhound. The aristocratic borzoi is Russia's wolfhound, and is certainly one of the most distinctive of the hound breeds. The greyhound, Saluki, and silken shag-coated Afghan come from the Mideast and are of a very ancient lineage.

Larger hounds include the otterhound, bloodhound, foxhound, coonhound, and Rhodesian ridgeback. These dogs, bred to run in packs, are generally easygoing (compared to the individualistic terriers) and are usually quiet and gentle with children.

Smaller breeds include the huskylike Norwegian elkhound, a robust, outgoing, and very ancient breed, and the beagle, the hunter's rabbit dog, which often makes a good family pet. The Basenji, the barkless Belgian Congo native dog, is in this hound category but is no groupie. It is probably the most individualistic and independent of all breeds—and in this respect, the most catlike. It is generally difficult to train because of its independence. The hounds in general are harder to train than other breeds because they were originally bred to work alone with the hunter following behind.

The easygoing basset hound is the comic of the dog world with his chubby legs and forlorn, droopy face. Very easy with children, it may frustrate some owners not because it is stupid and seems hard to train, but because it is a hound: affectionate, basically nonaggressive groupies bred to work with their noses and not under the direct control of their masters.

The dachshund—long and silky, short and smooth, and wire-haired varieties—is the badger hunter of Germany. Although classified in the hound category, its temperament is closer to the terriers'. It makes a wonderful pet, but doesn't always have the same easygoing nature of the hound breeds when around children. There are miniature varieties of the dachshund, too, and in temperament they are not unlike the toy breeds described earlier.

Sporting Breeds

There are three types in this category: the tall, keen-nosed pointing breeds (65 pounds or so); the retrievers, who are of a similar size and are excellent swimmers; and the smaller spaniels (35 to 45 pounds), who are quick in finding and taking game birds. Unlike the more independent hound breeds, these sporting breeds were bred to work in very close association with the hunter. Hence, they tend to be easier to train, and many of them make the transition to life as nonhunting pets relatively easily. In fact there are some breeds, like the Irish setter and the cocker spaniel, that have been bred exclusively for show and as pets for many generations. Like the hounds, these sporting breeds are usually good with children, but before you decide to bring one into your home, be sure, if you don't intend to hunt with it, that it is not from an active hunting lineage. A good bird dog cooped up indoors or in a backyard will not adapt well to a sedentary life.

The silky-coated setters include the Irish, English, and Gordon setters, with these first two breeds having been excessively overbred as "show pets" in this country to the point that many of them are purely decorative, very dim "sweet nothings." These seemingly insensitive remarks are not meant to demean any particular breed but rather to help you decide which breed you may like and to point out what breeding has done to many dogs. A "sweet nothing" of a dog may fit in far better in your home than its more active and outgoing working counterpart.

After the setters, who "set" on the prey, there are the pointers— including the pointer, German short- and wire-haired pointers, the Weimaraner, and the Hungarian Vizsla.

Other sporting breeds are retrievers, and in this category we find the Chesapeake Bay, flat-coated, golden and Labrador retrievers. The golden retriever is my first choice of the larger purebreds as a family dog—sweet, gentle, and so understanding and patient with children.

More active and in a way half terrier and half hound in temperament are the smaller spaniels such as the Welsh springer, the Brittany, and the English cocker spaniel. The smallest is the American cocker spaniel, whose popularity a few years ago was followed by a sudden decline in its numbers since overbreeding resulted in unstable, hysterical temperaments and genetic defects.

Choosing a particular breed dog involves something more than selecting a brand of automobile. You have to live with it, and it is going to become an integral part of your life and family. Select wisely. Knowing something about the various breeds and their many attributes and limitations in relation to your needs, personality, and life-style is a first step in the right direction. Getting a dog is akin to adopting a child *and* getting married; so for your sake and for your dog's, don't buy on an impulse. Know your breeds first!

2

Comparing the Cats: A Catalog of Fine Felines

For many people, there are just three kinds of cat—short hair, long hair, and Siamese. While the latter is probably the most popular of the pure varieties, there are many other types which differ as much in personality (or puss'nality) as they do in coat and color.

While I am a proponent of mongrel dogs, I have nothing against their feline equivalent—the "alley cat," or mixed breed. But choosing a pure variety of kitten can be a good insurance that what you are getting will grow up to have a very characteristic personality as well as physique and coat type.

The different varieties have such a wide range of personalities that you choose the type that would best suit you, just as you might choose a dog.

If you want a friendly, regular cat, you could do no better than adopting one from your local humane shelter. You will have all kinds to choose from—short and long hair, ginger or brown tiger-striped, blotched tabbies, calicos and tortoiseshells, silvers, greys, blacks, whites and piebalds or blotched ones.

This variety of color contrasts with the more limited variation in size. Compared to dogs, cats are much more uniform in body size. This may well be because they have not been domesticated nearly as long as the dog. Also, for the six thousand or so years they have lived with man they have not been selectively bred like the dog to perform

25

different tasks. Their prime task was to keep down the rodents, for which they are already perfectly built, so there was no need to make them bigger or smaller, swifter or stronger.

It is generally believed that the principal ancestor of the cat is the Kaffir or Libyan desert cat. Yes, all domestic cats are of a desert origin. This is why they still love to toast themselves in the sun and why, like most desert-adapted animals, their urine is so strong. They conserve water by concentrating their urine.

Before we consider some of the special varieties of cat, you should ask yourself if and why you really want a pure breed. As I say, they are often very special in their ways and sometimes quite demanding. If you have never had a cat, or you want just a good solid character around, adopt one from the humane shelter. Then, when you have learned something about cats, you may be ready for something more exotic and out of the ordinary.

Please, don't get a purebred cat just to have something unusual in your home—a conversation piece or status symbol. Some cats don't like that and others will soak it up and become spoiled and spiteful or demanding and demonstrative pests.

Also, don't raise your kitten—purebred or mixed—with the attitude that cats are distant and aloof or unfriendly and untrainable. I know people who believe these things, and they say, "Well, look at my cat, he's indifferent and unsociable." It's hard to convince people that their expectations are a self-fulfilling prophecy. Give a kitten lots of attention, play, and simple training and it will be quite a pet: affectionate, respectful, and responsive. Dull or insensitive people often seem to have cats (and children) who are like them. I wonder why they have cats (and children) in the first place!

A major reason for owning a purebred cat is because the owner is a "fancier" and would like to go to cat shows and, perhaps later, to start breeding cats. This is an enjoyable hobby, and the cat-show people have my respect. Neutered cats can be shown, and there are special classes for mixed-breed cats—not so for their canine counterpart, the mongrel, in dog shows.

Don't think you can make money from such a hobby. Most good "cat people" rarely break even.

A pure variety will cost you anywhere from $100 to $300 and up. You may, if you don't plan to show your cat, purchase one with a slight "defect," i.e., a pet-quality kitten. A little kink in the tail,

One of the best varieties of cat is the "mixed breed." Your local Humane Society is the best source—they'll have a wide range of coat types to choose from *(H.S.U.S.)*.

slightly below standard in size, coat, or eye color are insignificant flaws that may ban a cat from competition but not from making a fine pet.

Do, however, avoid getting a kitten with some serious genetic defect such as a severe squint (which is common in Siamese). The best place to find the right purebred kitten for you is a local cat show. Talk to the owners, some of whom will be breeders and may have or be expecting a litter for sale shortly. Avoid pet stores, since few can guarantee the health of the kitten. There's nothing to compare with the good care and attention that the average cat breeder will give to his or her cats. Don't be too surprised if the breeder turns you away. Many cat breeders are very particular as to whom they give their kittens, and not without good reason sometimes. Your personality may not feel right to them and they may advise you of another breed that would suit your temperament, life-style, or family better.

Siamese

The first purebred cat I had was a Siamese, Igor. A fantastic companion and teacher. This breed is perhaps the most doglike of the felines. Indeed, dogs and cats do come from a common ancestral root millennia ago. The doglike quality of the Siamese includes this breed's predilection to play ball, to catch and retrieve. It also trains easily on the leash and enjoys going for walks.

Of all the varieties of cat, the Siamese is the most vocal. It has a penetrating "meow" that some people find disturbing. Neighbors may think you are strangling your child!

Because of its vocal ability and responsiveness, the Siamese is quite talkative. Igor and I used to have "conversations," especially on long drives in the car.

Siamese cats are mischievous pranksters. They are highly intelligent and dexterous, some being able to open doors, pull down window blinds, and switch on lights without any training. They just observe you and learn through mimicry.

The Siamese is a very demanding cat, and if you don't have the time and attention to give it, you should not have one.

Siamese are very handsome cats, with startlingly clear blue eyes and a coffee-cream short body coat. Their extremities—ears, facial "mask," paws, and tail—are of a different color. With age, and in a cold climate, the cat will become darker all over, the body turning to a deep coffee color. There are different varieties of Siamese, distinguished by the color of their extremities: the seal point is the most common one (dark seal brown ears, paws, and tail). Other varieties include the lilac point, chocolate point, and blue point. A longhaired variety is called the Balinese. (Breeders have recently crossbred Siamese with the American short-haired variety to produce color-point shorthairs. These look like Siamese but have different colors on the extremities.)

All Siamese kittens are creamy colored all over and do not develop their coloration for several weeks. Full color is attained around one year of age.

Persian

Until recently, the Siamese was the most popular variety in the United States, but now the long-haired Persian is at the top of the charts.

In contrast to the Siamese, the Persian is a gentle aristocrat, finicky, discreet, if not modest. Reclining on a favorite cushion with fur flowing in languid waves, this variety strikes at the essence of exotic indolence. But beneath this outer veneer purrs a long, sweet-natured creature who enjoys a quiet house and an indulgent owner.

The outer silky appearance is deceptive; underneath is a chunky, firm body. Those who enjoy the svelte ripplings of the lean body of a panther would better choose a Siamese or Abyssinian than a Persian. And if they are not prepared to groom the cat thoroughly each day, they should not have a Persian. The Persian needs constant assistance to keep its coat free from snarls and knots. Some are quite lazy about their coats—or could it be that they just don't know where to begin, so why bother?

People who are very touch oriented and like to pet an animal will enjoy a Persian, as the Persian will enjoy them. They are also basically quiet and relatively sedate cats suitable for people of similar disposition.

A good-quality Persian has a blunt, rather pushed-in face not unlike a pug or Pekingese. This gives them a somewhat aristocratic and lordly, if not disdainful, demeanor. Their large, round, and widely spaced eyes give them an endearing quality, especially as kittens, who have almost owllike faces.

Avoid buying a kitten whose face is too pushed in or whose brow is too prominent: A look at one or both parents is a good way of double-checking. Facial deformities can lead to eye problems including squints and chronic running tears. There are over thirty different coat colors and patterns, the five basic ones being solid (e.g., white, blue, chinchilla, etc.) smoke, tabby, shaded, and particolor. The Peke-faced Persian has its own separate class and is acceptable in shows when it has a red-colored coat.

Other Long-haired Breeds

Cross a Siamese and a Persian and then, with luck and perseverance, you will get a very beautiful creature who possesses the best qualities of both lineages. This hybrid is called the Himalayan. Blue eyes set in a graceful sea of cream silk with extremities dipped in darker tints of the Siamese make the Himalayan a strikingly handsome feline. The long coat needs plenty of attention but doesn't snarl and matt as easily as the Persian's fur. Its voice is less raucous than the Siamese, although it will still "talk" with its owner. It is less of a devil and trickster than the Siamese and less reticent and more outgoing than the Persian.

Himalayans are sweet and gentle like Persians but less finicky and much more active. This breed of cat is for someone who wants something in between a Persian and a Siamese. Because of their good looks and easy but lively temperament, this breed is gaining a wide popularity.

Angoras

The Angora, or Turkish Angora, may be one of the oldest varieties of domestic cat. It has a silkier coat than a Persian, is slightly leggier, and has a very different head. It is more triangular than the Persian, with a longer nose, more pointed ears, and sometimes rather slanting eyes. It comes in only one color: white—so look out. Many pure white cats are congenitally deaf. The eyes may be blue, amber, or odd-colored (one blue, one amber).

Angoras are purportedly aristocratic but not overly aloof. They combine an affectionate nature with a subtle spiritedness that contrasts with the rambunctiousness of Siamese and the self-indulgent indolence of Persians. But as with a Persian, one must be prepared to work daily with the cat's coat.

Birmans

This is another long-haired variety. It is said to be the sacred table cat of Burma. Superficially it resembles the Himalayan, but it differs in being less stocky and in having white mittens; otherwise it has the "points" of the Siamese. The eyes are blue, sometimes purplish. In temperament, the Birman is easygoing but full of life. It is said to be gregarious and generally sociable toward people.

Maine Coons

This cat has *no* raccoon ancestry, in spite of its name. It may have developed as a cross between the early settler's European shorthairs and a longer Angora type. It lived a relatively free and independent life, and the forces of natural selection created its characteristic qualities more than any deliberate breeding by man. Now, however, it is a recognized breed and strict standards are kept.

These are large, robust cats, highly intelligent, active, and good hunters. It has a bushy tail and a coat somewhat shorter and coarser than the Persian. Coat color can vary, tabby markings and parti-colors being popular. The eyes are usually amber and sometimes green.

This breed tends to mature more slowly than others, and the females have fewer heats in the year, i.e. they are more "wild" in many ways. Polydactilism (excess toes) is quite common in this variety. The Maine coon cat makes a good pet and is a hardy animal, especially in cold climates, and is a good ally to the farmer or storekeeper who needs a good ratter.

Other Short-haired Cats

If you want a really "wild"-looking cat, the Abyssinian is the one of choice. Its sandy sable coat color makes it look like a miniature version of a mountain lion, and it moves like one, too. The coat is short, and each hair has three distinct color bands to give the wild tint of a rabbit. Some have a reddish tint. Graceful, agile, and affectionate (but *not* a sweet cuddles) the Aby is a cat person's cat. Some claim that they are the most intelligent of cats, and that they are as dexterous as a Siamese but not so vocal. They are neither shy nor retiring cats and are inquisitive and responsive toward strangers: good ambassadors indeed for cats. Like the Siamese, they are trainable, too.

Anyone who wants a wild animal but, for reasons I have emphasized before in my books, realizes they shouldn't get one, the Abyssinian should provide a satisfactory alternative. Wild-looking indeed, but a super "pussycat" inside.

Burmese

You may want a black leopard instead of a miniature mountain lion, and the Burmese is a good approximation. A dark rich and lustrous coat and golden eyes and high hindquarters give it a slinky low gait. It is a live and alive cat, alert and always ready for fun and games. It is especially easy (and understanding?) with children.

Deceptively, for its size, its body mass is compact and heavy. But it is agile and very dexterous.

Burmese have a way of winning people over like the Aby but even more so; Abys, like most cats, can sometimes be picky about who they accept. But the Burmese is an open and affectionate cat and has a certain irresistible presence few can ignore.

Russian Blues

This variety has the most incredible short coat, most like seal fur. The coat is a blue-grey double coat with silver-tipped guard hairs and is so plush that one can make patterns on it with a finger. Its eyes are a clear emerald green, making this cat one of the most striking symbols of man's ingenuity.

In spite of its aristocratic appearance, the Russian blue is not a nervous or high-strung cat like some lines of Siamese can be. It is affectionate, playful, relaxed, and easygoing. It is hard to find and fetches a high prices today *if* the breeder feels you would be a suitable owner for his or her creation.

Manx

This breed is born with no tail. It originates on the Isle of Man, a small island off the west coast of England. Since the hindquarters are higher than the shoulders, the Manx looks like a miniature lynx or bobcat. But it lacks the "wild" color of the Abyssinian, even though it has a wild type double coat. The short coat can span the whole gamut of colors—calico, tabby (stripes) bicolor, solid colors, etc.

The Manx has a very distinctive bunnylike waddly gait, and with its powerful hindquarters is an avid and agile jumper—tail or no tail! It is said to be a superb ratter, since this was its main employment on the Isle of Man.

Manx are self-reliant cats and will take no nonsense from other cats or dogs. Even so, they are very affectionate and are said to be good with children. Some, however, may be on the wild side and not enjoy too much cuddling and play.

American Shorthairs

You may be surprised to see a cat like your neighbor's or one you saw in the alley the other day at a cat show, being displayed as a pure breed. But these homely-looking cats are indeed purebred with set standards for body conformation and coat coloration. Coat colors span the whole range: white, black, cream, red, blue, chinchilla, smoke, silver, tabby (tiger-striped), and mackerel patterns, in various colors, and also tortoiseshell, bicolor, and calico. An "exotic" shorthair has also been developed that has some of the coat length and texture of a Persian.

Breeders of cats like to play the creation game by manipulating certain gene combinations and mutations, and often they do a beautiful job. Other varieties you may see at a cat show include the odd-looking rex, which has a very short curly or wavy coat; the tobacco colored Havana brown, the spotted Egyptian Mau, the Korat from Thailand, the bobtail from Japan, and a hairless cat called the Sphinx! Indeed there is a plethora of classical cats, but whether you want a fancy feline or a regular cat, it is a good idea to have some knowledge as to what types are available. And most important of all, to know which cat you are best suited for.

II

Training is Really Education–For Your Pet and for You

3

Training and That Essential Bond of Affection

If you love and respect animals, then you may be uncomfortable, as I am, with the idea of imposing your will on a dog or cat to make it conform to your wishes. I personally deplore the spectacle of the lion tamer "controlling" big cats in the circus ring, as I do anyone forcing his or her own will—and ego—on an animal in order to make it perform acts that are alien to its nature.

But how different is the sight of an equestrian guiding a horse through a routine that both enjoy, or a handler interacting with a lovingly trained dog! Both horse and dog obviously enjoy their subtly restrained freedom and the gentle but firm control of their trainer. This partnership is perhaps one of the consummate experiences that human and nonhuman animal can share.

Such a successful relationship between sensitive owner and sensitized animal results from an animal's willingness and motivation to learn. A classic example of the subtlety of this relationship is the story of Clever Hans, a German circus horse. He seemed to perform extraordinary feats of arithmetic, adding and subtracting and stomping out the correct answers with his hoof—but it was an almost imperceptible signal from his trainer that actually told him when to stop stomping. Clever Hans even outfoxed those who tested him in the absence of his trainer: He could sense, by minute changes in their posture or expression, when he had stomped out the appropriate number.

Dogs and cats can also respond to the most subtle and insignificant cues that we give them through eye contact, tone of voice, body posture or gestures. In their communication with each other, animals employ signals given in similar ways—they stare, growl, hiss, crouch, arch their backs, and so on—so they readily learn to respond to our human signals, provided these are not confusing or complicated. In the initial stages of training, signals must be clear and consistent. A trainer/owner should express his or her commands simply, directly, and within context—and should never make exceptions (such as "letting kitty walk on the table just this once," or "feeding Fido table scraps only for tonight"). If rules are changed arbitrarily at the owner's whim, a confusing double standard results, which can make an animal delinquent and unhappy. An animal, like a child, needs consistency in its relationship with its master/parent, and lack of it will only lead to confusion, conflict, and neurotic behavior or worse.

A more common problem, affecting pets and children alike, results from a teacher's excessive expectations and insistence on excellence. Rather than fostering cooperation, schools today set up such competitive situations that nervous breakdowns are not uncommon among young people in high school and college. In the same way, overzealous training of dogs (and horses) can lead to nervous breakdowns in the animal world. The rule is to proceed slowly in training, and stay within the limits of the animal's developing abilities. Try not to make the task too much of a challenge to your pet's level of competence and comprehension. Don't expect to be able to teach an independent animal like a cat to "sit," or a puppy to retrieve a ball for you before it has learned to answer to some simple calls.

In order for training to be effective, it's necessary to have an animal's attention: The animal must be interested in the training procedures and willing to please its master.

To have and hold a dog's attention, the owner must establish a close social bond between himself and the dog early in the animal's life, ideally when it is between six and eight weeks of age. A dog that has not been bonded to its master will be less trainable, since it has no real interest in pleasing him or her.

If your dog is inattentive, don't conclude that it's "slow" or is brain-damaged. Certain breeds—the collie and German shepherd, for instance—are simply more attentive to their owners than other dogs; they are alert to every command, and even if their master is involved in an ongoing conversation with someone, the inadvertent use of a word signal may suddenly bring the dog to attention.

Trainability, whether in dogs or cats, is more related to dependence than intelligence per se. My hand-raised wolves and coyotes are extremely bright but difficult to train because they don't share the same degree of dependence (probably genetically instilled) as the domesticated dog. But domesticated breeds vary in their degree of dependence, too—compare the trainability of a dependent shelty or toy poodle with that of an aloof and independent Afghan hound or Basenji.

By contrast, cats are generally less attentive, at least for the extended periods necessary for complex training procedures. Compared to dogs, cats are independent and solitary creatures and, as such, less socially motivated to please mere humans. Siamese cats, though, are notoriously trainable, not because they are more intelligent or affectionate but because they're more dependent than other varieties of cat.

But no matter how emotionally attached an animal is to its trainer, the training is difficult unless the trainer is in complete control. Control means establishing a dominant relationship over the animal; and this, combined with affection (an indispensable element, since an animal with a strong feeling for its master will perform more conscientiously), sets up the master as a leader/parent figure. Such a dominant relationship is easily established with a dog, since it naturally responds to its master as pack leader. (This, incidentally, is another reason why cats are not as trainable as dogs—they don't form packs in the wild and therefore don't respond to a pack leader. Control through dominance is extremely hard to achieve when dealing with the cat species.) But if a dog is overindulged and ruined by permissiveness, it may attempt to assume the number-one position itself and will be virtually impossible to train. That's why "making exceptions" is taboo.

As far as the training process itself is concerned, learning is accomplished through conditioning and association. Associative learning comes first: The animal learns that it will receive some form of reward (or punishment) when it performs a certain act. Conditioning comes next: A specific signal or command (such as "Fetch!") is added to the action (the retrieving of a ball) and the reward that's given when the animal responds correctly (perhaps a pat on the head and warm praise).

It's a good rule to begin training at the associative level and then "shape" the animal to develop a conditioned response. For example, your cat always jumps onto the dining room table, or your dog barks excessively. First, use mild punishment (a swat on the behind, a squirt from a water pistol, or a firm shake of the dog's closed muzzle), so that the act has a negative association in the animal's mind. Then interpose the conditioning signal, which in all likelihood will be a voice command ("Get down" or "Quiet"), and follow with punishment. Eventually—and this is the beauty of conditioning—punishment won't have to be given (except, perhaps, occasionally for reinforcement); the command signal will be enough, since the animal has now been conditioned to respond to the appropriate word or gesture. The same procedures hold true when training an animal to perform some positive action, such as retrieving or shaking hands. First, arouse the behavior you desire through play or some other appropriate manipulation: for instance, as you toss a ball playfully for your dog, sooner or later the pet will retrieve the ball and bring it back to you. When your pet gives a correct response in this way, immediately reward it with food or petting. Then, once the animal has made the pleasurable association, include a verbal command to accompany it. Gradually the animal will realize that "Fetch" means a specific thing.

A great asset in training dogs is a long, light leash and a chain collar—which, like the bit in a horse's mouth, must be used only with extreme care and gentleness. This will aid in guiding a dog into the actions you wish it to perform. Eventually, through conditioning, the leash and collar can be discarded, and yet the psychological control will endure.

As far as rewards are concerned, B. F. Skinner, the American psychologist, has done much research in controlling and predicting animal and human behavior; his studies have indicated that consistently praising or rewarding an animal for performing a task well is not always the best method. What is more effective is *occasional* reward. A dog or child will work harder if praise or reward is fairly frequent but given at unexpected intervals.

These learning principles I have mentioned can be applied to almost everything you want to train your pet to do or not to do. But remember always to be patient; don't push the animal to learn too much too fast. If it's being trained to "come" or "fetch," never punish it when it does something wrong. Mild scolding (which to an animal can be simply no praise) or clear disappointment ("Oh, you goofed again!") works well. Too often a person punishes a dog for not coming on command, and soon the dog refuses to come at all when called!

In another type of learning, an animal is brought closer and closer, step by step, to perform a particular act at a given time and place. This is a slow, trial-and-error process, such as repeatedly placing a puppy on its newspaper or a kitten up against its scratching post. Consistency, patience, and praise for doing the right thing in the right place is essential. Again, avoid punishing an animal for poor performance; it will be confused, think that the act itself is wrong, and become inhibited from doing it at the *right* time and place.

For both human and animal, fear and anxiety are the most likely causes of impaired performance. Whereas a little tension or anxiety can spur on a pet's efforts, too much will act as a block. When an animal is afraid, it needs very gentle and persuasive handling. If an actual phobia develops (such as fear of strangers, of thunder, of riding in a car or going into a show ring) you need to desensitize the animal, or help it to unlearn its behavior. How is this done? The animal is repeatedly exposed to the fearful situation, but at the same time it is given extra-gentle handling, frequent rewards, sometimes even *mild* tranquilizers, if needed. Through this desensitization process, the animal gradually *un*learns its phobic reaction.

I have not taken you, primer fashion, through ways to stop your dog from chasing cars or snapping at children, or to inhibit your cat from clawing you or the furniture. Nor have I spelled out the details of training—sit, come, fetch, heel, and so on. But if you follow the basic principles that I have outlined and have established a bond of affection with and control over your pet, you should be able to train it to do almost anything within the limits of its inborn potentialities.

A well-trained animal is a better creature to live with, because it is well-mannered and adaptable. It's also far healthier mentally than a pet that simply vegetates and is merely fed and petted. Training is education. An animal enjoys using the obedience skills it has learned. And you will enjoy sharing these experiences with your pet.

4

Puppies Are Smarter
Than You Think—
Start Training Early

It is commonly thought that young puppies can't learn much of anything except their names. Many dog-training schools even refuse to take pups under six months of age. But the truth is that a young puppy is a highly responsive creature with an incredible capacity to explore its environment and learn new things every day.

There is, in fact, a critical period between eight and twelve weeks of age when a puppy's inclination to explore and to acquire knowledge is set. If experiences, simple training and handling are denied or limited during this early period, the puppy will actually have a lower IQ as an adult dog! Just as head-start programs with pre-schoolers result in greater learning abilities later in life, so simple training early in a puppy's life can lay the foundation for learning more difficult tasks later on. One reason that many people don't always get the best out of their pets is that they mistakenly delay this early training.

"Training" can begin on day one of a puppy's life. My research with newborn puppies has shown that if aniseed oil is applied to their mothers' teats at birth, they will follow a Q-tip soaked in the oil twenty-four hours later—while pups *not* exposed to this substance will avoid it. This means that learning or conditioning begins very early in a dog's life. Its sense of smell is well developed at birth;

A puppy needs much supervision and training early in life and should learn to respect its owner's wishes and property. It will be less likely to destroy things if it has its own chew-toys *(H.S.U.S./ Frank Thorne).*

any learning that involves this sense is possible from the very beginning. And, although the newborn puppy is born deaf and blind, in several days it will be able to recognize and discriminate between different sounds and sights—and then it can begin learning with these two senses as well.

A sense of balance and a sensitivity to touch are also well developed at birth. Some newborns are tense and timid, some relaxed and cuddly—but whatever a pup's personality, you should accustom it from an early age to being held and handled. Handling socializes the puppy during its first few weeks of life, and the better socialized a puppy is the more trainable it will be later. This is an important rule, because such a pup will work for petting and voice rewards, and won't need food as an incentive to behave.

Also, the early formation of a strong social bond with a master will make a pet more willing to please, to be conscientious and attentive during training. Studies of puppies who had little or no human contact during the first few weeks of life show that such animals are fearful of man and literally impossible to train. Research on guide dogs for the blind brought out another important point: If a puppy is kept with its mother or with a littermate until about twelve weeks of age, it will be less trainable than a pup raised more or less exclusively with people from the time it is six to eight weeks old.

Thus, the basis for trainability is the social bond—or attachment to man—which is best established with a puppy around six to eight weeks of age. This must be followed by a period of what I call "enrichment," when the puppy is between eight and twelve weeks old. During this time your puppy should be exposed to as many novel situations and experiences as possible, ranging from meeting strange people and riding in an automobile to exploring the woods and walking on a leash down a busy street. I get many letters from people who suffer from the fact that their pets were never "socially enriched" as puppies. One woman complained that her dog was racist! Growing up in a lily-white suburb, it had seen only pale faces: when she moved to the city, her animal barked ferociously at any passing strangers of another color. Some dogs that grow up in a home without men become fearful when a repairman or a male visitor comes to the door.

Training per se can begin as soon as you get your puppy (ideally, when it's between six and eight weeks old). Don't push too hard at first; around eight or nine weeks of age, many puppies tend to be somewhat fearful. Gentle handling, gradual exposure to new experiences and small doses of new training each day will help the puppy cope with fear and uncertainty and bond it to you with responsive trust and willing dependence.

When you first pick up the puppy hold it securely, supporting it carefully under its chest and abdomen. It should quickly learn not to struggle when handled in this way. This simple act is a subtle way of asserting dominance.

Accustom a puppy to wearing a collar and leash. Allow it to take *you* for a walk first, then gently pull it toward you, saying "come," and pet it (a potent reward). Once the puppy is used to the leash, you can then train it to "sit." Place your foot on the leash, and pull it so that the puppy will feel gentle but firm downward pressure on its collar. Once the "sit" is accomplished, release it with the word "come," and pet it when it does.

After a few days, introduce the command "stay." Using a longer leash back off, and if the puppy gets up to follow you, step forward and tug it down into "sit" again; then back off with a raised hand and the command "stay." Eye contact, an important element of control, must be maintained at all times. Subsequently, "sit," "stay," and "come" can be practiced with the leashed puppy perched on a box a few inches off the ground, so it becomes accustomed to a different situation. And when the puppy is older (twelve to sixteen weeks), carry out this same training alongside a quiet road, and the dog will learn some traffic sense early in life.

A puppy will often chew things, such as a book or a good pair of shoes. When that happens, don't shout a long stream of verbal commands—that will only confuse it. Simply establish eye contact and utter a growling "no." Follow this up with a firm grasp of the pup's shoulder scruff (the skin at the back of the neck), and open its mouth and remove whatever it's chewing. Then close the puppy's mouth and shake its muzzle gently but firmly, and repeat the command "no" three or four times. With this uncomplicated conditioning procedure, the animal will anticipate a scruff grasp and muzzle shake every time you say "no." And, eventually, the simple command of "no" will turn off unwanted behavior. (Occasionally, though, reinforce your words with a scruff grab and muzzle shake.)

Excessive barking is difficult behavior to control but, in my experience, if inhibited early in life with this "no" sequence, you're less likely to have an uncontrolled adult barker.

Housebreaking is, perhaps, the most difficult of all to deal with. A mother dog will lick her newborn pups to stimulate defecation and urination until about the fourth week of life when the pups are old enough to emerge and walk a few yards away from the nest. From that point on, puppies soon develop the habit of going to one particular spot to relieve themselves.

Such behavior is linked with the other natural rhythms of sleeping, walking, eating, and so on. When a puppy wakes up, it's usually ready to urinate and possibly to defecate—just like a person. A while after feeding, it is most likely ready to defecate. To housebreak a puppy, it's essential to get in tune with these natural rhythms and to anticipate when the pet should go outdoors or be placed on its newspaper on the floor.

Training a puppy to the outdoors presents no problems if you remember always to take puppy to the same spot—the odor that lingers from previous visits will remind it just what it's there for. Training it to use a newspaper can be more hazardous. Often, a puppy will then refuse to do anything outside, but will wait until it gets back indoors to the newspaper—or to the place on the floor where you used to put its newspaper! The poor puppy has to *unlearn* the habit of going on the newspaper, or going indoors at all. It can be very confusing to be punished for using the newspaper when a few weeks earlier the puppy was rewarded for the same behavior!

You can ease this "transfer" to the outdoors by placing newspaper somewhere in the yard. But as some puppies seem to be extremely slow in learning to make the transference, patience is essential—and so is an awareness of when the puppy is most likely to want to relieve itself. Consistency in discipline is also imperative. Never give in "for just this once." The puppy will get confused or in the future will try to manipulate you by whining and being solicitous and submissive.

If and when the puppy messes the floor, pick him up and point his nose or head close to where he has messed. Don't strike the puppy or rub his nose in the mess. Say in a gruff voice, "You bad dog, that's for outside." Keep on saying this the whole time you're indoors and as you are carrying him or leading him out. Then, outside, say in a pleasant voice, "Good dog, that's for outside," and give him plenty of petting—especially if he has then defecated or urinated outside—so that messing outside is connected in his mind with a pleasant experience.

You have to be patient in establishing the habit. It may take weeks. Meanwhile, until the puppy has become housebroken, keep it in the kitchen so that if there is an accident, the linoleum and not the rug will suffer.

Owners who, for some reason, can't take a puppy out on a regular schedule and must confine it indoors most of the time often complain about how difficult it is to housebreak the animal later on in its life. People who don't have the right facilities to housebreak a pup and can't allow it access to the outdoors would be better off with a cat that needs no training. Cats instinctively use a litter tray, whereas dogs need to roam as they mature, to investigate scent left by other dogs on trees or posts and to mark these with their own urine, or "calling card."

It's also important to get an early start in eating habits. Training has a profound effect on later food preferences, so a puppy should be weaned at an early age to a well-balanced commercial diet. This way it won't want filet mignon later on but will eat the standard dog food, which is better for it. Feeding should be on a regular schedule because dogs are creatures of habit, and it's natural for them to want consistency. Discourage anyone from feeding your puppy scraps from the table. And give it food from your hand only when you are specifically training it or coaxing it to try a new food.

When your puppy reaches twelve to sixteen weeks of age, an evening a week in "puppy classes" can be a tremendous help for both of you. Check with dog-owning neighbors and in the Yellow Pages for a reliable dog-training school.

Just as with humans, animal bad habits become harder and harder to change as life goes on. So begin training early—and get started out on the right foot with your puppy!

5

The Courteous Canine: Basically Obedient Is Basically Better

If more owners spent a little time in teaching their dogs basic obedience, a lot of the pet problems that I get in the mail wouldn't exist. Surely we would have fewer young adult dogs being dropped off at humane shelters for destruction. A dog doesn't come already trained. He needs schooling as much as he needs love and good food. Obedience training puts you in control of your dog: You are number one. If your dog respects you as his leader, he won't be a socially maladjusted upstart who disobeys and always wants his own way. Nor will you have a bored animal whose intelligence and abilities have been repressed or frustrated by lack of challenge. Good obedience training means educating your dog to develop his best attributes; it also means he will learn good manners, too—to respect your wishes and not act like a selfish, spoiled child like many overindulged pooches do with their parent/owners. Corrective therapy (remedial obedience training) is harder to instigate after a dog has been raised the wrong way. To start things off right, basic obedience training should begin at around six months of age. Be patient and understanding and don't rush your dog too fast: Overtraining can be as bad as no training at all.

First, some basic rules for you, before you try to rule your dog. Never hit your dog, for he will learn that an upraised arm is a threat and this will lead to difficulties later. Punishment is effected by a scolding tone of voice, praise by a friendly, warm voice and a pat on the head if he is close. A harsh "No" is enough if and when your dog does something wrong, along with a firm push on the body to make him assume the position you want him to assume (sitting, for example). It is of critical importance that you discipline your dog at the right time. Never scold him after he has come back to you, otherwise he will associate coming to you with being punished. Then he won't want to come when called or when he has (or thinks he has) done something wrong. If he does something wrong during training, call him back to you, get him under control, but *don't* punish him. Simply start all over again. And if *you* begin to get frustrated and lose your temper, stop the lesson at once.

Initially you should start to train your dog in a quiet place where there are no distractions such as other dogs or people. A well-fenced yard or large basement is ideal. But this does not mean that you work with your dog off the leash. Until he has mastered all commands, all training is done with him on a long leash so that he is always under your control. And before you start working with him off the leash, take him to a busy place, like a park or shopping center, where he can learn to cope with distractions.

Each lesson should last about ten to fifteen minutes for a young dog and up to thirty minutes for an adult. Shorten the length of the lesson if he loses interest or gets restless. Always end each lesson with warm praise.

Most trainers use a leather or chain choke collar, not to forcibly choke the dog but to snap it to attention. A quick, firm pull on the leash (made of leather or canvas webbing) will tighten the collar, then immediately let it slacken. The choke chain is used not physically to overpower your dog but to help you assert your will over the dog's and to ensure that your control over him is quick, timely, and, therefore, effective.

First, call your dog's name to get his attention, then give the command "Sit," "Heel," or whatever you want him to do or to learn. If he goofs up, go back and repeat something he already knows how to do so that you can appropriately praise him and help him feel good. No matter how frustrated you may get, always end a lesson on a "high" note in this way. Remember, in training your dog you must also be trained to be patient and understanding. I much prefer this kind of reward training to more brutal methods where the dog is subordinated and punished until it has learned some new command.

The first things a young dog of three to four months of age can be taught are "No" and "Ok." "No" must always be said harshly and with his punishment. You can teach a young dog the difference between "No" and "Ok" by using a dog biscuit. Place it before him and as soon as he tries to grab it, shout or growl "No" and push him away or grab the biscuit yourself. Then put it down and say "Ok" and allow him to eat it. After several repetitions he should quickly learn the difference between "No" and "Ok."

On the leash, with choke chain, discipline is given by shouting "No" and briskly pulling the leash to pinch his neck with the choke chain and then releasing the tension. A better name for this training collar would be a training or pinching collar and not a choke chain. But the latter name serves as a warning because it can choke the dog if not put on properly.

If the training collar is put on incorrectly it won't snap and release when you pull and relax the leash. The free end of the chain that attaches by a ring to the leash should pass over the dog's neck, not under it. When you are facing your dog, this free end must pass over his neck through the ring and hang out on the right side of the dog.

Please, when you take your dog for a walk, don't keep pulling him with a "No" and a "Heel" command every time he stops to sniff something. Sniffing things and marking trees and hydrants with urine are important and enjoyable activities for your dog. Given him time to "read the newspapers," so to speak, with his nose, for where every dog has marked before him, there is something for his nose to read. During his training sessions, however, no such sniffing should be allowed at all.

Basic obedience training involves teaching the dog the first six basic commands in the following order: heel, sit, stay, stand-stay, down, and come.

You should reckon on taking at least a week to ten day days to teach your dog each command, giving him ideally two daily training sessions, morning and evening. If you only give one lesson in the evening, keep the time and duration regular. Always start off with a quick repeat of what he has learned already. If you do decide to put in an extra lesson on weekend mornings, keep the duration of the lesson the same. Some people try to "catch up" by making a lesson longer if they missed one, or they spend more time at it on weekends. This is to be avoided: Stick to a regular time duration even if you can't keep to a fixed schedule.

Another important word of advice. Don't use *any* of the command words in other contexts. For example, if you don't want your dog to get onto a sofa, don't say "Down." Simply say "Benji, no," emphatically. "No" should be the one disciplinary signal for all general purposes. Nor should you stop him from jumping up on someone by shouting "Down" or "Sit." "No" should suffice and he should be conditioned to this during training. When he does something wrong, a tug on the leash and a sharp "No" will soon teach him that a "No" means disapproval and that he must immediately stop what he's doing. When he does obey you, don't ignore him. Thank him with a pat. Don't get him hooked on food reward either unless you always plan to carry bags of food around all the time. Then what happens when he's not hungry? He will be less likely to obey you, obviously.

Heel

Once your dog is accustomed to a leash and collar, you can begin the first step in training. It is important that this be the first step because you don't want your dog pulling you all over the place and literally taking you for a walk, as is so often the case with larger or more active dogs. Hold the leash across your body in front, in your right hand, and have your left hand holding the leash near the collar. With a brisk command, "Benji [or whatever his name is], heel," start forward and snap the leash quickly to pull the dog close to your left side. If he starts to pull ahead or drag behind, repeat the procedure—name, command, and snap the leash. Soon you won't need to snap the leash: He will heel to order, staying by your left leg. Praise him each time he assumes the right position. Later, vary your pace, walking, jogging, turning, and moving in circles. Always start off walking with your left foot. This way your dog will learn to follow the leg on his side. While you are walking with him at your heel, praise him constantly and don't keep the leash tight. Have a little slack so that if and when he lags or moves ahead too much, you can correct him quickly with "Heel" and then a quick jerk. Having the leash tight all the time will not only tire you, it will give him an insensitive "hard neck," like a horse who develops a "hard mouth" if its rider keeps tugging on the reins and pulling on the bit in its mouth.

When you come to a stop and he is to sit, always stop on your right foot and bring the left foot up to it. This will help your dog to guide on your left leg.

Once he has learned to heel, you can move on to teach him to sit. It is a good idea always to go back and repeat the previous commands he has learned in the course of training. So after ten to fifteen minutes of teaching him to "Sit," spend a few minutes on "Heel." This will increase his confidence and enjoyment. And don't forget to praise him after each session.

Sit

Every time you stop walking, your dog should immediately assume a sitting position. After calling your dog to heel, walk a few paces and then stop. Call out, "Benji, sit." Then switch hands so your right hand is holding the leash close to the collar. Pull up gently but firmly on the leash while at the same time you push down on the dog's rump with your left hand to get him into the sitting position. Give him plenty of praise, then call him to heel again, and walk a few more paces before repeating this exercise.

He will soon learn to sit on command by your left leg once you stop walking and give the command to sit. You won't even need to use your hands to put him in the correct position. Eventually he will sit as soon as you stop without you having to give the command. Make up some variations: running, walking in a circle, around detours, and, of course, at the edge of the sidewalk by the road.

Stay

This follows naturally once your dog has learned the sit command. Stand facing him and put him into the sit position with your hands and they say "Stay," backing off a few paces. At first he will try to follow you, so you will have to approach him and put him back into the sit position with the command "Stay." Hold one hand up in front of his face when you say "Stay" and keep your hand up for a few seconds. Then drop it and say "Ok" and let him come to you.

When you leave your dog in the stay position, always step off with your right foot to bring the left foot up to it. This will help your dog to guide on your left leg.

Praise him at once. If he sits and then immediately gets up to follow you, don't punish him. Simply start all over again. It is a good idea to try to project a mental picture to him, of what you want him to do. Some trainers adhere to this psychic or telepathic method, believing implicitly in its effectiveness. Never give your dog a negative command such as "No, don't do this or that." He will only get confused. Keep all commands positive: "Do this, do that," etc.

Once he has mastered the stay signal, you can increase the time he must remain in the stay position for up to three minutes. You can also try increasing the distance between you and your dog at this time—but don't overdo it. Control must never be broken. Never try to push your dog too hard or too fast. Otherwise he may pick up bad habits which will be difficult to unlearn.

Stand and Stay

Now that he knows what "Stay" means, he is ready to learn to stay in a standing position. This is especially useful when you need to groom your dog, clean his ears, or have him examined by the veterinarian.

To teach this, call him to heel, then, when you stop walking, stop him from automatically sitting by cupping your left hand under his right groin and pushing gently and firmly upward. Just as you start to do this, say "Stand" and repeat the command. As soon as he does stand, praise him and take him through the familiar heel and sit so he will understand the difference.

Once he knows "Stand," you can tack on the "Stay" part because he already knows what "Stay" means. Make him stand, and then back off on your right foot and place yourself to the side or in front of him with one arm raised in front of his face and say "Stay." After he has held the position for a few seconds, go up to him and praise him, first saying "Ok." Increase this up to two to three minutes. Then you are both ready for the "Down" lesson.

Down

This is taught by first telling your dog to sit. Then approach him and lift his front legs up and slide them forward so that he goes into a lying down position. With one hand pressing down on his shoulders, repeat the words "Down" and "Stay" four or five times then release him, say "Okay" and praise him. Keep on repeating this lesson until he goes down on command without your needing to handle him.

Then, with a long leash (for control) get him to stay down and stay as you walk off or around him.

Many trainers like to teach the sixth and most important command last of all, namely "Come." This is because by the end of the training sequence you will have full control over your dog so that there should be no difficulties in always getting him to come when called.

Basic obedience training can lead dog and master to the excitement and enjoyment of obedience competitions; the more advanced obedience classes may bring out some hidden talents in your dog *(H.S.U.S./Tom Morrissette)*.

Come (or the Recall)

Call your dog to heel and then, after a few paces, stop. He will go into the sitting position. Then you should step to one side or backward, calling "Come" and at the same time giving him a brief jerk on the leash. Praise him as soon as he comes to you and make several repetitions. After this, with your dog on a long leash, make him sit and stay, and they say "Come," encouraging him with a slight tug toward you on the leash.

Once he has mastered these six commands you can next try working with him without a leash. There is nothing more impressive than seeing a well-trained dog with its owner being put through its paces without a leash. Most dogs enjoy a daily workout, and you should do your best to find the time and put in a little effort to teach your dog basic obedience. In Czechoslovakia, I believe, it costs $75 per year for a dog license, but it's free if the owner and dog have had a course at obedience school. This law, which would certainly not be inappropriate in the United States, especially for owners of large breeds and protective guard-dog types, is clearly designed to ensure that dogs will be under proper control by their owners at all time. Local townships in this country have a bad enough time even enforcing leash laws. While we may never make it mandatory in this country for people to obedience-train their dogs, owners do have a moral obligation for two reasons. A disobedient and uncontrollable dog can be a hazard to traffic and a danger to passersby on the street or in the park. A dog that has had no training has missed something in life, too. Obedience training will bring out the best in your dog and help establish a special bond of mutual respect that love alone can never do.

6

Pet Peeves: Corrective Training Is Easy— With Patience

THE PROBLEM DOG

People give up on their pets for many reasons, either having them destroyed or trying to find another home for them. Sometimes they are simply abandoned. But however the pet is disposed of, there is usually a common underlying reason. The pet exhibits some undesirable behavior the owners can't correct, so they get rid of the pet instead. Perhaps such people shouldn't have had a cat or dog in the first place. Or perhaps they had very unreal expectations about how their pet would grow up. Without *any* obedience training, many dogs will be misfits, less adaptable to one's home and life-style than a pet that has had some training. Without training, many dogs will bark a lot, jump up, chew things, destroy household items, fail to stay housebroken, steal food, chase cars, bicyclers, and joggers, and may even bite people. Such annoying behaviors are often grounds for getting rid of the pet.

A high percentage of the fourteen or so million unwanted cats and dogs that are destroyed each year by animal shelters are from homes whose owners say "they are too much trouble." One or more of the above behavior problems is often the "trouble." Eliminating the undesirable behavior by corrective training is relatively easy and well worth the effort—if you really want to keep your pet, that is, and don't just want an excuse to get rid of it. Only too often, mother is left to feed and care for the pet, and she has enough to do without having to take time out to train the pet. Someone else in the family should be able and prepared to take this responsibility. She is the one most likely to feel the brunt of the pet's troubles, too, being around the house with it most of the day. As for owners who go out to work all day and leave the pet at home, that's another problem and will be discussed later.

So before you give up on your pet, try out, with patience and perseverance, some of the following corrective training methods that may be appropriate for your particular pet problem.

Excessive Barking

The dog who barks at the slightest noise outside, barks for attention, or barks for barking's sake can be a pain in the ear: if not to the owner, then to neighbors at least. There are various steps you can take to rectify this. If he barks and whines outdoors, a cup full of cold water thrown in his face, preceded by an angry "No; quiet," should suffice. Indoors, a water pistol squirted in his face or a sudden noise, like a hand clap or loud bang on the table or door, again preceded by "No, Quiet," should silence him. After a few repetitions, "No; quiet" without the physical stimulus will most probably be quite effective. If it is, you will know you have conditioned your dog. But conditioning needs occasional reinforcement and that means giving the physical punishment once in a while as well as the verbal command. Some dogs respond well to the shock and jangle of having their metal choke chains thrown on the ground right beside them when they are barking. You may want to set things up to train your dog by having someone walk around outside, on the apartment floor, or even knock on the door. Let your dog give one or two barks and say "Ok, good boy" and pet him. Once he knows that you have heard the noise he should understand that he must be quiet. If he continues to bark, then you discipline and condition him as described above.

Some dogs won't respond to conditioning no matter how much you persevere. Bad breeding may be at the root of the problem, but of course it's too late to do anything about that. You have various options to consider before giving up your pooch. If he barks a lot when left alone, try leaving the radio or TV on. He may like the sound of company and the noise may help by acting as a kind of sound barrier so that his barking is less obvious to the neighbors. A slap upward with your palm given to his lower jaw like an uppercut punch is another shock method that is worth trying, again preceded by "No; quiet." You will have to repeat any of these techniques several times over a week or two (hopefully less) before you begin to get some results. By all accounts, it's best never to switch from one technique to another. Be consistent until one technique doesn't seem to work, then try another. Also, *never* let him bark excessively for any reason. Never give in, or allow him "just this once" to get away with it—and *this holds true for all corrective training.*

You could put a muzzle on him while you are out. A muzzled dog can't bark very well, and if he accepts the muzzle without obvious distress after two or three days' habituation, you may have the problem solved. If not, then the next step is to buy an antibark collar. They really do work well on some dogs, generating a small current that gives the dog a mild shock whenever he barks. Try one, and if he accepts it after a few days (and doesn't become hysterical, as some sensitive dogs will) you have your problem solved. And you've saved your dog for just a few dollars, too. Don't forget that another dog barking close to the dog wearing one of these collars could set the shock mechanism off, and this could cause all kinds of problems.

The final and most radical step is to have your dog's vocal cords removed by your veterinarian. Inhumane as this may seem (and *may* be—the psychological consequences of devocalizing a dog have not been evaluated), it is surely a better option than having your pet put to sleep. This is a virtually painless operation, done under a general anesthetic. Your dog will still be able to bark—he won't be frustrated as he might be by a muzzle or shock collar, so this method could be considered more humane than the other two. Devocalized dogs make a kind of throaty "woof" that has little carrying power and so isn't likely to disturb your neighbors.

The Jumper-upper

The menace to small children, a clean dress or suit, or a new pair of hose is the dog, big or small, who jumps up. There is a time and place when a dog should be allowed to jump up, if at all, and that is when he is invited to rough-play with someone who is prepared both in mind and apparel.

Some dogs are incessant jumper-uppers; this, even between dogs, is bad manners and may be infantile, aggressive, sexual, or specifically playful. When directed toward their owners, jumping up is usually a combination of infantile attention-seeking and playful greeting. If not discouraged in puppyhood, it can be a problem; even if *you* tolerate it, visitors may not, and a big dog can inadvertently knock over and injure a small child or an elderly person. So what to do with a canine "jack-in-the-box"?

One technique is to obedience-train your dog to learn the command "Sit."

If your dog is obedience-trained, you must not use the command "Down" when he jumps up. "Down" should be used in the specific obedience-training context. So choose another word like "Off" and preface it with a punishing "No."

As soon as you have said "No; off" in the most angry and disapproving voice you can, snap your dog under the chin with your palm. If a few repetitions of this won't work, your next play takes a little judo. As soon as your dog jumps up, seize his front paws and hold them stretched up. Then walk and push toward him so that he falls over backward. Or, as an alternative, step on his hind feet. As soon as you stop, say "No; off." He will most likely try again, so you will have to keep at it until he understands that jumping up is unpleasant for him and is not approved of by you. He still needs his strokes, though, so you must bend down and pet him with lots of praise when he does stay down. Small dogs are often jumpers because they don't like to be ignored, and once in a while they like to be face to face with people. So get down to their level once in a while and give them a fair chance to be friendly and kissy-face.

The Chewer (and House-wrecker)

After the teething period of puppyhood, at which time a pup will crave anything to chew, chewing can become a constant problem. Some dogs are never content unless they have something to chew on whenever they feel like it. The dog should be deprived of all chewable objects for a couple of days. Then put before him two items he likes to chew. The latter should be a rawhide strip or "bone" or an uncooked beef soup bone. The other object could be anything he has recently chewed but shouldn't have (a shoe, book or whatever). If he takes the permissible object, you say "Ok, good boy" and praise him. If he takes the forbidden object, you scold him severely with a "No; drop it" and take it away from him at once, placing it back on the floor with the permissible object. This exercise should be repeated several times each day.

The next step, if your dog doesn't make the connection, is to sit back and figure out just *why* your dog is chewing things in the first place and *when*. Knowing the when can give you an answer to the why. If he chews while you are out, as is often the case, he's either bored or frustrated and this is his way of getting back at you. You can't explain or reason with him that you have to go out to work or whatever, so what to do?

Confine him in one room and remove all chewable "no-nos" except his own chew toys and leave a radio or TV on for company. If he's still chewing the door and sofa, you can either put him in a holding cage or purchase a comfortable soft leather muzzle. Some trainers suggest taping a piece of torn drapery, carpet, or sofa into the dog's mouth for a couple of hours. This should set up a specific aversion, but he may then go on to chew something else, like a chair leg, and you can hardly put a chair into his mouth! Spray repellents to keep your pet from chewing things are a waste of money. Most probably the noise of the spray scares your dog off more than anything else. If you want to give chemical warfare a try, however, diluted tabasco sauce on table and chair legs is worth a try. Look out for teething babies, though!

The Food Stealer

Some dogs are real food snitches, will steal off your plate when you aren't at the table or even swipe a defrosting chicken. The worst thief of all is the pooch who grabs a cookie or sandwich right out of a child's hand. A dog's native intelligence tells it to respect what belongs to another dog: A dog knows that stealing is stealing. He *does* have a conscience. If, however, you encourage the children to feed him from their own hands (rather than putting all offerings into his food bowl), the dog may mistakenly think he's being offered something by the child and grab it right out of his or her hand. This could lead to accidental bites, too. So rule number one: Don't set up the wrong expectations in your dog by having low-to-the-ground children hand-feed him, otherwise cookies, ice cream, and sandwiches may never be safe.

Rule number two: Never feed your dog from the table or from your plate. Your plate, no matter where it is, is taboo, as is any food on the table. Any dog will have the common dog sense to know that what's on the table and on your plate is yours and not his—if you consistently follow this rule.

The kitchen counter, though, may seem more like common ground, especially if you fix his food there as well as your own. Still, he is capable of learning that he may eat only from the floor and only out of his food bowl.

In order to cure a thief, you have to catch him at it. So you must set your dog up for this one. Place a goodie on the edge of the table and hide around the corner to ambush him. If you can't hide yourself, fix a booby trap of pots and pans and string attached to the sandwich or chicken. When you see your dog grabbing the food or hear the clatter, move in fast. Yell a punishing "No! Drop it." Caught in the act, he should submit at once and seek either cover or forgiveness. You can add further shock by throwing his choke chain on the ground by his feet just after the verbal reprimand. If after several repetitions he still steals, you can work in the next corrective procedure. Place several small pieces of meat on a plate at the edge of the table. As soon as he reaches up to steal a piece, repeat the verbal reprimand. Then place the plate on the floor next to his food bowl; remove all the meat and put one piece on the plate and one in his bowl. Use the same verbal reprimand and a clip under the chin if he goes near your plate. Praise him and give him another piece of meat when he eats from his own bowl. Several repetitions of this should teach him which is his and which is yours. Anyone in the house who subsequently feeds the dog off his or her plate should eat out of the dog's bowl for a week!

The Biter

Believe it or not, but there's a dog-bite epidemic in the United States today. An estimated one million people are bitten each year. Some are killed. The most common victims are children and the most common area bitten is the face. The cost of medical care for dog bites exceeds $100 million per year. Knowing some of the reasons for this epidemic can help the dog owner reduce the chances of his or her dog biting someone. Some breeds of dog today are emotionally unstable (a consequence of mass production, overbreeding without good quality control). If you have a dog like this who is unpredictable around people, play it safe and always have a muzzle on him when you take him out. The same goes for a dog who is afraid of children. Training generally doesn't help these kinds of people-biters and putting a muzzle on the dog at appropriate times is a responsible and humane action—better than having the dog put to sleep.

For the fear-biting puppy, try clasping it close to your body (wear gloves and a leather jacket and keep your face out of reach) until it ceases to struggle and bite. Such nonviolent body-contact therapy works well for both violent children and puppies. They soon learn that they have nothing to fear about being close to someone or being touched. After this passive wrestling match is over, talk gently to the animal and stroke it soothingly.

The biter who is more amenable to training is the kind who bites out of sheer cussedness. He will nip or bite to get his own way, is selfish, has no manners, and believes that the entire world centers upon him. Such dogs are often the product of overindulgent and overpermissive rearing. When they mature, they assume the number-one position in the home. The best "cure" for a dog who bites the hand that loves it is a dominance fight, with the fight rigged in your favor. With a small dog, wear gloves and a thick jacket. When it snaps or growls, shout "No, bad dog" and seize its muzzle and shoulder scruff in each hand and hold the dog to the ground until it ceases to struggle; in other words until it submits. Another alternative, for larger dogs, too, is to follow the verbal "No, bad dog" with an uppercut to the lower jaw with the palm of your hand. This is a very effective "shock" treatment. If this doesn't prove out, the next step is to use a choke chain and leash. As soon as he growls or snaps, pull up on the leash so that his front feet are off the ground and shake the leash from left to right. This would be like a larger dog giving yours a good shaking. Keep saying "No, bad dog" and make up to him later when he submits and asks forgiveness. You owe it to your dog, and to other people who may be bitten, to be tough with him and maintain the number-one position. You are then in control. Take no chances, and if in doubt, apply a muzzle.

The same holds true for dogs that are overprotective of their territory. You may like this, but the mailman or some innocent visitor or child who gets chased or bitten won't. If you can't control such a dog and make it obey you, you shouldn't have it. For precautions, put up warning signs—"Danger—Biting Dog"— around your property and keep him muzzled when outdoors. Castration will help reduce such territorial-related aggression in some male dogs.

The Car/Bicycle/Jogger Chaser

This behavior problem most likely originates from the dog's need to chase prey. Regular exercise and play (tug of war with an old towel, and chasing a ball) will help reduce this drive. The most effective remedy is a long leash and choke chain. Give the dog plenty of rope to begin to chase, then pull him back sharply with a loud "No, bad dog." If he is obedience-trained, pull him into "heel" and "sit-stay." Another method is to have an ally who acts as jogger, cyclist, or motorist and once the dog starts to chase, he stops, turns and throws a jug of water into the dog's face and shouts "No, bad dog." You repeat this as you pull on the leash to check your dog. As in all corrective training procedures, several repetitions may be needed and would be advisable.

The Unhousebroken

Finally, the dog who suddenly becomes unhousebroken can pose a serious problem and is a common reason for a person's getting rid of a pet. Sometimes there's a medical problem—a bladder or kidney infection or bowel disorder. It's worth having your vet check things out. Lazy owners who won't take their dogs at least four times a day are asking for trouble. Forcing a dog to hold things in could lead to other problems—bladder trouble, constipation—and restricting water, especially in an older dog, could aggravate an existing kidney disorder. The dog has to drink and urinate more to compensate for its disorder.

There are other causes, too, often emotional in origin. Your dog may resent being left alone for extended periods and make this his way of getting back at you. If this is the *when* of the problem, use the appropriate remedies described earlier for the house-wrecker. A holding cage or backyard or patio pen may be the only solution. Be sure to scold your dog verbally and tell him that you don't approve. But don't rub his nose in the mess.

Sometimes male dogs will raise a leg and urinate in the house. This can sometimes be corrected by regular exercise and opportunity to mark his territory outdoors.

Scolding him when he does it is all very well, but the trouble is, you can't always catch him in the act. Take him to each place that he has marked and reprimand him, then take him for a walk and shower him with praise when he performs appropriately. Do this three or four times a day for at least seven to ten days. When in the house, never let him out of your sight, so if he does make a mess, you can catch him at it. Keep him confined in the bathroom, basement, or in a holding pen when you can't watch him all the time and never give him the freedom of the house unsupervised until he is once more housebroken. As a final resort, having your dog neutered may stop him from lifting his leg in the house. It's a better alternative than getting rid of him.

So if you have a problem dog who fits one or more of the above categories, give him a fair trial run at corrective training. A little time, patience, and perseverance can work miracles. Dogs aren't dumb—they are intelligent creatures and amenable to training therapy. After all, it may save his life and at least make life easier for everyone in the home, including your dog.

THE PROBLEM CAT

Cats, in contrast to their cousin, the dog, are generally not much of a nuisance either in the home or for neighbors. They don't bark excessively, chase mailmen, or knock little children over. They come with a built-in instinct to use the litter tray and don't have to be housebroken or taken on long walks. Compared to the average dog, the cat is a paragon of self-contained virtue and self-reliance. But not all cats. Some finish up being destroyed because of some behavior problem that the owner was unable to cope with. Others are simply abandoned to fend for themselves, often a fate worse than a quick, humane death. Both such steps are often quite unnecessary because cats, like dogs, are intelligent creatures and amenable to corrective training. At the very least a cat with a behavior problem deserves some attempt on its owner's part to rectify things, and there are surprisingly a number of corrective measures that can help unite cat and owner once more. How sad it is for the bond of affection to be broken by some undesirable behavior, such as clawing or urinating, when very often the animal isn't wholly responsible and the problem can be easily resolved.

Some owners or particular family members seem to seek an excuse to get rid of their pets, picking on any little quirk as grounds for separation. Others are clearly at their wit's end as to what to do with the beloved pet whose behavior is driving them up the wall. Even if the behavior problems and remedies that I'm going to describe don't fit your particular pet problem, have heart and faith. Some of the corrective behavior measures are appropriate for other problems, too, which could well be of help to you.

The Scratcher and Biter

Cats swipe with their paws and scratch more often than they bite. This behavior problem can have a number of causes. Sometimes the cat is fearful of being held and/or petted. Some may tolerate being petted but will scratch and/or bite if attempts are made to pick them up. Possibly as a kitten it was handled roughly or did not have enough human contact and tender loving care. The cat may appear to crave contact but at the last moment change and hiss, scratch, or run away. There are two logical courses of action to take depending upon the severity of this touch or handling shyness. If the cat will tolerate, and obviously enjoys, being petted but not picked up, best to let things be and live with it. Never try to pick it up. For the more extreme schizoid type that wants to be petted but freaks out at the last moment, grooming with a brush may be an effective substitute and later lead to hand contact. Cats normally groom each other, and to want such petting from a person is quite normal. If the brush substitute fails, more drastic steps may be taken. Forcibly—gently but firmly—seize the scruff of the cat's neck and hold it down, talking to it gently all the while and stroking it along the back with your other hand. As you stroke, gradually release your hold on the back of the cat's neck and eventually it may stop running off and stay to be petted. Several repetitions of this should teach the cat that it has nothing to fear; restraining it by the back of the neck is like forcing it to see that there are no grounds for its paranoia.

Then there is the cat who, when petted, suddenly lashes out for no apparent reason. But the reaction is a defensive reflex and cannot be controlled, because when the cat's stomach is being stroked it is lying prone or on its back. With such a cat one simply avoids stroking it in such places when it is in certain body positions.

Another type of biter often misunderstood is the *love biter*. The cat suddenly seizes your hand or arm without a prior hiss or swipe and may hold on for a few seconds. Such behavior is acceptable if the cat doesn't bite too hard. In fact, with one of my cats, an amusing game evolved from this; if he bit my nose, I would bite his paw! The hard biter who gets carried away should be disciplined with a growling, emphatic "No" and a brisk pat on the nose with the palm or fingers. Don't say "No, Sam" (or whatever his or her name is) because the cat's name should be used as a calling signal and affectionate word while being petted and should not be associated with discipline or punishment.

The Ambusher (or Human Hunter)

The cat who waits behind the door or sofa for someone to walk by and then rushes out to grab or swipe at ankles and legs isn't a psychopath. The cat is suffering from play deprivation, specifically prey chasing and catching. Under the confines of the home, there is no natural outlet for this drive for those cats who don't find a ball of wool a suitable prey substitute. "Therapy" for this cat problem can take a number of directions. First, try stalking and chasing the cat yourself. It may enjoy this, especially early and late in the evening. Remember, when you are playing with your cat and initiate the play, you can set the rules—and that means no clawing or biting hard. A loud "No" and a puff in the cat's face or a flip on the nose is effective communication your cat should have no difficulty in comprehending.

Next, try creating a good play-prey substitute for your cat: a stuffed sock, a catnip mouse, or "cat mobile" (wire and ball to swipe at on a wooden stand). A ball of wool on a string that you can pull can be very satisfying to a cat who would otherwise have no interest in a stationary ball of wool.

For refractory cats, the only solution may be declawing, and this will be considered in relation to the next common feline behavior problem.

The Claw-raker

Many cats are sent to the local animal shelter for adoption or destruction because they claw upholstery, drapes, and carpets. Some owners give up without trying any form of corrective training, while others have tried everything and have given up. Have faith: there are remedies to try. First, train your cat to use a scratching post. You should put two or three up in the house—a two-inch by four-inch vertical board covered with carpeting (or a strip of clawed drapery) plus a flat board angled against the wall, one foot wide and two and a half inches thick covered with similar material. Every time the cat starts to claw in the wrong places, say "No," pick it up and place it in front of the board or post. Make clawing movements with your hands then lift the cat up and coax it to claw. A little catnip tea (catnip soaked in boiling water) rubbed into the material may act as an added incentive. When you aren't around to correct the cat, keep it in a "safe" room (bathroom, kitchen, or basement) with a scratching post for company.

Step two, in cases where more severe discipline is necessary, entails doing all of the above and using a water pistol to squirt your cat once or twice in the face (preceded by a loud "No").

Step three is to trim your cat's front claws way down and to keep them trimmed. It will then do less damage and you can continue to train it to use a homemade scratching post. Trimming a cat's claws takes experience and usually two people and good nail clippers. One person holds the cat and the other squeezes each toe to extrude the claw. Have a dry run first and get used to handling your cat and positioning the claws. Then trim one claw with a quick snip, just in front of the pink "quick" (so it won't hurt or bleed). If all goes well you should soon have all the nails trimmed. A cat, like a child, will learn that having nails trimmed isn't going to hurt. If you are in doubt, ask a friend to help or go to your vet, who will certainly know how.

The final step (other than getting rid of all materials your cat may damage) is to have the front claws of your cat removed surgically by your veterinarian. This is especially needed for those cats who become hysterical when they have their nails clipped and for those who can still rake things badly even after their claws have been trimmed and all prior training has failed.

This operation is done under a general anesthetic and is relatively painless. The cat will be sore for a few days afterward but should heal quickly. You should use shredded paper in the litter box until all the toes are healed because the litter will stick to the toes, dirty the wounds, and cause infection.

Declawed cats rarely if ever develop any direct psychological problems after being declawed. They will still rake and scrape with their front paws and satisfy their need to rake things. Such cats should never be allowed out, though, for without front claws to defend themselves they would be at the mercy of other cats and dogs. All in all, this is a fair and humane alternative to getting rid of your cat.

The Sprayer

The cat who backs up against the wall or furniture and lets out a squirt of urine is marking its territory. Indoors this is unusual and abnormal, outdoors (in its territory) quite normal. When the cat feels insecure it will spray more to make itself feel more "at home." The more its home smells of itself, the stronger will be its sense of place and identity.

Such spraying occurs in two patterns. First, in the maturing cat whose "ego" is developing, it may start to mark the house in various places. Since this behavior is related to sexual maturity and may be triggered by the sex hormones, the best solution is to have the cat neutered. This holds for both male and female cats, but is more common in males. It is such a deeply ingrained behavior that corrective training (or using repellent sprays) rarely if ever works.

The other spraying pattern is caused by some emotional disturbance. A newcomer to the home (another pet or a child) may make the cat feel somewhat left out, and so it compensates by laying its mark down in various places. As though saying, "I live here and this is my place." Such behavior deserves empathy and understanding. Extra attention and affection may be all that the cat needs to feel more a part of the family.

The Unhousebroken Adult

Spraying or simply squatting and urinating or defecating out of the litter box are even more complex and common behavior problems. When a cat suddenly becomes unhousebroken, you should first have it thoroughly examined by your veterinarian. It would be sad to destroy the pet when, in fact, a chronic bladder problem was the cause and could have been cured by appropriate medication.

There are nonmedical reasons, too, for this behavior and once a medical cause has been ruled out, some detective work may be needed. As in the spraying described earlier, a cat may avoid its litter tray because of some emotional problem. Even a subtle change in relationships between two or three cats in the house could lead to one feeling pushed out. This one may then become unhousebroken until the emotional cause is rectified. This is why the owner must do some close observation first before trying corrective training.

Reshaping an unhousebroken cat to use a litter tray can be easy. All that some need is their own extra tray in a new place where they have been "letting go." Others require a larger tray, a different type of litter, or three or four litter trays in various places. Thoroughly deodorizing the soiled areas on the floor first with a chlorophyll-containing agent (*not* Lysol—it is poisonous to cats) may help break the cat's habit of going in those places.

Other cats require more rigorous restrictions. After deodorizing and cleaning the marked area, confine the cat to a holding cage for ten to fourteen days. Provide it with litter box, resting board, or box and blanket. Let it out to exercise and play only under constant supervision. This way the cat will be forced to use its litter tray since it won't mess in the only other place that it has in the cage—its sleeping area.

Although seemingly inhumane, this treatment can break the cat's bad habit of not using its litter tray. One should realize that long after some emotional trauma has passed, the abnormal behavior will persist as an ingrained habit. This has to be broken.

Patience and perseverance with the unhousebroken cat are essential. Even having a rug cleaned, buying new furniture, or moving to a new home can trigger such a change in normal toilet behavior. Give the cat time to readjust emotionally; confining it to a cage with litter tray can be the key to success. Don't forget to take the cat out for frequent but supervised exercise and plenty of petting and grooming, otherwise further emotional problems may develop.

The Plant Eater

This is a common vice in house cats and frequent grounds for "divorce." There are some solutions that can restore the relationship.

The plant eater may need its own supply of fresh grass. Cut some from outdoors (and wash it well), and for the winter grow some indoors for your cat to nibble on as it pleases. As for your own plants, arranging inaccessible shelves and hanging pots is a partial answer. Another is to set mouse traps to snap around the pots if the cat goes near. The idea is to scare but not hurt the cat, so be sure to fix the traps so they will just make a noise. This is also a good remedy for those cats who like to dig into the soil in the pots.

I have found with my own cats that a verbal command "No; down" followed by a couple of squirts from a water pistol will work wonders. The only limitation here is that you have to keep a constant eye on the cat while you are around to catch him at it. If need be, confine the cat to a plantless room while you are out. Only a few "water shock" treatments are needed as a rule.

I hope that if you and your cat share one or more of the above problems you will now have the conviction that a resolution of the problem is not impossible. Like any marriage, there are rough times and one has to work on the relationship when problems arise. For various reasons, some people give up too easily, and this is more so when it comes to people and their pets. I wish more people shared my optimism toward all relationships—with people and other animals. With a little good counsel, solutions can be found for seemingly insurmountable problems.

DON'T GIVE UP!—SOME FURTHER REMEDIES

Here are some more all-too-common pet behavior problems and some possible courses of action. Problem cats, like the food snitcher, the vomiter, the kittenish nurser, the wool chewer, and the nymphomaniac, can be helped. So can the dog who is a stool eater, a "scooter," a yard digger, a paw chewer or is afraid of thunder storms.

Cats first: One of the most annoying traits is their proclivity for jumping up onto the dining table or kitchen counter while food is being prepared or eaten. Since my cats are clean and healthy, I don't mind this. Like many cat owners, I accept the fact that cats enjoy getting up on tables and counters to say "Hi" and to see what you are doing. Sociable cats don't like to be left out of things and, provided they are well mannered, I don't see anything wrong. Some cats, however, don't have the best manners and will, like my greedy Abyssinian, Sam, try to snitch food while you aren't looking. And worse, with particular delicacies, like fish or shrimp, they may even try to grab it off your fork.

Just as one dominant cat will hiss and swipe at another who dares to come close to snitch a bite of its food, so you can mimic cat body language to deter your thief. A quick direct stare, a sharp, loud "No" and "Down," and a hand swipe toward the cat's face or a light tap on the nose—in that sequence—works well. A few cats, instead of just jumping down, will crouch, close their eyes, and remain still. This is the passive-submissive posture a cat may use to try to manipulate you into accepting its presence. Don't give in: Pick the cat up and put it on the floor. A swift cat who has succeeded in grabbing a morsel of food will most likely take off and hide somewhere safe so it can eat in peace. You must corner the cat and take the food away. Never feed the cat on the table or kitchen counter, otherwise you will be training it to expect food, and if not fed, it may become a snitcher. Do look out for the cat who gets into the trash can or bag, especially after chicken bones (which could kill it).

The vomiter, who coughs and gags and throws up, may have been into the garbage, so be sure to keep all attractive but potentially dangerous scraps out of the cat's reach. More usually, the vomiter has a furball to get rid of. In the process of grooming themselves, cats normally swallow a considerable amount of fur and it is natural for them to regurgitate the material that accumulates in their stomachs. Regular grooming, together with a weekly dose of mineral oil or a lubricant laxative and tonic such as Laxatone, which you can obtain from your veterinarian, will help this problem. This behavior "problem" cannot be corrected by training since it is a normal activity. Recurrent vomiting and loss of condition, however, requires veterinary attention.

For some cat owners, the kittenish nurser can be a problem. Whenever they pet the cat, it "regresses" and becomes infantile, drooling, nuzzling, and kneading with the forepaws and sometimes even using its claws as it ecstatically "nurses" against your body. First, try to accept this as normal social behavior. Your adult cat still sees you as a "parent," and this behavior then is not really abnormal. If the cat gets too carried away and starts to claw you, it can be inhibited by disciplining it in the same way as a mother cat would in weaning her kittens: a direct stare, a stern "No," and then either pushing the cat away or tapping her lightly with your "paw" on her nose.

Be consistent in your disciplinary intervention whenever the cat gets too excited and begins to rake you with her claws as she makes alternating nursing pushes with each front paw.

Related to this behavior complex may be the more serious problem of wool chewing, especially in Siamese cats. Too early weaning may underlie both of these problems in some cats. Others may be insecure, bored, or naturally more prone than other cats to regress as adults. Nursing (drooling, sucking, and chomping) may turn into chewing, and sweaters, drapes, and blankets soon get destroyed. Possibly some chemical (e. g., lanolin, natural wool oil) or the soft texture of the material (which is like a mother cat's mammary area) turns on the cat's infantile nursing behavior. In my experience, no amount of corrective training will deter a wool chewer. One must play it safe and remove all items that might be attractive to the cat except her very own blanket. Try to motivate her with toys to chase and retrieve—a toy catnip-filled mouse, and a cat-mobile of balls hanging on a wire or string to swipe at. Declawing and removing teeth will not help one iota. Sometimes, because boredom can be a contributing factor for a single cat, obtaining another kitten companion can work miracles.

Last, but not least, the nymphomaniac. Unlike female dogs, female cats can have recurrent heat cycles over several weeks. Owners who don't realize this often think their cat is hysterical. The aroused queen will call frequently, and with a raucous Siamese, this can make the owner hysterical too. Pacing, rolling, and excessive licking and grooming are additional signs. There is no effective "cure" for such a cat except pregnancy or spaying. The latter is to be advocated since nymphomanic cats may, if not fixed, develop more serious problems: cysts on the ovaries, uterine infections, and mammary gland tumors at a later age.

Now for some other common dog problems that can be easily resolved with a little understanding and patience.

The coprophage, or stool eater, is probably the most distasteful pooch (no pun intended) you could ever meet. Petting such a dog is one thing, but the idea of it kissing you! This behavior in a young puppy is not uncommon. It's part of natural puppy curiosity and they usually grow out of it. In an adult dog it is a bad vice for which there is neither a simple reason nor remedy. In a caged or otherwise confined dog it may be caused by boredom. Regular exercise and play objects, such as a piece of garden hose or a green stick to chew on, help in many cases. Adding a little raw liver to the diet, or some digestive enzymes which you may obtain from a health food store or from your vet, are also supposed to help some dogs. A liberal sprinkling of brewer's yeast in the food can help some cases also. For the "incurable," corrective training is best implemented by keeping the dog on the leash and appropriately inhibiting it with a pull on the choke chain and a sharp "No, bad dog" when he turns around to get at his just-voided stools. Don't correct him until he has had a couple of sniffs first since this is natural and all dogs seem to like to check out what they have just passed.

I often wonder if some dogs who occasionally let loose in the house eat up the mess because they feel guilty. As yet, though, we have no evidence to confirm this possibility!

The scooter is disconcerting to many dog owners. This refers to the dog who drags his posterior over the lawn or carpet. Many people think this means that the dog has worms and so they buy worm medicine. This is not the usual reason and worming the dog is the last thing you should do. Too many people worm a dog for almost any reason, and most times they are way off the mark and can do more harm than good.

The scooter is relieving some irritation around his hind end, and this is a perfectly normal thing for a dog to do. If it is persistent, however, you should take your dog to the vet. The most common reason for scooting is overactive, infected, or blocked anal glands, which require veterinary attention.

The yard (and garden) digger has something in common with the dog who is kept indoors and wrecks the house. He resents being left alone for extended periods and discharges his frustrations and resentment by digging up the yard, lawn, shrubs, etc. Wait in hiding until you can catch him at it, then rush outside banging a pan and shout "No, bad dog." Take him to the hole and show it to him and repeat the harsh words several times. Then fill the hole in. Several repetitions of this (or, alternatively, using a pan of water to throw in his face as water shock therapy) will be needed. Be sure that he has plenty of play objects to keep him busy and don't expect to inhibit your dog from this vice if you never take him out for exercise. Other dogs just enjoy digging for digging's sake and no amount of inhibitory training seems to help. A concrete run or a wire running line to confine him to one area of the yard may be the final answer. You could put down attractive "crazy" paving or bury strips of storm-fence wire mesh in the area to which he is confined. Don't forget that many dogs dig shallow pits to lie in and keep cool in the summer. Be sure that your yarded dog has adequate shade, shelter, and water at all times. If you never take him out for play and exercise, you are unfit to own a dog.

An increasing behavior problem in dogs is paw chewing. A dog with this problem will sit and lick and chew his paws until they are red and raw. Frequently there is a fungal or bacterial infection that requires veterinary treatment. But the dog who chews and chews in spite of all treatment most probably is doing it out of sheer boredom. Yes, some active dogs begin to mutilate themselves if they are cooped up indoors all the time. If you can't take it out regularly for one reason or another, your dog may well be happier in another home where its needs can be better satisfied.

The paw chewer may develop what I call a "sick game" with its owner. Because paw chewing gets the owner's attention, the dog keeps on chewing its paws in order not to lose that attention. Since this is often the case in the chronic paw chewer, it should be ignored when it begins to chew its paws, and then remotivated with active games, long walks, etc.

Last but not least, what can we do for the poor dog who is afraid of thunderstorms? First, if you are afraid, too, you will have to solve your own problem since your fear most likely affects your dog. A change in barometric pressure can affect an animal such that it will soon learn to anticipate a thunderstorm; it may also sense the ionic charge in the air. Nevertheless the flash of lightning and crashing of thunder can be extremely disturbing and analogous to the effect of fireworks, which your dog may also fear.

By far the most effective treatment is to obtain a mild tranquilizer from your vet. Medicate your dog when a storm is predicted (and if it doesn't come, don't worry, since the drug won't be to your dog's detriment anyway). When the storm comes, talk to your dog reassuringly and if you can, make a tape recording of the storm. Play it back to your dog in a few days and flash the living room light on and off occasionally. Try him without the tranquilizer if he can take it. After several storms, tranquilizer treatments, and tape recorder sessions, he should be gradually becoming desensitized. The final phase is to give him half the usual dose of tranquilizer and then none at all. When the storm comes, behave as though nothing unusual is happening. Keep the curtains drawn, a radio on fairly loud as a sound barrier. Don't pay too much attention to your dog or he may become anxious again. Since you presumably groom him regularly, groom him thoroughly and, if possible, get him to play with you later. At all costs avoid comforting actions and tone of voice, and if you are afraid, do your best to hide it!

Even if your pet doesn't have any of the specific problems described above but has some other behavioral disorder, it is quite likely that one or more of the corrective-training procedures I have described would be quite appropriate for your animal.

Above all, when a pet does develop some behavior problem, try to put yourself in the animal's place. Discover *when* your pet acts up and *how* he probably feels. Then you may know *why*, and therein you may discover the seeds of your pet's discontent, which you may have even planted yourself!

III

The Meeting of Minds

7

Games for You and Your Pet

Animals who play together, stay together: The same is true for humans, especially children. Both human and nonhuman animals have clear social preferences, selecting certain individuals to play with—often those most compatible in terms of age, size, and temperament. Playmates indeed.

Play does many things for a child or other young animal. It is not only an outlet for energy and a healthy form of exercise, but also has two important consequences which can lead to a deep understanding and appreciation among animals and between animal and man. Through play, one learns certain social rules—not to play too roughly and not to hurt one's companion. Since the latter may then stop playing, the other animal will soon learn to be more careful and aware of the needs of its companion. Conflicts will be avoided because play is pleasurable and rewarding. In a subtle way, therefore, the pleasure motive underlying play makes animals cooperate, because if they don't, they can't share the enjoyment of playing together. Additionally, play has a bonding function: Animals and people who enjoy playing together soon become attached to each other.

What I am suggesting here is that play is a very important, naturally evolved mechanism whose prime purpose is to bring individuals together in order that they may learn about each other.

Parents who take care of their child's needs but who do not play with them may not only limit their child's development, they may also never establish a close bond of affection with them. Love is expressed not only through caring but also through play—and with it comes good humor, respect, and mutual appreciation. The same is also true for people and their pets. An aged but still playful dog seems much younger and filled with joy and zest for life compared to one of the same age with whom no one has ever played. In _Understanding Your Cat_ I describe how play or the lack of it can foster or destroy the potential bond between cat and owner. It _is_ a self-fulfilling prophecy that cats are distant and aloof towards people if people never play with them when they are kittens.

Some people—overcivilized perhaps, or unsure, ill-informed or overly inhibited—don't seem to be able to play. Have they lost their zest for life, are they too serious and preoccupied to enjoy it, or have they simply forgotten how to play? People from some cultures and from different families are, like old dogs, more playful than others. Play therapy for adults, married couples, and parents and their children is an important and valid contribution to the well-being of many in our society today.

Knowing how to play with your pet, learning the various signals that must be given and the rules of the various games that two different species (man and cat or dog) can enjoy together, can break the "species barrier," as I call it. Once this barrier is broken, man and animal can enjoy each other and so establish a depth of relationship that is rewarding and fulfilling for both.

First, let me describe the various forms that play may take. Self-play is when the animal (or child) plays by itself. A puppy or kitten may chase its tail or appear to "hallucinate" and chase imaginary objects or take flight as though someone were chasing it.

Then there is play with some toy (inanimate-object play), which could be a ball, stick, leaf, or any suitable object. Play actions with such objects include chasing, catching and killing, guarding and hiding—all actions associated with hunting live prey. In developing creative playthings for pets one should keep these behaviors in mind. The toys should not break, splinter, or have sharp edges that may injure the pet. Materials should be nontoxic and of a size large enough so that the pet can't swallow them.

The third category of play is social play, and that means fun and games with a companion—animal or human.

Usually some clear signals are given to communicate playful intentions. Imagine if one dog went up to another and lunged at its throat without any warning. Such an action could be misinterpreted as an attack. It is very important to keep this in mind when teaching young children (and older ones, too) how to behave correctly and communicate with a pet. A child suddenly diving onto a dog companion while the latter is half asleep could be disastrous. Even if the child doesn't get bitten, it could scare the dog, who may eventually avoid much interaction with the child.

People can and should use the same language their pooches use to communicate their intentions to play. These are the rules of the game—or rather, for starting a game. Make eye contact with open eyes and a friendly grin (the dog's equivalent of an "open-mouth play face"). Then pant (the dog's equivalent of laughter, an important play signal) and bow down or squat, facing the dog. He may bark, wag his tail, grin, pant, and even reciprocate your bow and briefly bow in front of you.

That's it. You have said, in dog language, "Let's play." But what and how are you going to play?

First, though, we mustn't leave out the feline members of the family. Cats are more subtle, usually less demonstrative, in signaling their desire and intention to play. They don't bow like dogs but instead flop over onto one side (an invitation to groom or wrestle). Or else they walk by you and suddenly give a couple of frisky steps with the tail arched in an inverted U. This signal means "Chase me." Some cats will also approach you and either paw at your hand or foot or give a play bite and then flop over or frisk away to be chased. Some cats, especially Siamese, like to retrieve things, and they will, like many dogs, place some toy in your lap or at your feet: yet another signal meaning "Let's play!"

You might think that this last signal is one that an animal learns from its owner. This, in fact, may not be true. I have seen dogs, for example, romping together in parks and sometimes one will find a stick. The stick is used as a kind of "social tool," as a facilitator of various play themes. One dog with the stick approaches another and may drop it at the other's feet. This isn't an invitation for the other dog to throw it so the stick can be retrieved. The dog may be inviting

A game of chase-and-retrieve is fun for most dogs and provides them with necessary exercise as well *(H.S.U.S./Clyde Marshall)*.

the other one to take the stick; then the possessor of the stick is chased. Or the stick-giver may *dare* the other dog to take it. A tug of war, with each holding the stick, may follow, or the stick may be ignored as both dogs wrestle and play-fight with each other.

You can learn from your dog and acquire some variations on the stick game theme too! Although many dogs seem to enjoy countless repetitions of throw-the-stick, retrieve it, drop it, throw it again ad nauseam, variations on the theme are fun. When the dog drops it, "dare" him to pick it up again, or grab one end, back off a little and invite him to a tug of war, or to chase you to get the stick.

Tug-of-war games, especially with an old towel, are great fun and few dogs need much coaxing to throw themselves into this game. It's also a good therapeutic regimen for increasing the confidence of a shy or inhibited younger dog or puppy and one of a battery of tests that can be employed to test the strength and confidence of a pup.

There are many commercially available toys that you can purchase for your pet if you don't feel like making some yourself. No matter what or how many toys you buy, though (and the same holds true for children), they are no replacement for social play with you—owner and/or parent! Fluffy toys, catnip-filled "mice," a ball of string or old nylon stocking, a cat-mobile of hanging things to paw at are a must for most cats.

My own two cats especially enjoy playing hide and go seek. Provide them with hiding places—a brown paper shopping bag or cardboard box with a couple of holes in it are perfect—a place to hide in when chased, a place to lie in quietly, waiting to ambush!

Dogs and children also enjoy the hide-and-go-seek game, be it around the house, in the woods, or in the long grass of a meadow. Since most dogs won't "stay" when it's your turn to hide, it's best to have a second person hold the dog until you have gone undercover. (A dog won't give you a count of 100 and then say "Coming, ready or not!")

Cats, dogs, and children also engage in other forms of play in which the different species can involve each other. One is "playing scared." A kitten, for example, will approach a mirror, arch its back and then flee as though terrified, only to repeat the performance again. Kids like the "bogey man" game, and some dogs go berserk with playful glee when you pretend to turn into some kind of

Hide-and-go-seek and catch-me-if-you-can are games that both cats and dogs enjoy *(H.S.U.S./Alice Moulton)*.

intimidating ogre. But be sure you have given the right play signals first. Children and other animals might otherwise be scared or react defensively—with teeth or claws!

I remember as a child really enjoying a rough and tumble wrestle with my dad, especially when he allowed me to get on top and be the number-one tough guy. Animals, too, show this phenomenon: A high-ranking wolf or dog will allow a subordinate all kinds of social freedom during play and permit the underling to attack (playfully) and even assume some dominant postures. Such reversals of social rank during play and the endless repetition and variations in the sequencing of actions all point to the remarkable awareness that we share with our animal kin: that play is play (not serious) and it's fun!

A little more play in the world will make it a better place, and we can all start by getting down on our knees and playing. It is a key to our humanness, and to our animalness as well. Let the spark of play ignite a sense of fellow feeling in all people and their animal kin!

8

What Your Pet Is Trying to Tell You

Do you realize that when a cat rubs its head against you leg it isn't merely cleaning its face but is sending you a message? There are special scent glands around a cat's mouth and on each side of its head just below and in front of its ears; cats mark their close companions (both human and feline) with these glands as a friendly gesture. Dogs pant in order to cool off, since they don't have sweat glands as we do. But panting, as I've mentioned, is also a special social signal. It says, in effect, "I'm ready to play."

Animals communicate more through body language than through sounds. They have a rich and varied repertoire of facial expressions and tail and body postures that communicate mood and intentions. Recognizing these can help you understand what your pet is actually saying, not what you *think* it's saying. A woman recently told me that her dog embarrassed her by crawling woefully on its belly. "People will think I beat him or something," she complained. To break him of this behavior, she had scolded him severely, but this only increased his groveling. When I saw her dog, I gave him a few brief pats and kind words and then ignored what he was doing and told her to do the same. Soon afterward she told me her dog was behaving less like a whipped puppy. All it had been asking for was some small and affectionate recognition.

In another case a woman thought her dog had become psychotic

85

when it nipped her and ripped up the rug. It was simply having a temper tantrum: it was jealous because a young niece was visiting! Another woman wrote to me in despair about her dog, "who acts absolutely crazy the moment my husband comes home from work each night, hiding and trying to bite Jim!" Again, this dog was jealous at having to share its mistress. All she had to do was pat the dog on Jim's arrival and give it some extra attention.

Another commonly misinterpreted signal is a dog's urinating at someone's feet—especially at the feet of a stranger it is greeting. Most people conclude this happens because the dog is excited or frightened, when actually it's an act of friendly submission to the newcomer. Instead of being cross with your dog, pile on the love and attention, and in time he'll outgrow the submissiveness. (And in the meantime, try to keep all greetings safely outside of the house!)

The same misunderstandings occur with cats—perhaps even more so because their body language is even more subtle. I know a sensitive adolescent girl who was upset that her cat would close its eyes and yawn when it was around her. "I'm boring her," she wailed. Actually, the cat was saying "You're okay—and I feel okay. I'm relaxed with you." On the other hand, a cat being tickled on its stomach may suddenly claw at you angrily and run off. No, it's not going crazy; being on its back sometimes triggers a defensive-aggressive reflex, which seems to surprise the cat as much as it does its playful owner.

A cat who suddenly won't use its litter box is not being naughty for no reason. This is usually a sign of some emotional disturbance and a signal to you. Look for some change around the house—a new child? another pet? The cat may be signaling its desire for some love and assurance.

In some instances, it's best to take animal gestures at face value since, like young children, pets are unable to conceal their feelings and intentions. My neighbor's Siamese cat kept bringing things over to her feet. It never occurred to her to accept a simple explanation— her cat wanted her to throw these things so the animal could retrieve them! My neighbor thought that only dogs were retrievers and kept ignoring her cat's invitation to play!

Another common misinterpretation occurs when the owner of either species decides that a sulking pet is reacting to some trans- gression or slight by the owner. Sometimes, indeed, the pet is

Dogs communicate their needs in a variety of ways—we should look and listen carefully *(H.S.U.S./S. & J. Holberg)*.

emotionally depressed—but more often, prolonged sulking results not from being miffed but from being physically sick. Warning: When in doubt, don't play psychiatrist; see your vet.

Basically, all the signals a dog or cat gives are inborn, instinctive. How your pet communicates is pretty well fixed by heredity, but to whom the animal relates depends on its early socialization and emotional attachments. Signals in the animal world serve some specific basic functions. Some are for warning (the low growl of a she-wolf, for instance, sends her cubs into hiding) and for increasing, decreasing, or maintaining certain proximity with others. A dog's growl or a cat's hiss is meant to keep rivals at their social distance. And a silent baring of the teeth and raised back hair or an arched back and fluffed-out tail are meant to be intimidating.

Friendly signals include the purring of cats and the licking of dogs. Also as friendly gestures, both species will nuzzle and push with their heads like nursing infants. Displays of submissiveness in the dog include crouching, tail wagging, the lowering of the head, ears and tail, and the retraction of the lips to form a submissive grin. Paw raising, rolling over, and urination are also submissive gestures. The cat has a less complex repertoire of submissive gestures: It is often seen crouching or approaching like a kitten with hind end raised and tail erect.

Both cat and dog have a specific play-soliciting signal that is also seen during courtship: The dog bows (or lowers the front part of its body so that it seems to be bowing) and the cat rolls on its side. Eye contact is another channel of communication. A direct stare is a threat signal given by both cat and dog, while avoidance of eye contact is usually associated with fear or submission.

Vocal speech is only a small part of the human repertoire of communication. Some experts believe that as much as 80 percent of all human communication is silent—and that most is made with eyes, facial expressions, body postures, and gestures. And animals are acute observers of our body language. Some people interpret their animal's awareness as extrasensory, but it is simply observational learning. My cats know when I'm in a hurry or getting ready to go out; they have learned to read some of my actions and habits.

Most of the time we communicate with our pets using this human body language. In fact, it is primarily because of the close similarity between the silent language of man, cat and dog that all three can

A wolf and a dog bow to each other, signalling their readiness to play—an action or "display" that we can mimic to communicate with our dogs *(M. W. Fox)*.

communicate so well with each other! For example, an uptight person will scratch or adjust hair or clothing; a nervous cat will briefly groom itself; a dog may scratch itself or look over its shoulder. The following listing shows you the body language that is shared by dog, cat, and human.

To assert rank: Humans, dogs, and cats all assume an erect posture and a direct stare. All attempt to look bigger—humans draw themselves up and inflate their chests, cats arch their backs, dogs raise their hackles.

To indicate aggression or pose a threat: Humans, dogs, and cats purse or tense their lips in an aggressive pucker, and humans and dogs snarl and sneer. Humans hunch their shoulders, the hair on the backs of cats and dogs rises. Humans, cats, and dogs lower their heads and stare directly at the object of their emotions.

To indicate submission: Humans, dogs, and cats crouch, lower their bodies, avoid direct eye contact. Humans and dogs often retract their lips in a submissive grin.

To show playful intentions, a friendly greeting: Humans and dogs open their mouths, making a "play-face" or grin; humans and dogs indulge in arm/paw raising and hugging/nuzzling; dogs pant, humans laugh, cats purr. Dogs bow playfully, cats roll onto their backs. Dogs act as though they intend to bite; humans may pretend to strike or cuff gently; cats may bat out with their paws.

Is it possible to use some of this "animal language" on your pet? It's fun to try a Dr. Dolittle on your cat or dog, but beware—a strange Pekingese nearly took off my nose some years ago when I was trying out a canine bow and playful panting! And one evening a friend decided to walk and call like a mountain lion as a demonstration of animal behavior—and one of my cats remained on top of the refrigerator for a full day after witnessing this incongruous change in human behavior.

However, you might get quite a charge out of "playing" with your dog in his own language. On your hands and knees and face to face, "bow" with the forward part of your body, grin and pant, and you'll be surprised by the reaction. At a friend's house the other night their dog became very excited when I entertained it by communicating in dog language rather than human body talk. I kept giving him a canine play signal by bowing my head and shoulders with an open-mouthed, smiling, panting face. The dog, normally shy, started to play as never before. My eight-year-old son, Wylie, tried it and flushed with excitement. "You're right, dad, it really works!" he exclaimed. "It's the first time that I ever talked to a dog in his own way!"

9

The Beasts and the Children: What Kids Should Know for Blessings All Around

I can't imagine childhood without a pet, whether it's gerbil, gold-fish, or kitten. As a boy, I took in strays and lovingly cared for them, and I vividly remember the setters and terriers and sheepdogs who were my playmates and friends. A dog, sometimes more than parents and peers, can give a child that deep sense of companionship and unconditional love that we all need sometime in our lives.

Child psychologists have recently demonstrated the effectiveness of using pets in therapy to draw out withdrawn and emotionally disturbed children. In a comparable way, a pet can play a vital role in the life of an average child. Every youngster sometimes feels unloved or insecure—and a pet is always accepting, is generally consistent in its behavior and can give a child a sense of relating and belonging.

In return, it's important for a child to understand a pet's body language, emotions, and needs, so that the creature is seen as less of a play object and more of a companion-animal, with its own rights and values. I believe that the child who is allowed to treat an animal like a toy, to be discarded for another with more promise (or less work), will have exploitative, superficial relationships with people, too. By truly caring for a pet, a child develops a sense of responsibility that carries into all social relationships—even marriage and parenthood.

But before getting a pet for your child, make sure that *you* want it, too. Though many children and adults may dream of a Lassie who can do everything just right without training, there's no such animal. And neither is there justice nor common sense in foisting a pet on a child and saying, as many parents do, "Now remember, he's all yours—and your responsibility. Leave me out of it." The fact is that you *must* be involved. The sharing of responsibility and concern for a pet will create a closer relationship with your child. One father told me that he had felt increasingly distant from his adolescent son—until the boy got a puppy for his birthday. Father and son then had something to share, for "the old man" knew a good deal about dog training.

If a child is very young, you're better off postponing bringing in a pet. Most children before the age of three tend to treat animals like stuffed toys and think nothing of picking Puppy up by a leg or grabbing Kitty by the tail. These little ones will poke, prod, and tease an animal in the same way they'll poke at an electric socket or reach for the knobs on a stove—just to see what happens. Unfortunately, this detached curiosity is potentially sadistic when it's applied to living creatures. I remember bringing home a sick little pup from the laboratory, and my children, then three and six, nearly pulled it in half, each demanding "my turn to pet Suzie." I had to step in to save the terrified puppy, and I immediately laid down ground rules. Many dogs and cats seem to understand about tiny tots and will tolerate a good deal of abuse from them, but others are less accepting and patient. Constant vigilance and supervision are necessary.

What if the pet is already in the family before the child is born? Then you must remember that your dog or cat may become jealous of the newcomer—yes, "sibling rivalry"! Somehow, despite the demands of a new baby, you'll have to give extra time and attention to your pet so that it doesn't feel rejected.

Kittens, gerbils, rabbits, mice, and similar pets are good for children age three or more, but I personally would wait until the child is eight or nine before buying a puppy. This is because there is a lot more to caring for a dog than simple feeding and cleaning. A child must have the maturity to assume such responsibilities as exercising and training the dog.

Preparations for a pet's joining the family should be made before

Young children should be supervised when around your pet. Not all dogs and cats are as gentle and understanding as this dog *(H.S.U.S./Jeff Greiner)*.

Children should be taught how to hold, care for, and understand their pets—and to respect their pet's rights *(H.S.U.S.)*.

its arrival. Have your child think about a place for the pet—a safe corner of its own, where it can sleep (or hide) and be alone if it chooses. Together, examine the toys that are lying about and that could injure a puppy or kitten if chewed or swallowed. Explain to children that they must be consistent in their behavior toward the pet—always gentle and firm, loving and understanding. Point out that regularity in feeding, walks, play, and other routines is as essential for the pet as is their own regularity in going to bed, having meals, and so on. In fact, some children who object to parental discipline begin to comprehend and accept it once they see that a pet, too, must be supervised and disciplined for its own safety and for the welfare of others.

Set down a few basic rules of health for the young pet owner. Hands must always be washed after cleaning out the pet's cage or after playing with the kitten or puppy—especially before mealtime. And the animal should not be kissed on the mouth.

Though it's certainly tempting (and makes a pretty picture), the new pet should not be allowed to sleep in the same bed with your child. Youngsters may feel they are comforting a small animal this way, but they are also making it dependent. Also, a small animal may fall off the bed during the night and hurt itself. When the animal is older and this habit persists, the child stands a chance of getting ringworm, fleas, mange, tics, and other infestations from his or her bedmate.

I am frequently asked what kind of dog one should get for a child. *Don't* get a fragile toy or miniature breed. An active little terrier, however, is fun and tough. A mongrel is ideal. Children don't need purebred dogs, and a mongrel is usually reliably adaptive and even tempered.

Once you get your child to accept the responsibility of caring for the pet, there are many valuable lessons to be learned. Children see that a pet needs a good balanced diet—which is not necessarily comprised of its favorite food. And some of a child's anxieties about earlier toilet training are quickly relived and relieved with the job of housebreaking a pet.

As the animal matures, another important learning experience occurs as a child makes honest and realistic observations about sexuality. The need of a tomcat to roam, the menstruallike discharge of a bitch in heat, and even the forthright action of two dogs copulating in the yard are natural events that children can comprehend.

Caring for a sick pet is another experience that encourages empathy and compassion. The death of a pet, however, is a harder thing to face. But in our culture, where we are so often psychologically and intellectually ill-equipped to face death, I believe that a pet's death must be seen by parents as an opportunity to deal with a difficult subject in a sensitive and meaningful way. Parents may well find that the loss of a pet draws the family closer together, not only in mourning but in appreciating everyone and everything here and now.

Just as you must protect a pet from a child, it's of utmost importance that you teach children what to do if *they* are threatened or attacked—and, better yet, how to avoid these catastrophes. If threatened by a roughhousing animal, they should keep an eye on the dog but not stare. Staring could be interpreted as a challenge. Above all, a child should not run but should walk very slowly, acting nonchalant and relaxed as though the dog wasn't there.

The snarling dog with bared teeth who seems serious about attacking is something else. A child should try to get to safety by backing away immediately and slowly and seeking refuge in a store or house or familiar parked car (perhaps even scramble on top of the car). If grown-ups are around, ask—or *call*—for help. And if a bite of scratch *should* occur, tell your child to report the injury to you right away—since wounds should be immediately and thoroughly cleaned and the animal observed for possible rabies.

If your child doesn't have a pet, I urge you to give him or her one. Encourage your children's involvement by presenting them with handbooks and articles on care and behavior and exposing them to films and television programs on the subject. And learn and enjoy *with* them. If a good relationship with animals is developed in childhood, a reverence for all life will be carried on into adulthood.

10

Calculating Cats?
Devious Dogs?
Why Does a Pet Misbehave?

One of my kittens, Sam, an Abyssinian, used to climb to the top of the dresser in my bedroom and deliberately knock things to the floor, creating a loud clatter that was calculated to make me get up and feed him. Even more dramatic, when my friend disciplines his poodle, the dog will often run into the bedroom and defecate, usually on his master's pillow. Misbehavior? Of course. Why? Sheer cussedness.

This is only one of the basic reasons why a pet or child will misbehave. By "misbehave," I mean do something of which the owner or parent doesn't approve. The idea as to what is socially acceptable behavior is based on the values, needs, and wants of the owner or parent. It's generally a one-sided judgmental situation. And unless it's improved through empathy and understanding, we have unhappy pets or children.

How often, for instance, the normal and natural frustration of young animals and children is misinterpreted as misbehavior! A young dog confined indoors all day is like a child being forced to study behind a desk twelve hours a day. Both are bound to "misbehave."

The second reason for a cat or dog misbehaving is that its natural traits or tendencies don't fit in with the owner's expectations. Certain traits are so ingrained and instinctive that the animal

96

literally cannot be inhibited from expressing them. For example, it's difficult—sometimes even impossible—to stop a tomcat from spraying furniture, a dog from barking excessively, or a pet from stealing food from the table. All these are natural beahvior. Or to put it another way—natural "misbehavior," to be filed uner the heading of animal-human incompatibility.

It's also natural for a puppy or kitten to explore, to investigate, occasionally to upset or destroy things, very much like a child. This natural, inquisitive drive should not be inhibited because through it an animal or child learns about its environment (far better simply to remove breakable things).

Another reason for misbehavior—and this one is in many ways similar to sheer cussedness—is to attract attention. Here the pet engages in some form of social manipulation in order to get its own way. Recently a woman wrote to me about her cocker spaniel, who gives her painful nips when she engages in conversation with others. The dog is simply trying to get attention. An even more unusual case was reported a few years ago by two German veterinarians. They treated a dachshund who for a period of time had a gastrointestinal disturbance. A medicine resembling paragoric was given to the animal, and eventually the owners were manipulated into feeding the dog a teaspoonful of medicine every evening to make it settle down. The dog would bark and solicit their attention until it received its medication—and their pats and reassurances as well. A possible interpretation was that the pet was addicted to the morphinelike drug—but certainly the attention it received was an important factor.

This kind of manipulation also occurs when a dog who is left alone for extended periods attacks the draperies, sofa, chairs and carpet. This could be a combination of attention seeking and sheer cussedness. You should remember that punishing a dog is a form of attention. Some pets, I am sure, have an almost sadomasochistic relationship with their owners; even painful discipline can be rewarding, because at that time the pet is receiving the undivided attention of its beloved master.

The fourth and the most important reason why a pet will misbehave is that it's *emotionally disturbed.* Jealousy is a common emotional disturbance. Just as the birth of a sibling can trigger jealousy in a child, so can the introduction of a new pet or a baby into the household upset a pet. The jealous reaction can range from sulking, refusing to eat and temper tantrums, to destroying furniture, nipping the owner and occasionally biting the newcomer. One of the most bizarre cases reported is of a dog who had seizures whenever its owners engaged in a marital squabble. As soon as they left the room, however, the little dog would immediately "recover" and get up and follow them!

Disturbed cats show a more limited range of symptoms than dogs. The most common "misbehavior" here is for a cat to stop using the litter tray and to urinate or defecate in all parts of the house. This behavior can persist long after the triggering emotional situation has passed. For example, a new cat in the neighborhood that is more aggressive and dominant could cause this sort of behavior in your pet. Also, be on the alert for a changed relationship in the home, such as the introduction of a newcomer, the death of a companion pet, or the death or absence of an owner.

One of the reasons I am turned off by the usual dog-training manuals and cat-care books is that they simply do not give the owners sufficient information about the emotional needs of their pets. Discipline and training alone are not enough for a child or a pet. Both need a much deeper level of empathy and understanding.

Before you discipline a pet for misbehaving, make an effort to understand what the animal is trying to communicate by his action. For instance, chastising a dog that has run away—out of frustration or sheer cussedness—is no way to get him to stay with you. After you've chased a dog halfway around the neighborhood, bring it home to a reward rather than a punishment—even though it's difficult to keep your cool at such times.

Similarly, though declawing is one solution to the cat who ruins furniture, trimming the claws is a more humane alternative. Also, consider remotivating the animal by giving it something else to do—a toy to chase and pounce on, for instance. Or furnish it with an actual clawing board made from a strip of carpet with a little catnip underneath.

The key to "training" a pet who misbehaves is patience. Cats don't respond naturally to a pack leader; they're solitary animals, so there's a natural biological limitation to the degree of attachment and allegiance they'll give. This also means there's a limit to how much a cat can be "trained." (Some varieties of cat are more dependent than others, however. This is true of the Siamese cat, and for this reason the Siamese is the most trainable. You can easily teach a Siamese cat to walk on a leash and to retrieve things.)

Johnny Carson said recently that he has little time for cats because they just sit on top of the television and don't do tricks like a dog. Many people with this attitude do favor a pet that is more outwardly directed and easily trained as dogs are. And the more trainable and well trained the less disobedience and misbehavior problems you're likely to have when the animal matures. This is very important to remember about physically powerful dogs, and I emphasize that anybody who has a large dog, such as a German shepherd, a Saint Bernard or a Doberman pinscher, should be a licensed and competent handler. This could certainly help reduce the number of bites and even deaths that occur because of canine sociopaths and delinquents.

Dogs have been domesticated for thousands of years, and in this process of domestication they have been made more dependent on humans for their well-being. However, if a puppy is raised with very little human contact, it will not become emotionally bonded to people. And being less dependent and socialized, it will be much harder to train than a puppy that's had a great deal of human contact during its formative weeks. This is one problem you'll have with a dog that has been in a kennel, a pet store, or a humane shelter for a prolonged period. Having been around other dogs instead of people, he'll be a misbehaver—less concerned with pleasing his owner and more inclined to puppy-pleasing high jinks. The key to trainability is this emotional link between animal dependence and human affection—not intelligence per se.

When you are communicating with your pet, keep your commands simple. Cats and dogs have a capacity to learn a few words, such as *no, down, sit,* and so on, but a volley of words can be confusing. Eye contact between animal and human is also important. A direct stare is a way of asserting dominance, so before you give a command to your pet, establish eye contact and then give a verbal command. With a dog this can be facilitated in various situations by a choke chain and a long leash. Cats can also be trained to the leash but, except for the Siamese, it's not usual. One way of controlling a cat over a distance is to use a water pistol. Establish eye contact, speak your command—*down* or *no*—and then give your cat a quick squirt with the pistol.

In training pets, always be consistent in giving reward or punishment. Inconsistency leads to confusion, and under such circumstances the pet may, like a child, begin to manipulate, to solicit your attention and affection in order to get away with its mischief. I remember one elderly couple who had a large German shepherd that would absolutely not respond to a single command unless it felt like it. This dog was literally number one in the household and was in many ways reminiscent of a human adolescent delinquent. If the owner is not seen as the "pack leader," such pets easily take over a home. And because of overpermissive and overindulgent rearing, they can become psychopathic to the extent that they have no social inhibitions and will bite people to get their own way.

You should remember that as young male dogs mature, they go through an adolescent crisis before they reach full sexual maturity; during this period they will often test the owner. If they can intimidate the owner and get the upper hand psychologically, they may well win this fight for dominance. From then on it's a quick road downhill. The relationship has been turned upside down; the dog rules the household, and everyone has to cater to its every whim.

It's been said by some authorities that it's impossible to discipline a cat, that a cat has no conscience. I would say that training is possible for a cat, and that a cat *does* have a sense of right and wrong. What a cat doesn't have is the same manner of expressing that conscience. We all know immediately that our dog has done something wrong when we come home and—instead of greeting us—it slinks under the table. A cat won't behave this way, unless it was terrified by the plant, pot, or lamp that it upset during your absence.

Children have to grow and learn what they can or cannot do in society. They learn this from their parents and from their peers at school. The experiences that a puppy or a kitten has with its owner and its littermates is no less critical in influencing later social behavior. The way to instill self-control in children and pets alike is to raise them in an atmosphere of unconditional affection and consistent discipline.

11

Your Pet's Emotional Problems (and Their Solutions) Start with You

"Now, remember," Mrs. Browne said, "she doesn't drink plain water—just a mixture of equal parts of milk and boiled water that's cooled until it's just warm enough. Don't forget to heat up her snacks, too: her tummy always gets upset if the food comes right out of the fridge. And here's her favorite pillow, blanket and stuffed toy. She won't go anywhere without her furry puppy doll, and she won't go to sleep without it."

No. I wasn't being given charge of someone's spoiled child: it was a small dachshund that was being left for a couple of weeks at the veterinary hospital's boarding kennels. As a student in England, I was used to such doting dog owners and their pampered pets. Yet it never seemed quite real. Could a dog be so human—or neurotic (the difference is often not very clear-cut!)—that it wouldn't drink plain water, eat regular dog food or settle in its clean and warm kennel without all these accouterments?

However much I wondered, though, I had to follow the owner's instructions to the letter, or we might have had a sick or even a dead dog on our hands. A pet as overpampered as this one could lapse into an acute depression when separated from its owner and its familiar routine and toys.

"Do take care of him—he's all I've got in the world, and he does think he's human." This was another familiar parting remark from

101

anxious owners. When a cat or dog is owned by a lonely person, is kept indoors most of the time and has contact with very few people or other animals, it may well become conditioned to being treated like a human being—or, more specifically, like a spoiled child. Indulging an animal's every whim and raising it without consistent discipline can create an overhumanized and overdependent pet. And it is the overdependent pet that is most prone to develop neurotic patterns of behavior.

Basically, a neurotic reaction in man or animal is a sometimes harmful behavior designed to get another's attention. Because of some underlying emotional insecurity (such as fear of rejection) or overdependence (created in the pet by the owner), the normal need for affection and security becomes abnormally intensified. A need to dominate others—whether it's an animal's need to control its master or a person's need to control other people—may also stem from this neurotic insecurity. In both man and animal excessively solicitous "infantile" behavior (for food or for affection and indulgence) as well as attention-seeking aches and pains and even more drastic psychosomatic reactions are all associated neurotic reactions.

Neurotic symptoms may be expressed in various ways. Mrs. Browne's dachshund was a real candidate for separation depression and associated anxiety reactions. Worse, such a pet may be nonresponsive or even hyper-aggressive to a well-meaning caretaker unless it's treated as if it were a child. Such anxious behavior in itself may not be neurotic—for instance, it's not unnatural for a dog to be afraid of strangers or new situations—but if it will respond only when effusively spoiled, then it is a neurotic brat.

Also, when a humanized animal refuses to interact with its own kind—when it's consistently fearful, aggressive, or indifferent— then something is surely amiss. Again, some of this may be due to an understandable unfamiliarity with strange dogs. Real neurotic reactions, however, are more enduring, compulsive, and sometimes intensified when the parent/owner is present.

Such socially maladjusted pets also may have the added problem of being sexually attached to people, and will not breed with their own kind. And if bred (under considerable restraint, a not uncommon breeders' practice of "enforced rape"), they may refuse to nurse their offspring. Another problem of the overindulged animal occurs when the pet considers itself number one in the household and feels socially superior to its owner: the result is an animal very difficult to live with. And the pet who is top dog in a household will relate to outsiders with the same assertive I-want-it-my-way attitude. To the unfortunate professional trying to groom or examine the animal, the result can be bites and scratches. I remember trying to examine a pooch's slightly inflamed eye. My kind words and coaxing were to no avail; the dog growled, snapped at me, and literally started to chew up its master in a terrifying frenzy. Without a complaint or reprimand, the owner allowed this to continue until the neurotically spoiled dog had vented its frustration.

I should add that canine delinquents that are allowed to become number one in the house are not always neurotic. Some simply have such cool and confident personalities that they are what I call top dogs. The neurotics are those who overreact with frenzied anger or fearful hysteria when they're challenged or even gently restrained.

Even parent/owners who are not particularly overpermissive can be caught up in a neurotic bind with their animals. For instance, hypochondriacal pets often have hypochondriacal owners, and nervous, high-strung owners will often have nervous, high-strung animals. As to whose symptoms came first, the answer is not so easy, since the neurotic reactions of one person or pet often occur in relationship with those of another, thus producing an ongoing cycle.

Cats and dogs, like children, are adept at manipulating others so that they can get their own way. A dog may sulk or even have a temper tantrum or seizure when reprimanded by its owner. When a pet (or child) overreacts in such ways, it causes guilt in the parent/owner; appeasement follows and the pet or child wins. The "neurotic" behavior is thus reinforced or rewarded. A colleague told me that when she mildly reprimanded one of her very dependent dogs, who was playing too roughly with a pup, it became so upset that it actually had an epileptic fit.

Another good example of social manipulation is the dog who, when disciplined, later urinates or defecates in the house, even on the bed, out of spite. It is simply getting back at its owner. A more common way in which cats and dogs manipulate their owners is in their eating habits. Some pets will test their owners to see how far they can go in getting the kinds of food they like best. They'll go on a hunger strike, refusing to eat the sensible balanced diet that the vet recommends. (A word of caution, though: A sick pet may go off its regular eating schedule, so don't put down *all* eating problems as neurotic. If in doubt, consult your veterinarian.)

I have seen obese creatures who have manipulated humans to the point where the owner honestly believed that "poochy" or "pussy" would eat only the best steak or the finest tuna. Those shortsighted owners have shortened the lives of the pets they love, as such diets are simply not adequate. Resisting the meows or pawings of a begging pet is admittedly difficult—but give in and the pet's manipulative behavior is rewarded. Is this desire for food always neurotic behavior on the pet's part? Not at first but, if continually indulged, yes. Once an animal becomes overdependent, any change in routine can trigger neurotic reactions: a pet may suddenly have diarrhea, forsake its previous toilet training, go into a depression or rage or even develop lameness and pretend to have a bad leg.

Dogs—so much more emotionally dependent than aloof cats—are especially adept at developing emotional disorders and/or psychosomatic problems when they're frustrated. These neurotic reactions can be motivated by any number of situations in which the pet feels ignored—say, the appearance of a "rival," such as a new baby or potential suitor, or a new professional or social project that receives the "undue" attention of the pet's owner. I know a poodle who whines excessively and scratches itself furiously whenever there are visitors in the home, breaking out in what looks like hives. Another pooch all but mutilates its front paws when ignored. And if the owner fusses sympathetically over such quirks in his pet, the neurotic pattern will simply be perpetuated.

Sometimes a person may unwittingly reinforce neurotic behavior out of ignorance. A good example was one woman who heard her dog's stomach grumbling and immediately fed him. Eventually, the dog was eating all day, simply because the owner had misinterpreted normal digestive sounds in the abdomen as a sign of hunger. The more she fed the dog, the more these sounds were heard, and the fatter the dog became.

Or consider this very common occurrence: An owner accidentally steps on her pet, who starts yelping and whining. To comfort him, she gives him a small snack. With one such simple association, a quick-witted animal will soon be yelping or limping again for more food and attention.

Because many people don't really know what is best for their pet, quack pet profiteers can easily stir up guilt and prey on consumers with pitches that imply "if you don't give our product to your pet, then you obviously don't love it." Fear of loss, like the fear of rejection, also affects a human's attitude toward a pet. A person's desire to keep the affections or attentions of another often leads him or her to lavish great attention on that person or object, and the smothering concern of an owner must make life difficult for many pets. The practical solution, as always, is to learn about pet care and behavior by reading good magazine articles and books (such as mine, naturally)—and, if in doubt, to call on your veterinarian for help.

We have seen how a doting owner can make a pet neurotic, as well as how a manipulative pet can make an owner feel guilty, anxious, and neurotic in return. But in addition to such relationships there are people who have deep-seated fears or phobias about animals. A traumatic experience in childhood—a dog bite, for example, followed by a series of painful antirabies injections—can create such problems. A fear of snakes may become so irrational that a person literally can't enjoy a walk in the country. Then there is a general fear of animals—zoophobia—where an individual has unfounded fears of being injured by an animal or catching some animal disease. More specific neurotic reactions, such as ailurophobia (the fear of cats), may be reinforced by the reactions of animals toward that person. Often a cat will immediately pick out and approach the one person in a group who is terrified of felines. Similarly, people who fear dogs will often "spook" a dog to behave aggressively or fearfully.

Persons suffering from such animal phobias should seek help, and today there are effective desensitizing programs being conducted by trained and experienced clinical psychologists to help people overcome their general or specific neurotic reactions towards animals.

Basically, animals can make us more responsible, humane and understanding. But neurotic problems do arise in man's relationship with animals and when they do, the burden is on man to be a responsible human and allow his pet to be a healthy animal.

12

Like Master, Like Dog: How People Affect Their Pets (and Vice Versa)

I received a phone call recently from a lady who was most upset about her old collie dog. She had been attacked and almost killed by an intruder in her home, and the dog slept through it all! She said that she didn't like her dog after this episode and thought, because it was the same breed as Lassie, that it naturally should have leaped to her rescue and saved her.

Her tone of voice over the telephone told me more about why her dog didn't do anything to help her than her verbal commentary did. I asked her if she was a self-confident, assured, assertive, and outgoing person: She confirmed this long-distance diagnosis. It was, however, harder for her to accept that because she had this kind of personality the dog probably thought that she could take good care of herself and so didn't bother to come to her rescue.

That an owner's personality will make many dogs less protective of their owners—or, conversely, more protective—is a very significant fact. It is something to consider, therefore, when one decides to buy a particular breed of dog. Its breed temperament and your personality could interact to produce a canine personality that you may not like, or find very difficult to handle. More of this later: Back to Ms. X and her sleeping collie.

She was particularly irate that her dog, of the same breed as TV's Lassie, hadn't instinctively known what to do. I pointed out that while some dogs do display amazing insight sometimes, and can rescue or protect people from danger without prior training, training *is* important. Thousands of hours are spent training Lassie to do tricks (and don't forget the trick camera art, too); Ms. X had never given her dog any training.

The lesson here is: Don't let your expectations get a hold over you. You will usually wind up disappointed in others (people and dogs) if they don't live up to your expectations. Ms. X doesn't like her old dog anymore, but to a great extent she is to blame.

Another important consideration, other than the owner's temperament in this case, is the effect of socialization. Most dogs are raised to be friendly toward people. While they may bark at someone knocking at the door, they are taught to be friendly to strangers who are in the house. Such a socialization training process early in life can act as a strong inhibitor of aggressive/defensive reactions toward strangers who may have criminal intentions. Training a dog to attack can be extremely difficult because of this socialization training, causing conflict and confusion in the dog's mind.

Then, the very next day, I had a long phone conversation with another dog owner. Ironically her dog, a young male Irish wolfhound, was becoming so aggressive toward visitors that very few friends came by anymore.

She sounded like a nervous and very apprehensive person and I asked her if she was somewhat shy and anxious. This she confirmed with obvious surprise at my apparent clairvoyance.

I assured her that I was not all that psychic but rather it was her dog's protective behavior that was a reflection of her general timidity. The "treatment" suggested was a course of assertiveness training for the owner and dog obedience school for both of them.

The old adage "like master, like dog" clearly needs some modification after considering the above two anecdotes. What seems to happen so often in relationships between two people or between the dog and its master is that one partner acquires certain traits that are supportive of the other's needs and deficiencies—like the shy woman who is attracted to an assertive and self-confident spouse, or the timid owner whose personality creates a supportive but complementary opposite in his or her dog.

This intriguing phenomenon warrants serious consideration and has great practical significance when you are deciding what breed of dog you want to buy. Understanding that your dog behaves in certain ways *because* of you will help you cope with and find some solutions for undesirable traits in your pooch.

First, sex differences are significant for people and dogs. A male dog is often more possessive and protective with a female owner than with a male owner.

More than one unmarried girl has written to me describing the all-too-common problem: a male dog who won't let a male human visitor into the apartment, or who keeps trying to get between his mistress and her male visitor.

A female dog might be less jealous and more understanding; hopefully she would not compete with her mistress for the boyfriend's attention. But this does sometimes happen. For example, when I take my two dogs for a walk in the park, Tiny, the female, is quite aggressive toward female dogs when they approach me. But when my wife takes them out, Tiny is far less possessive of her and is consequently less challenging toward strange female dogs!

Relationships become even more complicated when the sexuality of both of my dogs comes into play. Tiny wants to greet and play with male dogs, but her male dog companion, Benji, is just too jealous and possessive to allow this. Conversely, Tiny doesn't like Benji to be friendly toward female dogs.

Such reactions, likes and dislikes in our canine companions, are, therefore, not restricted to their own kind. Being socialized to people, they will similarly show specific likes and dislikes toward people which are influenced by the sex and temperament of their owners.

One single woman had a female golden retriever who was suspicious of all male humans but got along fine with other women. Dogs raised exclusively with women, irrespective of their sex, will generally be more wary of men. This can get the woman owner into difficulties, especially if her dog is a male—since the element of sexual jealousy and rivalry toward a human male may erupt. If she has a very protective breed like a German Shepherd (or an individual dog of any breed that is defensive), and that dog is a male, she may be compounding her problems even more. And worse still if she is of a shy or anxious personality type. An outgoing, self-assured young woman should have fewer problems, but, irrespective of her personality, it would be a good idea to attend obedience classes with the dog in order to establish control over it.

Don't forget, too, that the dog's jealousy over attentions being given to a male human visitor, to one's husband, or even to one's child, needs understanding and sensitive handling. Reassure the pet that it is still loved and isn't being pushed out. More than one dog has barred entry into the bedroom when it felt put out by its mistress's apparent neglect of its emotional needs!

Unsure, apprehensive, and socially shy men and women can affect their dogs in many ways. Most predictable is a "transference" to the pet, such that the dog becomes wary and shy of strangers. This will usually occur if the dog is timid by nature. A more assured and self-confident owner would be more likely to bring out the gregarious streak in a naturally timid pet.

The former personality type could produce a very defensive and protective dog if its lineage was outgoing and assertive. "I just can't control my dog" is a common complaint from such people. Obedience school is the answer.

A confident extrovert will often have an outgoing pooch—a real match of temperaments—just as the more anxious personality type may have a nervous and unstable dog. But the domineering kind of person can produce another canine personality—an obsequious, servile type.

Some breeders of Scottish terriers told me of some pups they imported from England. Great little Scotties they were, but a total flop in the show ring. Any time anyone looked at them, they would cower—not fearfully but submissively—and wag their tails obsequiously. Their breeder in England unknowingly altered the basic temperament of these outgoing, feisty little terriers because his personality was extroverted and boisterously (but not unkindly) assertive.

Just as a shy or anxious person should think twice before owning a powerful dog that may become overprotective, so a boisterous and domineering extrovert would do better without an overly sensitive and passive kind of dog. An ideal "middle-range" breed of dog would be a golden retriever, but be warned: A shepherd or Doberman may be overprotective *or* sensitive and passive by nature. We can, therefore, make few generalizations about breeds. Although the various breeds do have certain temperament characteristics, individual differences within breeds are considerable. We should, therefore, consider temperament on an individual basis for both man (of various races) and dogs (of various breeds).

I recently received a long letter from a distraught parent. Her dog was so protective of the children that she couldn't let the neighbor's children play with hers until the dog was locked up indoors. This is important to bear in mind. If your dog is protective by nature, do be careful: It could mistakenly protect one of your children (or you) and do serious injury to a playmate (or house guest). The dog can't be held responsible. To be responsible pet owners we do have to be on the alert and aware of these idiosyncrasies in our dogs' personalities.

It is really remarkable how dogs attune themselves to the personalities of their owners. Even sudden emotional changes in the owner can affect some dogs. Recently in the park I met a woman who was obviously afraid of my dog, Tiny (who was on the leash). Her behavior made her large male dog bristle all over and, snarling, it attacked Tiny as we walked by. Previously we had met this dog alone in the park and he and Tiny had played together.

What this all seems to boil down to is that people who have problems handling their dogs may have some personality problem themselves. An unsure or nervous horseman will probably make his horse stumble or balk at a low fence. Similarly, our emotions and personality have a direct and often profound effect on our dogs.

It is also just as important to remember that in certain places, as in certain social contexts, your dog may be difficult to control or behave in a way you don't like. In a car with a nervous driver-owner, the dog may become hyperactive, behave fearfully or show clear signs of apprehension which may look superficially like carsickness. Also your dog when on the leash may behave quite differently than when off the leash. Attached to you (by the leash) it may be more defensive or aggressive. Your dog may be more protective in the backyard when you are there with him, but quite relaxed in the house, then protective again when there is a stranger visiting. Keep these differences and individual idiosyncrasies in mind—it will make life easier (and safer) for all people.

Understanding our pets can be like a mirror to understanding ourselves. If we don't like what we see, we should not always blame our pets (or our children) but rather attempt to discover what in ourselves might have contributed to the problem. We are not, of course, always to blame, but irrespective of blame is the element of responsibility. The more we understand, the more responsible we may be and closer to fulfilling the ancient injunction "Know thyself."

13

Family Feuds or Household Harmony: Your Pet's Feelings Make a Difference

Many pet problems don't just involve the pet alone. Relationships between members of the family and the pet, and among each other as well, can create emotional and behavioral problems in the pet. Sometimes the owner is quite unaware of the fact that his or her relationship with another member of the family, or with a visitor, can have profound effects on the pet. Just as a cat or dog is affected by tensions between two family members, so, too, are children. Being aware of this can make us better parents as well as more sensitive and empathetic pet owners. By understanding a pet's (or child's) disobedience or jealousy, and restraining the urge to punish, you replace crass ignorance with responsible compassion. This will also help the pet (or child) become less of a pest (or brat), as the case may be, for when they are understood, harmony and togetherness are just around the corner—as distinct from resentment, hurt feelings, and the continued tension of unresolved conflicts.

One owner consulted me over the following problem. He loved his dog, but wanted to kill it because his wife kept using the dog as a barrier between the two of them. She would ignore the husband and shower affection on the dog whenever the two had an argument. The husband became so jealous of the dog that he felt the only way to reach his wife was to get rid of it.

The husband was lucky that the dog did not become aggressive toward him. Another example will suffice to lay the groundwork for a more detailed analysis of some of the common types of pet and family disharmony. Again, a husband problem. This time it was a happy marriage but, as the dog matured (a male, as is often the case) he became more and more attached to the wife, possessive of her, and resentful of the husband's paying attention to the wife. The dog would try to stay between the two and as close to his mistress as possible. The couple allowed this pattern to develop and never intervened to correct the dog until the inevitable happened. One evening the husband was not allowed into the bedroom. The dog lay on the bed, next to the man's wife, snarling menacingly.

Unconscious Wishes

This case history brings out the first important point to consider. The wife, in the second case, could have had an unconscious wish to make the husband jealous or to break up the marital relationship, which was unapparent (at least to the husband if not to the dog!). In the first case, the wife's intentions were quite obvious to the husband but, in my experience, not necessarily obvious to the wife. This being the case in many instances, the wife cannot understand why her husband kicks the dog or pushed it roughly off the bed. She may come to see her husband as being mean to the dog and not know why he is acting that way in the first place. Unconsciously she may want him to abuse the dog so that she then has grounds for an argument. Pity the poor dog in such awful real-life family triangles. Pity also the child who may be drawn into similar pair-bond tensions.

Unconscious or deliberate as the case may be, one family member may create a monster out of a loving and trustworthy pet in order to get back at someone else in the family. I often wonder if this is why such people sometimes show so much guilt and remorse when the "monster" has to be destroyed.

A former student of mine used to leave her dog at her mother's while she attended the university, which was conveniently near her mother's house. The dog, a friendly mutt, would chew up her mother's furniture and drapes but *never* did this when she left the dog alone at her own house. The dog even "attacked" some of her own furniture that she had given to her mother. I asked the young woman if she didn't get along with her mother. With some surprise she replied, "No, I don't like her and I resent her control over me." The dog was aware of this tension and of his mistress's dislike for the mother, was consequently unhappy being left there, and "got back" at the mother by wrecking her home. The mother was always kind and patient with the dog; a pity she wasn't that way with her daughter. My analysis was confirmed a few weeks later. The dog attacked the unfortunate mother, but inflicted no serious injury. Obviously the only hope for a resolution was for the daughter to clear up her feelings of resentment toward her loving but overly controlling mother, or "cop out" and never see her or leave the dog there again.

Jealous Lover

Interestingly, it is more common for a male dog to become overattached to the wife and act like a jealous lover toward the husband than for a female dog to become "bonded" to her master and resent his mate. This may be because a mature male dog is constantly sexually potent (and arousable), while a female only has two brief seasons in the year. A bitch is more likely to be a jealous lover when she is in heat than for the remaining ten months of the year, but there are exceptions. Another possibility is that the human female produces a body odor that is more attractive to a male dog than a man's odor is to a female dog. Dogs certainly can and do recognize the difference between human male and female.

The bedroom scenario described earlier is one form this jealousy may take. A more subtle form is the dog's ignoring the affection and attention of the husband and resenting any form of discipline. Such reactions are not confined to married couples. Singles find that "swinging" together can be disrupted by a jealous lover pooch: He wants to swing, too, and strategically between the couple at that. I have had countless phone calls and letters on this problem. "What can I do—my dog won't let my boyfriend touch me," or, "Help, I've got this great girl but I can't get near her because of her dog, whom she insists on taking just everywhere with her—and I mean everywhere!"

For the lover or husband to have it out with the dog and establish his dominance and rights is easier said than done. It not only takes courage and knowledge (reading *Understanding Your Dog* will help) but acceptance by the wife or girlfriend. She may unconsciously like things the way they are or she may not even recognize that there *is* a problem in the first place since she doesn't get those cold stares and occasional snarls from the dog directed at *her*. So talk it out with the lady first and then work things out with the dog. I've discussed before how to establish your dominance over a dog and it would be needlessly repetitive to spell it out here. You will not succeed, though, if your female partner does not support you in spirit and action.

Top Dog, Bottom Dog

It is not unusual in marital relationships for the dog, male or female, to ignore the wife and to dote on the husband. Usually this is not because of a sexual attachment to the master but rather because he is seen by the dog as the pack leader. The dog focuses all its attention, respect, and affection on its "lord and master." The wife, who is regarded as subordinate to the master, is virtually ignored, even though she may be the one who grooms, feeds, and exercises it. The husband who doesn't lift a finger to care for the dog may sometimes get the brunt of his wife's jealousy. Unconsciously the husband may encourage this to the point that the wife becomes subordinate to the dog (in the dog's eyes) and may be threatened, bitten, and physically dominated by the dog. I know of one case where the wife was actually killed, and another who divorced her husband after the dog held her at bay all day behind the sofa. Funny as this may seem to some, it is one of the sicker games where pet and family therapy is needed. The veterinarian should be alert to these possibilities and whenever possible suggest a family therapist consultation.

What to do in such cases is obvious. The husband, as pack/family leader, must discipline the dog to obey and respect his wife, and he should support the wife whenever she attempts to control the dog. How similar this is to a parent siding with one child against the spouse as in *The Diary of a Mad Housewife*!

The "Sick" Game

A dog, just like a child, can develop a variety of behavioral and psychosomatic disorders because of family problems. Two forms are to be looked out for. The most common one is the dog who acts sick or behaves in such a way as to monopolize the attention of one or more members of the family. The dog may learn that chewing its paws or tail, scratching excessively, vomiting or defecating, or even acting lame on one leg, hooks the concerned owner's attention. Medication is given, frequent trips to the vet, etc. The best cure is simply to ignore the dog for a while. Very often the problem quickly resolves itself.

The second and more subtle sick game is sometimes harder to spot. It is result of conflict between two family members which affects the dog (or child) and leads to the development of a variety of problems. One dog, for example, used to have a mild seizure every time the wife and husband had a fight. Eventually the dog began to have seizures whenever he saw the wife carrying a suitcase, which she would often grab and pack after a heated spat with her spouse! Other symptoms include flight, hiding, anxiety, guilt, and possibly psychosomatic problems such as diarrhea, urticaria and other skin problems, asthmaticlike coughing attacks, and becoming unhousebroken. The remedy here is to resolve family feuds, and, when an argument does erupt, assure the dog (or child) that he or she isn't to blame, is still loved by all, etc.

Sibling Rivalry

It is quite common for a pooch who has been the one and only "child" of a young couple to react like a jealous sibling when the couple have a real child. One must be alert to this potential problem. It is best resolved by giving the pet extra attention, affection, and reassurance until it accepts the new family member as a companion. Another related problem can develop later: *overprotective parent*.

Some dogs, particularly female and especially those of the more protective guard-dog variety, may become so attached to the child that they will act protectively and not allow neighborhood children to play or to engage in rough-and-tumble and tag games. Be on the look out for this. Since this protective instinct is difficult to inhibit, if attempts to instruct the dog that all is okay do not work, then it would be advisable to keep the dog appropriately restrained and under constant supervision. Sometimes a dog will challenge the father or mother or sister or brother who disciplines or bullies another child of the family to whom the dog feels particularly protective. Often this is not without good reason and the dog may be instigating an appropriate intervention which clearly demonstrates that dogs do have a moral sense of what is right and wrong, fair and unfair. This is not unlike a wolf's intervening to stop one wolf in the pack from bullying another.

Redirected Aggression

As in the wolf pack, chicken flock, and human family, a tiff between two individuals may result in the subordinate, or loser, venting his anger on a third, weaker and more subordinate individual—like the husband who was put down at work by the boss and who comes home and takes it out on his wife, the children, or the dog. Sometimes a child may redirect his or her aggression after being disciplined by a parent, and take it out on the dog or a younger sibling. Perhaps this is what happened recently in California: A pit bull terrier (unfortunately bred to fight by a sick segment of humanity that enjoys illegal dog fights) was locked indoors. The master didn't want it outdoors with him. A while later he went indoors and found that the dog had killed their young child—a good example of redirected aggression in a frustrated dog.

I haven't said much about cats mainly because they are more independent and less pack/family-oriented than dogs. Consequently they are more self-reliant and somewhat aloof from such family-related problems. They are not immune, however. Any sudden change in behavior in a cat—fear, hiding, eating less food, spraying in the house, or suddenly becoming unhousebroken—should be looked at in relation to any possible change in the family structure. The birth of a child, the addition of a new cat or other pet, could bring on one or more of these problems.

Loss of a Family Member

Cats, and especially dogs, can be affected adversely when one member of the family dies or when one goes on vacation or away to school. Depression, refusal to eat food, and even death may follow. Don't forget that the loss of a companion animal could cause such acute emotional reactions in the remaining pet.

What our pets seem to be telling us in the above categories of family-related problems is that they aren't dumb things requiring only feeding, exercise, and an occasional play period. They are (or should be) an integral part of the family. They are sensitive to subtle and often unconscious emotional influences and relationships within the family. They differ in fewer ways than they are similar to us—especially to our children. In the final analysis, a family pet is kin, and its rights and needs should be understood and respected by all members of the "family of man."

14

"Incredible Psychic Feats": The Super Senses of Pets

Recently there was a newspaper account of a dog's "incredible psychic feat." Shep was on vacation with her owners when, on the day they were due to return home, a distance of some 350 miles by road, she was nowhere to be found. Like many young couples who enjoy a trailer-camp vacation, this couple had taken their pet with them, and Shep had been allowed complete freedom to roam around the adjacent woods and hills. They spent hours searching and calling and finally, heartbroken, they had to leave, but first they gave the local police a full description of their pet.

Vacations often end this way—a pet roams too far and gets lost, or perhaps is caught in a trap, shot, or led far astray by joining up with one or more local dogs.

Several weeks later, however, a very weary, footsore, and emaciated Shep appeared at her owners' door, wagging her tail and barking furiously. Overjoyed and amazed, her owners called the local newspaper, and Shep's incredible psychic feat hit the headlines.

This was not a psychic feat, however. Many animals have the ability to find their way home using their well-developed senses or supersenses, rather than some mystical extrasensory power.

Salmon returning from the oceans are able to find their way precisely to the river where they were hatched, even to the exact region of the river where they were born. They are able to do this because of their acute sense of smell: They essentially become imprinted with the distinct chemical qualities of their natal waters.

No less remarkable is the homing ability of pigeons. When released many miles from their home coop, they are able to navigate their way home using the sun as a compass. Research has shown that racing pigeons have an exquisitely accurate sense of time. Some part of their brains (an internal "clock") is set to accord with the position of the sun over their coop—to local time, therefore. Any distance from their coop the sun will be in a slightly different position, the greater the distance, the greater will be the difference between home time and the time (or position of the sun) where they are released. Some pigeons are better at computing fine differences than others and thus make excellent short-distance racers. In addition to this sun-time sense, some pigeons are able to use geomagnetic influences to navigate as well. Other birds, especially those that migrate thousands of miles, such as ducks, geese, swifts, and swallows, use celestial as well as solar cues to navigate by: Yes, incredibly they can read stars and keep on course!

Shep, I believe, found her way home by using the sun as a directional guide, and a number of other pets, both dogs and cats, have made similar incredible journeys home. This seems to be a natural ability in many wild animals. One wolf we released from captivity in Alaska with other members of a pack decided itself to come back home—it returned some 250 miles to its cage across a bleak and difficult Arctic terrain.

Why more lost pets don't eventually find their way home can be attributed to many factors, including their being shot, trapped, run over, killed by a larger animal, or taken in and cared for by people. Domestication and generations of dependence on man may well have affected the homing mechanism. Experiments with animals have shown that after a while, they are able to reset their internal clocks to a different local time when moved to a new locale. If Shep had reset her clock to local time at the vacation site, she may have never made it home, unless she had two clocks. Migrating birds may have two such internal clocks, one being activated around the time when they are ready to migrate, which is set to accord with the local time of their destination.

Such incredible abilities have been researched in cats. Test animals were transported in boxes through which they could not see and were set free in the center of a complex maze. Older cats tended to emerge from the maze exits that faced the direction of their homes!

The sense of smell is superbly developed in dogs, and, compared to man's, it is a supersense. Apparently the dog can detect molecules of odor that a biochemist's spectrometer cannot even pick up. A trained dog can find a few pennies buried a foot under the ground or pick out even small amounts of marijuana from a mountain of mail. Dogs can also be trained to locate buried mines and other booby traps. Dogs have no difficulty discriminating between the scents of identical twins. More certain than fingerprint identification, each person, to a dog, has a different odor. Much like bats can "see" in sound, dogs "see" with their noses. Without such a supersense, it is hard for human beings to enter into this dimension, but at least one should be understanding and patient as one's dog stops to sniff everything when out for a walk!

Until recently, there was some mystery about the fact that Saint Bernard rescue dogs in the Alps could easily locate a person buried several feet under the snow, but not a corpse. Some interpreted this as being due to a cold body emitting less odor, while others thought there might be some psychic factor involved. Recently, however, researchers have shown that the dog's nose contains highly sensitive infrared detectors, and only warm bodies would produce an infrared (heat) cue.

It would seem, therefore, that the more we know about the nervous system, the better we can explain so-called psychic or extrasensory phenomena in terms of physiology. Two well-known examples of this are the sonar abilities of bats and dolphins. Bats and dolphins have evolved radarlike systems with which they can locate solid objects in front of them. They emit a pulse of sounds and pick up the echo that bounces back if there is a solid object in front of them. This ability is so highly developed in bats that they can literally see in sound: They are able, from the echo, to decipher the actual shape of the object in front of them. Their ears have become their eyes.

Not all the incredible feats of animals can be explained physiologically. One day, though, when we know more about how the brain and senses function, what is regarded today as psychic and extrasensory may be understood.

Take, for example, the story of an English dog who suddenly appeared at his master's side in a trench in France during World War I. Somehow the dog had crossed the English Channel (probably on a boat carrying troops) in order to be with its master. How can this, and other less dramatic but no less amazing feats of psi-trailing be explained?

Psi (or psychic-) trailing is quite different from navigating back to home base. It refers to an animal's ability to locate its owners who, for example, have moved some distance away (say to a new home) and had to leave the pet behind.

Dr. J. B. Rhine, former director of the parapsychology laboratory at Duke University, followed up on a number of alleged cases of psi-trailing in pets. A high percentage could not be verified because the animals in question had no identifying cue such as a collar, tag, scar, or body anomaly. I was once taken in by a Siamese cat who appeared at the door very emaciated but answering when I called its name—"Igor." When allowed in, he settled in his usual favorite spot on the sofa. Igor had been missing for several days and it was good to have him home. Then, a few more days later, the *real* Igor returned home! Both cats looked and behaved exactly alike, although the one that wasn't the real Igor did seem a little shy; but this we had attributed to the stress that he must have experienced while lost.

Many cases like this Dr. Rhine discredited; although admittedly some could have been authentic, proof was lacking. Even so, those animals that were able to find their owners by psi-trailing did so by using some sensory mechanism that remains to be understood. Journeys of anywhere from 300 to over 1,000 miles have been reported. What cues could the animal use to find its owner in some distant place it has never been before? Odor can be ruled out, since the people traveled either by air, rail, or road. The best explanation is that people, and probably all living things, for that matter, emit a kind of energy resembling that of a radio transmitter. The pet is able to pick up on this, some part of its nervous system serving like a radio receiver. This isn't too remarkable considering the sonar abilities of bats and dolphins.

Many dogs and cats have made incredible journeys to locate their families after being lost, or given away, when their owners have moved hundreds of miles. How do they "psi-trail"? *(H.S.U.S./ Ronald McNees).*

Research with people in the USSR, with one group sending a message telepathically and another receiving, had not only demonstrated this as a possibility beyond the law of chance, but has also shown that distance is critical. Receivers very close to the transmitters may have greater difficulties in picking up a message than one, say, 100 or 500 miles away. It is also thought that psychic waves (and the aura of the body may be related to this kind of energy) are emitted in pulses. One of the limitations in a lot of research on human telepathy is that people try to send messages—ideas or words or picture symbols. It might be far more affective to transmit an emotion or feeling. This would certainly be within the realm of an animal's communication. I wonder in how many cases of psi-trailing there isn't a child who really misses its pet (and vice versa) so the child acts as an emotional transmitter which its pet is able to receive and, even more incredibly, to home in on. Such directional sensitivity has not, so far as I am aware, been researched in man.

This psi-trailing may be simply one aspect of a more general phenomenon of psychic integration in highly social animals.

A missionary in Africa once reported how incredible it was that one of the tribal chiefs, a Bushman, pointed to the horizon and said that a sick man was coming. Two days later, a sick tribesman came into camp from exactly the direction the old man had pointed.

Australian aborigines, until the impact of Western religion and culture destroyed their way of life, practiced a trance state known as dream time. In this state of altered consciousness, which the subject practiced for an entire lifetime and which was handed down from one generation to the next, a man possessed clairvoyance. He could, for example, "see" a kangaroo behind a hill. The Sydney police used to use these aborigines as trackers. Given some possession of an escaped convict or lost explorer, they could follow the person's trail even if it was months old.

Are such "primitive" people closer to animals in their extrasensory abilities? Perhaps such abilities are dormant in us since we spend our lives constantly being busy, involved in trivia and distracted and anesthetized by pleasurable forms of entertainment. Time for reflection and inner contemplation is limited. Even so, we hardly need to develop these abilities since we have telephones, telegrams, letters, and soon will have video-phones. to close the distance between friends and loved ones so that we may share feelings as well as information.

Most people at least once in their lives have some form of psychic experience; often when relaxed and doing nothing, an intense feeling about someone else may occur out of the blue. Frequently dismissed as imagining, a letter a few days later or a phone call that night often verifies the experience not as imagined but as real.

The key to this, I believe, is empathy, and underlying it is attachment and love. Pets that are well attached and loved may therefore be able to empathize with their owners.

A friend of mine told me of a sudden change in behavior in her cat and dog one morning. Both behaved in an obviously disturbed way as though they had been shocked or terrified by something. Later in the day she learned that her mother, who doted on the animals, had died that morning.

Another often reported example is of the effects of the death of a pet on a surviving companion animal. At the time of euthanasia at the veterinary hospital, the pet at home may show a marked change in behavior indicative of emotional stress.

Some other recent reports of pets' psychic abilities add further weight to the naturalness of this phenomenon. An urgent letter from a lady in Philadelphia concerned her Siamese cat, who had been calling loudly for three weeks after the loss of their companion, a twelve-year-old German shepherd. This problem was easily rectified, but the background to the case is interesting. Three weeks earlier the shepherd was rushed to the veterinary hospital with an acute gastric torsion. Surgery was performed immediately, but the dog died on the operating table at 10:00 A.M. The vet called an hour later to tell the lady of the unfortunate loss but she already knew something tragic must have happened. The cat had started its frantic and painful calling at ten that morning.

A well-documented example of an as yet unexplained psychic ability in animals was related to me by a veterinarian from Cleveland. His wife always knew when to set the table for dinner because their dog would "tell" her when her husband was on the way home. The dog would become restless and wait by the door. The wife arranged to note the exact time when the dog reacted in this way and the husband kept a record of the time as he left his hospital. They discovered that the dog's behavior coincided with the doctor closing the door of his surgery. He always walked home from there, about fifteen minutes' distance from home; he left at no specific time because evening surgery could finish at any time. But the dog knew just when he left the hospital. Could he "feel" or "see" his master coming home? Perhaps such abilities are more commonplace in animals than we may think, and the possibility remains open that many species, wild and tame, may be interconnected somehow in this way.

A psychiatrist friend told me of his next-door neighbors in the Bronx who moved across the city to Queens. My friend took their dog, since they could not take him to the new apartment with them. But the dog ran off after they left, and a few days later his owners found him on the street where they lived in Queens, looking for them.

Their dog had never been there before. How he crossed the city and located them amongst all those millions of people, busy streets, and thousands of buildings boggles the human mind. The answer is perhaps elusive in its simplicity. Those who love have a connection, a link that transcends the physical, and possibly the mortal, framework of everyday reality, as we understand reality to be. We and all life may well be interconnected in a spiritual/psychic way in much the same pattern as we are spatially and temporarily in the material world. We are therefore perhaps dealing with a psychophysical field continuum. Our science, culture, and minds, however, only appreciate and understand the physical side of this *gestalt* of reality. Those who are concerned about pollution in the physical world might also reflect on the potential pollutants of destructive thoughts and feelings in the psychic realm!

We know little about these various phenomena in animals and human beings. I contend that there is nothing psychic or mystically extrasensory in these abilities, but rather they are part of the incredibly complex and fascinating dimension that unifies all things that are sensitive and capable of empathy and love. As Teilhard de Chardin, the great Jesuit philosopher observed, "The earth was made round so that it may be encircled by love."

Our pets are part of this circle, as presumably are other wild animals with their own companions. Little wonder then that psi-phenomena occur. But one wonders still . . . !

IV

In Sickness and in Health

15

Your Pet's First Days

For those who plan to get a new puppy or kitten, here are some basic first procedures to follow in buying one and bringing it into the home. Knowing the right procedures will greatly reduce the chances of ending up with a problem pet—or worse, a kitten or puppy that you really don't want to keep anymore because it is constantly ill, has a bad temperament, or hasn't adapted to its new home.

Before you even contemplate obtaining a new kitten or puppy, be sure to check up on local ordinances and on your lease if you are a renter. Some landlords don't allow dogs or even cats. Many local authorities enforce a leash law, require you to buy a license for your dog and have it vaccinated annually against rabies. So give city hall a call to determine what you must do to comply with any ordinances and when.

First, if you desire a purebred cat or dog, find a local breeder, visit their place and have a close look at the mother, and if possible the father, of the kitten or puppy you might buy. Parents and offspring should be friendly and in good health, and the breeder's facilities should be clean and tidy. Timid or aggressive animal parents could mean that the pup or kitten you buy would be like them. One of the worst cases I recall was of a woman who had a friend buy her a Doberman puppy from a local breeder. The owner herself never saw the parents but she decided to visit the breeder a year later because her dog was "crazy"—hyperactive, emotionally unstable, and unpredictable. What did she find but a very timid mother and an unmanageable and aggressive father. One should avoid buying a purebred pup or kitten without seeing one or both parents first.

If you do not want a purebred pet and would prefer a mixed breed instead, which is likely to be a very robust and even tempered animal, the best place to get one is from the local animal shelter. There's less need, I believe, in seeing the parents (and in fact, very often no one knows who the father is anyway). This is because, as a consequence of the genetic "mix," many of the potentially undesirable traits that surface through inbreeding in purebred animals are buried through "mongrelization." (This is called *hybrid vigor*.)

The better animal shelters will be able to give you an idea how big your pet will grow up to be. They should also insist that you return later to have the pet you decide to adopt neutered.

In selecting a kitten or puppy, be sure that it looks healthy and that its eyes and nose are free from any discharge. The animal should be bright-eyed, alert, and responsive to you. Puppies naturally tend to be somewhat "pot-bellied." This is not a sign of worms, but most pups do have worms anyway and should be checked for these internal parasites, which can stunt the animal's growth and sometimes cause serious health problems (see chapter 20 for further details and also for the shots your new pet should be given).

One really essential point that is often overlooked when obtaining a pet is to note carefully exactly what kind of food the kitten or puppy has been weaned on to. It's no use writing down "a tablespoon of canned food four times a day plus dry meal available all the time." You *must* note down the actual brand, because a change in brand could cause digestive upsets and worse, your new pet might refuse to eat it. The cardinal rule is to endeavor to minimize the amount of stress a pup or kitten is likely to be exposed to during its first few days in its new home. Any sudden change in diet would add to the stress of being separated from littermates and mother and having to adapt to very unfamiliar surroundings.

Ideally you should not get a kitten or puppy that is in the process of being weaned. Wait until it is over this stressful transition and only take it home when it is fully weaned. Then it will be independent of its mother for food—but it will still need its mother and littermates for companionship, warmth, affection, and play. Being deprived of all of this, the young kitten or puppy will naturally show some distress, so one must be understanding when the new pet cries and searches through the home. This is where the owner steps in and acts as a parent-substitute. Plenty of tender loving care should be prescribed during these critical first few days. Children should be instructed to be quiet, nor to run about the house—this could scare the pet and it might even get stepped upon—and to leave the animal alone *at all times* when it is eating and sleeping.

Sometimes an older pup or young dog will insist on raising its leg against the furniture for a few days. Try to ignore this behavior since it is a reflection of the dog's insecurity. Once he's settled down and feels at home, such behavior usually disappears.

The first night home can be the most difficult. Be prepared for at least one and possibly more sleep-broken nights. It's a good idea to get your new pet on a Friday or first day of a vacation for this reason. Puppies will howl and whine when left alone for the first time. If you give up and bring the pup into bed with you, you are likely to let him condition you into allowing him to sleep with you every night. So if you don't intend this in the first place, be firm and keep the pup in his sleeping place. This could be in the corner of the bedroom, but better still in the basement or kitchen. A warm "nest box"—a cardboard box with an old towel or blanket inside, plus a ticking clock or radio turned on at low volume for company—should suffice. I like to put an old unwashed sweater or T-shirt in the nest box. This way the animal gets attached to the owner's odor and will quickly find comfort in the surrogate company provided by the owner-odored garment. It is also a good idea to leave a low-watt light on for the first few nights.

If it's a puppy, keep it corralled in one corner with plenty of newspaper on the floor. Expect some mess to clean up each morning until your pup is housebroken.

A kitten should have a similar nest box set up but won't need paper on the floor. Nearly all kittens will instinctively use a litter tray if it is easy to get to. Best way is simply to place the kitten in the tray once every hour until it does something. From then on, it's plain sailing.

Because puppies and kittens receive some immunity from diseases by way of their mothers' milk, there's no need to rush a freshly weaned new pet to the vet's for a thorough checkup. No reason, that is, unless you are buying a purebred animal and the breeder or salesperson won't give you a 100 percent money-back refund unless you have the animal examined at once by a veterinarian. The animal you buy should check out healthy and free from any inherited birth defects. Some purebreeds need to be examined at a later age for such problems as hip dysplasia. I for one would demand a guarantee that the pup is free of all such defects and that if it is defective, I should be able to keep the pup (if I wished) and have the money back that I paid for it to defray future medical expenses. If prospective owners don't play tough like this, unethical breeders and pet tradespeople will continue to sell poor-quality animals,

A puppy or kitten ideally should not be allowed out until it has received protective vaccines against infectious diseases that it could contract from other animals *(H.S.U.S./Lennart B. Anderson).*

many of which will be unable to enjoy a normal healthy life as well as being an unwelcome burden to their owners.

Because the passive immunity from the mother lasts only a short while, and because its immunity may not be very strong anyway, it is essential to keep a new pup or kitten away from other animals that could be carrying an infectious disease. This means you must not take your pup outdoors (except in the backyard) until ten to fourteen days after it has been taken to the veterinarian and has received its first protective vaccinations.

Ideally, one should adopt a pup at around six weeks and a kitten at eight weeks and take it to the veterinarian for the first time a week later, after it has settled down in the new home. (But if in doubt about your pet's health at any time before this, take it to the vet at once.) Take along a stool sample at the same time to be checked for worms.

As to locating a good veterinarian, ask any of your neighbors who have pets, and if that fails, call the local humane society or check out the Yellow Pages for one near you. Arrange an appointment if possible to avoid clinic hours, since it isn't advisable to sit in the waiting room with other people and their sick pets because your kitten or puppy would be exposed to potential infection.

Because there are many hazards for a young animal in the house, check out the following: Remove or cover (under a carpet) any electrical extension cords that might be bitten; close all floor-level cupboards and drawers that contain household chemicals; open and close all doors slowly and walk carefully to avoid injuring the little animal.

As soon as your new pet comes home, let it explore the house. Follow it around just in case it gets into trouble or mischief. The more it is able to explore, the more likely it is to feel at home and settle down quickly. While a kitten can be allowed a free run of the house or apartment, a puppy must be kept in a fairly confined area until it is housebroken.

Don't try forcing the pet to eat as soon as it arrives. Excitement, disorientation, and apprehension may well make it uninterested in food until it has had a few hours in its new surroundings. Attune yourself to its rhythms. It is more likely to want to eat after it has been asleep for a while. Keep showing it where its food and water are located so that it will quickly learn to get a drink or a bite to eat whenever it needs to. After waking up or eating, a kitten or pup is ready for play and attention. Plenty of time should be allotted for play, grooming, and general petting and cuddling.

I like the idea of getting not one but two kittens, and many dog owners say that they have never done better than when they got two pups and raised them together. This is worth thinking about. Two animals can satisfy certain of each other's needs much more easily than most people could, especially when an owner must leave a pet alone at night or during the day. In addition, they will provide owners much enjoyment when they do their own thing together, such as play-fighting, reciprocal grooming, and playing hide and seek or tug of war. Owners who want more dependent and essentially "humanized" pets had best not get two, however, but stick to one instead.

Finally, before you go out and get your new pet, be sure that you know and will uphold your pet's basic rights. It is the responsibility of every pet owner to understand and respect these four basic rights of cats and dogs:

> —the right to a complete and balanced diet that will keep it in top condition at all ages
>
> —the right to regular health checkups, protective vaccinations, and proper veterinary attention when it is sick
>
> —the right to humane understanding of its psychological and emotional needs
>
> —the right to have a community-conscious owner who is aware of the social responsibilities of keeping a pet

16

Feeding Your Pet Right: What Looks Good to You May Not Be Good for Him

There are many myths about what we should and should not feed our pets. Some of these old wives' tales aren't harmful, but others could mean disaster for your animal. Cats love fish, dogs love bones . . . these are common assumptions. But the truth is that an all-fish diet could kill a cat and the wrong kind of bone has caused the untimely end of many a dog.

Some people believe that a meat diet makes dogs more agressive, although there is no evidence for or against this. On the other hand, shepherds in England once believed that meat would "soften" their hardworking sheepdogs—and fed them an all-cereal diet so deficient in protein that the dogs aged rapidly and developed a debilitating disease known as canine pellagra, or black tongue.

Of late, a new myth has evolved, based on the anthropomorphic thinking of pet owners and advertising executives. It goes something like this: If you really love your pet, you should give it the very best, and what seems best to humans is a nice-smelling, attractive product that looks just like human food. But the fact is that cats and dogs are basically carnivores and need a very different diet from ours. Even the best-fed cats like to go out and hunt, and dogs on the most extravagant diets can't resist picking through garbage cans. Wild cats eat insects, birds, lizards, and small rodents, and wild dogs will eat all these things plus carrion—the remains of dead animals.

135

True, you'd hardly want to open up a can of such food for your pet today. But the point is that "human-type" pet foods are aimed more at snaring pet owners than at nurturing their animals. A commercial diet that looks unappetizing to you may really be best for your pet.

It's obviously important to know if you're providing your animal with a balanced diet. A balanced diet is one that contains the right amounts of fat, carbohydrates, protein, vitamins, minerals, and trace elements necessary for growth and maintenance. An improper diet can cause just as many serious problems for animals as it does for people—it can lead to retarded growth in a young animal; low milk production in a lactating mother, and poor prenatal development while she is pregnant: skin diseases; obesity; and kidney and/or heart complications in later life. These are just a few of the problems that a veterinarian sees, primarily because people will not be sensible about what they feed their pets.

There are three important guidelines to remember in feeding your pet:

(1) Don't indulge its preferences or pleading, or you'll have a finicky, spoiled eater. Though it may go on a brief hunger strike, a pet will eventually eat, so don't give in by dishing up the special fare it wants. Don't let the pet train you—*you* train your pet.

(2) Don't feed your pet human-type foods. Synthetic foods that look unappetizing to you are generally better for your animal. If they're soundly balanced, that's what counts! Remember that it's ultimately detrimental to your pet's health and longevity if you feed it like a child and ply it with tidbits from the table.

(3) Start out right. Beginning in infancy, raise your pet on a set diet, one scientifically balanced and approved by your veterinarian. Food preferences are developed early in life: by establishing healthy tastes in a kitten or puppy, you'll be guiding it toward good health as an adult.

What to feed your pet: Of primary importance are a food's palatability and its attractiveness to your pet, and of course its completeness as a balanced ration. If your pet doesn't seem to like his dry chow, add moisture to make it more appealing—or add gravy and a few table scraps.

But don't think of your pet as human and pity it because it eats the same thing every day: Domestic animals will thrive on the same food day in and day out. Unlike omnivorous humans who enjoy a wide range of tastes and textures, animals do not need variety: in fact, they may find sudden changes in their diet extremely disturbing. A little variety—high-quality table scraps in small amounts and a little fresh grass, especially for cats kept indoors all the time—may be appreciated. The rule is to be consistent, and if you have to change the diet (because of sickness, increasing age, pregnancy or whatever), consult your veterinarian.

Pet foods should contain the following basic nutrients, in these percentages, based on the food's wet weight (this information is given on most petfood cans—and if it is not, switch to a label that lists the contents):

Adult cats need: water, 70 percent; protein, 14 percent; fat, 10 percent; carbohydrates, 5 percent; and a small percentage of ash and calcium.

Adult dogs need: water, 75 percent; protein 6 percent; fat, 1.4 percent; carbohydrates, 17 percent; ash, 0.3 percent; calcium, 0.3 percent.

The protein for both dogs and cats must be of high quality—meat or liver. If it's protein of low quality and made of connective tissue such as lungs, it will ultimately be poorly utilized in the animal's system.

Some foods should have a label warning that "this food is not a complete diet for your pet." But not all food companies are so straightforward (some would have you believe, for instance, that an all-meat diet is good for your cat or dog), and it is up to you as a responsible owner to check on just what your pet is getting.

Note that a cat needs more protein and fat than a dog: therefore, it's unwise to feed moist or semimoist dog food to a cat. Also, young growing animals require more protein. You can now purchase special "kitten" and "puppy" diets for them; in the long run, this is safer than trying to feed a young animal adult pet food with special supplements.

Beware of giving cow's milk to kittens and puppies: The high content of lactose—or milk sugar—can cause severe diarrhea. Also, do not give pets vitamins and other dietary supplements without veterinary supervision. Overzealous use of certain vitamins can cause serious problems.

There are basically three kinds of food you can buy for your cat or dog: moist (canned); semimoist (in a sealed pack); and dry. Most canned foods are not usually a fully balanced diet; check the labels, and if in doubt, consult your veterinarian. I give my cats and dogs canned food only as an extra supplement—their basic diet consists of portions of semimoist feed, with dry food always available.

Another note of caution: The drier the food, the more water your pet will need. Remember, cats and dogs don't sweat but, instead, keep cool by panting, and a lot of water is needed in order to regulate body temperature. Don't overfeed with dry food in hot weather; your pet may have a swollen mass in its stomach if it drinks too much after eating a large meal. Instead, cut its ration in half, and feed morning and evening.

There is much debate in veterinary circles about whether dry foods contribute to bladder problems (urinary calculi) in cats. Since there is no simple answer, it's best to avoid feeding your cat an all-dry diet. Some vets recommend adding a little salt to induce the cat to drink more and thus reduce the likelihood of bladder blockage with calculi or "sand."

Cats and dogs on an all-moist diet may develop dental problems—bad breath, brown "scales" on the teeth, and infected gums. That's why it's advisable to encourage cats to accept dry food as part of their diet, since dry materials do keep the teeth clean. Dogs may also be given dry food to combat this problem; also good are hard dog biscuits, or long "bones" of dry rawhide (rather than rawhide strips or chips, which may be swallowed). But don't give dogs small bones, which they might swallow, or chicken or pork bones, which can splinter and perforate a vital organ.

How much to feed: This depends on many factors. Read the instructions on the can or package carefully. Pets who are growing, pregnant, or lactating require more food of high quality, and smaller pets require more food per pound of body weight than larger ones. When more food is needed, avoid indigestion problems by giving less food more often. If you must change your pet's diet, do it gradually, mixing increasing proportions of the new feed with the food that it's used to. A sudden change in diet may cause problems ranging from a pet's simple refusal to accept the new food to actual gastrointestinal disturbances.

When to feed: Dogs and cats are creatures of habit; even in the wild they go hunting and foraging for food at specific times. So feeding time should be on a very regular schedule. A natural hour for feeding would be at your own dinner time, with dry chow left available throughout the day for whenever your pet wants it. (Snacks are not necessary, and should be used only as rewards during training.) If there is no set feeding time, your pet will be begging for food all day. The lack of routine can also lead to digestive upsets as well as constipation, for how will you know when to take or allow your pet outside?

Emotional problems may affect a pet's eating habits just as they do ours. Loss of a companion, for instance, or being left in a boarding kennel may cause *anorexia nervosa*—depression and a refusal to take food. Of course, you should have an animal doctor make sure the pet is not physically ill. More rarely, anxiety may cause compulsive eating, and the pet becomes obese. This happened to my parents' dog, who became jealous when I gave them a new kitten.

It is a fact that in some countries children are less well fed than most pets in the United States. Some people deplore this "waste" of food on animals. I share with them a deep concern for starving nations, but the point is not that our animals should be deprived of an adequate diet, but that the root causes of mass hunger—underproductivity, drought, and relative overpopulation throughout the world—must be rectified.

In the face of rising costs and the growing need for high-quality animal protein for human consumption, pet foods are becoming more and more synthetic, with ingredients ranging from soy protein to dry skim milk and cereal additives. Although not appealing to us (or to a pet conditioned to human-type foods early in life), pets of the future will have to accept such fare—and the future begins now. The scientifically formulated and well-balanced "additive" diets that are now available commercially are generally cheaper than other kinds of "meaty" pet food, and are usually better for your pet's health (poor-quality animal protein is in fact inferior to vegetable protein). If these foods are dry, adding a *few* (no more than 10 to 15 percent) table scraps (if you ever have any these days) or a similar quantity of a flavorful moist canned food, will make them more palatable.

Giving kitty nothing but canned tuna and pampering poochy with the best filet mignon or ground sirloin is love that kills. Despite our affluence, because of habit and ignorance American people—

and their pets—generally don't eat what's best for them. It's up to you to make your dog or cat's life longer and healthier.

17

Proper Care for Healthy Coat and Skin

Some of the most common pet problems—often the easiest to diagnose and the hardest to treat—are those affecting the skin. There are a number of cardinal signs that cat and dog owners should know, not so they can treat their pets but so they can get them to the vet as soon as the problem starts. The sooner the better; the longer the delay, the harder it will be to treat.

I am often reticent about giving detailed descriptions of various pet diseases to people because I fear that they may then be more likely to try home-doctoring themselves. Home-doctoring often does more harm than simply leaving things to "nature's care." Please resist the temptation and, whatever knowledge you acquire about skin diseases, let it be only to help your vet help your pet when it does have a skin problem.

But there are a number of things that you *can* do to reduce the chances of your pet's developing certain skin problems. The best "medicine" is preventive medicine: good nutrition and body care will help prevent certain problems in human health, and the same holds for pets as well.

"Natural" Skin and Coat Care

Wild animals generally have beautiful coats, especially in the winter. This is why there is such a thriving fur industry of winter-

141

trapped animals. I hope that before we go any further, you are not one of those people who still wears a wild creature's fur. Remember that in some countries people wear dog and cat fur, specially treated to look wild. If you can't imagine wearing your pet's pelt, then I hope you couldn't think of wearing a wild animal's fur—there's really no difference: A living being lives inside of it!

Now the living being inside your pet's skin isn't very wild. After thousands of years of domestication, various things have happened that may mean you will have to help your pet take good care of its skin and coat. In fact, a high percentage of pet skin problems are a consequence of domestication and of their present way of life. Some of the factors are physiological, hereditary, or environmental, while others have a nutritional or psychological basis. Then there are those disorders that are caused by various diseases and parasites. Any of the former factors, either singly or in combination, may determine resistance or susceptibility to this last.

The skin is like a mirror, often revealing the presence of some serious problem elsewhere in the body. For example, a patchy shedding or thinning of hair and certain changes in the skin could mean a malfunctioning thyroid gland or a tumor of one of the endocrine or hormone producing glands. Home-doctoring, such as applying "salve," psoriasis medicine, or other human medicine to the skin obviously wouldn't help since it's the thyroid gland and not the skin that needs treating. This is not unlike one pet owner for whose dog I prescribed a tablespoon of polyunsaturated vegetable oil to help its coat: It was fortunate that I soon learned that she was rubbing it into the dog's coat and had forgotten that I had said to put it in the dog's food! So remember that many apparently "external" skin problems are superficial reflections of deeper internal troubles.

Regular Care

Before describing some of the more common skin problems in cats and dogs and their preventive measures, it should be realized that many pets do need some assistance from their owners to maintain their coats and skin in good condition. *Heredity*—heavily influenced by man—may work against a cat or dog. For example, all long-haired varieties will need some help to keep their "man-made" coats in order. The Persian cat requires daily grooming—it should not be

Dogs with long hair—like this sleepy "doormat"—need regular grooming to avoid skin problems *(H.S.U.S./Roz Durham)*.

expected to be able to take care of itself. The fur mats and balls easily and the cat's small raspy tongue "comb" is simply not adequate to take care of such a long coat. Since dogs groom themselves even less than cats, long-haired dogs—like Old English sheepdogs and Afghan hounds—should also receive a daily grooming. Pay special attention to the feathers or long fur along the belly, tail, and legs. It's worth investing in a good-quality grooming brush (I like those with a rubber face and natural or soft plastic bristles). Get your pet used to being groomed right from infancy: Handling and restraint early in life is the key to easy handling in maturity.

Sometimes the pet's coat may seem to be very "smelly," and the owner thinks a bath may help. Unless the dog has been rolling in something obnoxious, regular baths are not necessary and are not substitutes for regular grooming. If your cat stops grooming itself, it may be sick. If your dog's coat seems to smell a lot, the odor could be coming from the feet, oil glands in the ears, or from the glands in the skin, which could mean an infection or dietary/metabolic disorder. If in doubt, see your vet—don't bathe a sick animal!

Strong "doggy" smell is natural in some breeds, like the Airedale, that have oily coats. One way to remove such odors from the coat is to rub in some talcum powder. This will absorb some of the oils, and when brushed out (best to do it outdoors) the odor will be removed as well. This is an effective "dry bath" for pets: Be sure to use a commercial brand of talc that is free of asbestos fibers, since inhaling this material can cause cancer.

Whenever I have to actually bathe a pet, I like to use a bowl of warm water with a mild baby shampoo and a sponge. It's less disturbing to spong-wet some pets than to "dunk" them in a bath—and much easier for a very large dog. A hose or several jugs of warm water should be given to rinse out all the shampoo. A ball of cotton wool should be put inside each ear to keep soap and water out of the ears.

A few other pointers concerning our pets' "domesticated dependence": A properly balanced diet is essential for general health and for a good coat. A poor coat could mean some dietary inadequacy or a nutritional drain because of worms or the demands of pregnancy or of producing milk for hungry offspring. The pet cannot choose naturally what its body needs and has to eat what it is given. A common deficiency in many commercial feeds is fat. This can be the cause of a dry coat and scruffy, dandruff-caked skin. As a sensible nutritional supplement for a 30-pound dog, I recommend one tablespoon of polyunsaturated vegetable oil in the food daily, plus a sprinkling of brewer's yeast (for B vitamins) and wheat germ.

Another domestication effect is excessive sheeding. Normally there is a seasonal cycle, but this can become upset when the pet is not in tune with the external environment: Being kept warm and indoors with artificial lighting in the winter, and air-conditioning in the summer could lead to irregular or even constant coat shedding. Regular grooming is as much as one can do other than avoiding overheating the house in winter and overcooling it in the summer.

Some pets never grow winter coats, and some breeds of dog, like the poodle, never have a shedding cycle but, like human beings, have to be trimmed regularly. A good stripping out and clipping will help many dogs feel more comfortable in the summer months. In the winter, other dogs may well need an "overcoat" put on when they go outdoors. Some breeds and some individual dogs don't develop the thick underfur to keep themselves warm, and if they are old and not so active outdoors, some protection from the elements is indicated.

You will notice that cats don't like to get wet as a rule. This is because they do not have "waterproof" coats, and this reflects their desert ancestry. A dog's ancestor, the wolf, has a fantastically waterproof coat—one shake after a swim or a rainstorm and it's dry. The oily guard hairs and underfur together make a warm and waterproof cover. Some dogs, like the poodle, have no guard or surface hairs, only fuzzy underfur—another product of man's domesticating intervention—so the coat will soak up water like a sponge. Pets with such coats should be protected from the elements: It's not silly sentimentalism, treating such a pet like a person—it's common sense.

In addition to general coat care, the ears and toenails of your pet will need regular checking. Nails may require trimming, especially in dogs that don't get outdoors and onto rough surfaces very often. Nail clippers should be used to trim them. Be sure to note where the pink quick is, for if you cut into it you will hurt your pet and the toenail will bleed. With dark toenails, in which the quick is difficult to detect, a simple guide is to clip the nails just in line with the pads: removing too little is better than removing too much. Pay special attention to the inner toe or dew claws. especially in long-haired dogs, since the nail quickly overgrows and may curl back and cut into the pad.

Ears should be cleaned with a little warm olive oil on a swab of cotton wool. Don't poke inside with a cotton swab. Very oily ears may be rinsed with very mild shampoo or a solvent preparation from your vet. Just as with the skin, though, don't wash healthy ears excessively (more than, say, once every two or three months). You may bring on a bacterial or fungal infection by altering the natural "balance" of the bacterial life that lives normally on the skin and in the ears.

There are some rather special areas of your pet's skin that you should know about. Cats have a bald spot or at least more sparse hair on the temples, just below and in front of the ears. These two areas are the temporal scent glands which the cat will use to "anoint" its friends. There are similar glands in the edge of the lips, and any dark secretion you see there is from these lip glands. The upper surface of the tail also has a scent gland and in some cats, especially males, it may secrete excessively and cause the tail hairs to be oily with a brown secretion at their roots. Similarly the scent glands on the cat's chin may lead to an acnelike condition. Soapy shampoo treatment to remove the excess secretions will help.

Dogs have a similar but smaller tail gland. Often this area becomes bald or rubbed short—usually because of the dog's habit of tucking its tail under when it goes to sleep or sits down. Heavy breeds should have a soft bed to allay the development of calluses on the elbows and heels. Such bald, scaly areas are no cause for alarm, unless the scaly area increases and is sore or itchy.

Both cats and dogs have anal glands with small openings for each gland on either side of the anus. In some dogs, and rarely in cats, these glands require regular emptying, especially when they irritate the pet and become infected, overactive, or when the opening or gland duct becomes blocked.

Good pet care generally means that your animal will have a good skin and coat. The routine care and preventive measures described here will help ensure that your cat or dog will stay in good condition. There are, however, a number of other skin troubles that good care cannot prevent. Good care may improve your pet's chances of a quick recovery or enhance its resistance. These other troubles, such as allergies, fleas, and hormonal disorders, will be discussed in later chapters on pet skin problems.

18

Fleas, Ticks, and Other Skin Problems: Don't Play Vet with Your Pet

The following description of various skin problems that your pet may develop is intended to enable you to take certain precautions and preventive measures, and to let you recognize when your pet is in trouble and requires veterinary treatment. No medicine at all is better than bad medicine. Let your veterinarian treat all diseases or disorders.

As a responsible pet owner, you should give your cat or dog a regular health check yourself (in addition to a thorough once-every-six months or so checkup by your own vet). On a weekly basis, when you groom your pet, you should examine its fur and skin thoroughly from nose to tail. Also check ears, eyes, teeth, feet, and genitals, and at least once a week be sure to examine your pet's urine and stools for any blood or parasites, and look out for signs of difficulties in evacuating too.

Fleas

The most common skin problem in cats and dogs is the ubiquitous flea. In some areas, such as Florida (an ideal flea climate), they are a serious year-round problem. To control fleas, one must understand their life cycle. They spend more of their life off the host (your pet and sometimes you) than on. While it's normal for a pet to scratch and groom itself occasionally, excessive scratching and shaking could mean fleas. Fleas can be found by stroking the fur back and looking for these fast-moving hoppers. They are dark brown in color and congregate especially around the neck, back, and rump of their host. They may also be spotted crawling on the shorter fur of your pet's belly. Sometimes you may not see a flea, but instead some tiny pinhead-sized black flecks of coallike dust in your pet's fur. Place a few of these on a piece of wet white paper. If they dissolve and turn brown-red, you will know that it's not dirt or coal dust but the feces of fleas—a product of their blood meals sucked from your pet!

It is important to understand the life cycle of the flea in order to control it. A fertilized female flea usually lays its eggs on the ground. These hatch into larvae after about seven days. The larva fattens and matures over a two- to three-week period and then turns into a pupa or chrysalis. This "incubates" for about two weeks and then bursts, and out crawls an adult flea that searches for a host for its first blood meal.

Thus, in controlling fleas, which will be more or less constantly developing and at various stages of development in your house (especially in shag rugs and floor crevices), simply treating your pet once for fleas isn't going to help. A new wave of hatching fleas bursting hungrily from their pupal "mummy" cases will soon be on your pet.

A thorough vacuuming of the entire house is the first step. Incinerate or seal in a garbage bag the dust bag from your vacuum. Burn, launder, or scrub out the pet's blankets or bed area. Then you should have your house fumigated by a professional. This may have to be done every month if you have a serious flea problem. Often two treatments in late spring and midsummer will suffice. Perhaps you have come home (with your pet) after a two- to three-week vacation only to be greeted by a swarm of hungry fleas crawling and hopping up your legs. Remember that it's the house as much as the pet that has to be treated. To avoid constant reinfestation of your house, you should also remember that your pet, if allowed to roam free anywhere outdoors, is more likely to pick up fleas and infest the house. (This is another good reason for not allowing your cat or dog to run free in the neighborhood.)

It is also a good idea to discourage your pet from sleeping with you or your children. An infested mattress may have to be burned.

Children developing chicken-pox-like spots all over may well be being eaten by fleas at night in their beds!

Finally, one must treat the pet. I like to use dips or powder preparations, applied every ten days or so (because of the constant reinfestation pattern of the fleas' life cycle). Sprays tend to scare many pets. Apply the medication especially along the back and neck of your pet deeply into the pile of its fur: It won't be able to lick it off so easily then. Be sure that the medication is safe for cats. Flea medications for dogs can be poisonous to cats. Some cats are also sensitive to certain fumigants, so keep your pet out of the house for as long as possible after the house has been fumigated. Flea collars can be useful on small-bodied pets but simply don't have enough effect (since they slowly vaporize around the animal) if it is very large. If you do use a flea collar, check under it each day just in case your pet is developing a sore neck, which is a sure sign of an allergy to the collar. This is quite common. The collar should never be buckled on tight: Always keep it loose. Never allow the collar to get wet, and if your pet does show signs of sickness, take the collar off at once. A flea "medallion" that dispenses a vapor and which can be worn on a regular collar is probably safer for your pet. In some areas, fleas seem to be becoming resistant to all kinds of insecticides. I have heard that dosing the pet daily with one to five grams of vitamin-B complex acts as a flea repellent. Combine this with a more frequent house fumigation and life may be easier for you and your pet. But this isn't the last word on fleas. There are two other problems that fleas can cause.

Flea Allergy (or Summer Eczema)

Your pet may become so hypersensitive to the saliva of the blood-sucking flea that the bites of even one flea may cause it to scratch and lick excessively. Soon a red, oozing hot spot may develop on the skin (especially near the base of the tail). Veterinary treatment for flea hypersensitivity is essential.

Tapeworms

There is one species of tapeworm whose life cycle involves the flea. The maggotlike moving segments of the tapeworm that you may see in your pet's stools contain eggs. These are eventually eaten by the flea larvae and develop inside it. Then when the flea is mature and is accidentally eaten by your pet as it grooms itself and bites at the fleas, the tapeworm enters your pet's body. The tapeworm hatches inside the pet's digestive system and gradually matures until it produces egg-filled segments that pass out with the pet's stools, thus completing the parasite cycle. I have spelled this out in detail because only too often I find people treating their pet for the tapeworm infestation and doing nothing about the fleas. The presence of fleas will guarantee reinfestation with this tapeworm, called *Dipylidium*.

Ticks and Chiggers

These are common problems for any pet or person who goes outdoors. Sometimes ticks will infest the house and fumigation is indicated. Regular dipping to kill ticks and use of a repellent collar will help keep their numbers down. Never use kerosene or hot match ends to remove them. A firm twist and a pull with tweezers will remove any that are attached to you or your pet. Preliminary soaking in petroleum jelly or linseed oil will help paralyze them and render them easier to remove. Usually the mouth parts of the tick, embedded in the skin, will come out, too: If they do stay in, apply a little antibiotic or mild disinfectant. They rarely cause any complications.

In some areas ticks carry Rocky Mountain spotted fever (in the Rockies and parts of Oregon and California), which causes a serious disease in man similar to sleeping sickness. Extra care should be taken so that your family and home do not become tick-infested. The brown dog tick and the Eastern wood tick are probably the most common and harmless to man. The former is the most likely to infest your home or kennels.

A female tick will lay anywhere from 10 to 2,500 eggs that will hatch after nineteen to sixty days. So-called seed ticks hatch out, and immediately seek a blood meal from an animal. Once fed, they live off their host and molt after one to three weeks into nymphs. They can live without another meal for several months. Mature female ticks breed while feeding on the host and soon after laying eggs expire. Ticks are very resistant to heat and cold and are difficult to eradicate outdoors. Clearing brush and weeds will help: They avoid open areas since they are susceptible to dessication. In a warm house, the brown dog tick can be active year round and the only answer is thorough cleaning and fumigating. A large heap of dry ice on the floor is said to attract ticks so that they can be easily collected and destroyed. Try it and let me know your results!

Ear Mites

An extremely irritating external parasite of cats and dogs is the ear mite. The microscopic mite lives in the host's ear canal, burying into the soft tissue folds of the ear. This can drive a dog crazy and it may soon mutilate its ears by scratching. Cats are less sensitive but will also claw their ears. Scratch marks and hair loss behind the ears are telltale signs. The animal may shake its head violently and rupture the tissues in the ear flap, causing a hemotoma or huge blood blister. If untreated, it will eventually dry up and the ear will literally crumple. The mites irritate the ceruminal or oil glands of the ear canal causing a copious secretion of brown-black, dryish, tarlike material in cats and a red-brown smelly discharge in dogs. This can be easily detected by gently inserting a cotton swab into the ear canal; never penetrate deeply into the canal.

Ear mites also give rise to a chronic thickening of the folds in the ear meatus or opening. They are then even more difficult to remove and, worse, secondary bacterial or fungal infections may develop.

Ear mites may become so irritating as to cause heat and swelling in the ear, and the pet will scream and bite defensively when handled. Convulsive seizures may even develop.

Unlike ticks and fleas, ear mites pass their entire life cycle of egg, larva, nymph, and adult in the host's ear. No treatment of the environment is needed. A thorough shampoo to remove any stray mites from the head, neck, paws, and tail may help eliminate the problem. As with mange mites (see below) the toes may pick up mites in the process of scratching and be one source of transmission from animal to animal. Bedding material should be burned.

Being alert to the early signs of ear mite infestation and seeking veterinary help immediately will prevent these serious complications. If you have more than one pet in the house and one seems to have ear mites, have all of them checked out. A cat may show no obvious symptoms but be the source of infestation for another cat or dog in the home that reacts more severely to them.

Ringworm

Fungal infections are most prevalent in younger animals. Hair loss in small circular or irregular bald spots on the body, legs, and face are symptomatic. The skin in affected areas is usually dry and scaly. Scratching and signs of irritation may not be evident. The infection can be contracted from the soil or from another animal. Ringworm can develop in people, especially children, and if this is suspected in your home, your veterinarian should examine your pet.

Mange

There are various kinds of mange. Like ear mites, they burrow into the skin and reproduce there, setting up considerable irritation. The animal may scratch itself raw, and the scratching will help spread the disease via its toes. Secondary skin changes may develop, especially bacterial infections and chronic thickening of the epidermis.

Follicle Mange

The most difficult to treat—because it buries so deeply into the hair follicles—is follicular or demodectic mange. The first signs may be a few small, bald reddish spots with silvery gray scales developing in the skin, especially around the face or legs. If untreated and the pet is in poor condition, it may spread rapidly. Many dogs are symptomless carriers of this disease. Stress (caused by worms, poor diet, and the demands of growth in a puppy) and/or an allergic reaction to the presence of this mange parasite may cause the problem to erupt.

Sarcoptic Mange

This form of mange is much more irritating to the dog, causing severe scratching and often rapid self-mutilation. Skin inflammation is intense, and hair loss may be extensive. The mites burrow deep into the skin and lay their eggs in these burrows. It can spread rapidly over the body and from one dog to another, often beginning around the edges of the ears. A red itchy rash on anyone in the house should be suspected to be an infestation of mange from the dog. Veterinary treatment as soon as your dog starts to scratch excessively and/or develops any redness of the skin is essential. With both forms of mange, the earlier the diagnosis and treatment, the better.

Cats are generally more resistant to mange but may develop a demodex form of mange especially around the eyes. The feline equivalent of sarcoptic dog mange is symptomatically similar but is caused by a different mite (*Notoedres*). Usually the infestation is confined to the ears and head.

Miscellaneous Problems

I have described some of the more common skin problems that one may encounter in pet cats and dogs. Mention of a few others will help put you on the alert to recognize when there is a problem that requires veterinary treatment. Excessive licking, grooming, and scratching can be due to allergies (to household materials, floor polish, foods, pollens, etc.). Some breeds such as shepherds, setters, and small terriers seem to be more allergy prone. Similar symptoms, sometimes leading to self-mutilation and red-raw patches of skin, can be a psychological itch-scratch vice in cats and dogs. Boredom may sometimes underlie excessive grooming and chewing of paws. Infected nail beds or cysts between the toes should be looked for also.

Swellings on the skin take various forms: an abscess, bite wound, oily cyst, buried grass seed, or a tumor may be the problem. An area that refuses to heal may mean that there is skin cancer developing or a hypersensitivity to sunlight. Very oily, caking yellow dandruff with a rancid odor, especially in spaniels, means seborrhoea. Often symmetrical areas of baldness, sometimes coupled with a darkening of the skin, can indicate a hormonal disturbance, frequently thyroid in origin.

I hope that this synopsis of skin problems in pets will not turn you into a hypochondriac but rather make it easier for you to spot a skin problem in your pet. And then you will know what should be done.

19

Emergency Aid for Injured Pets: Your Quick Action Is Essential

"If only I had known what to do, I might have saved him," sobbed a woman whose toy poodle had expired on my examination table. It had been mauled by two big dogs after slipping its leash and running away.

"We tried to save her—we did all we could," said another owner whose dog suffered heat stroke after being shut up in the car for an entire summer afternoon. The dog's heart stopped beating while I was examining it, and I could not resuscitate it. The owners had wasted too much time "letting it rest" and giving it aspirin before they brought it into the hospital.

What *is* the best course of action in case of an emergency? The following guidelines should help pet owners stay sensible and coolheaded when disaster strikes, and may mean the difference between life and death for your pet.

First of all, make sure that you have the phone number of the nearest veterinarian or animal hospital close at hand. Even at night or on weekends, most local veterinary associations offer off-duty emergency service. If such help is not available in your area, you should demand that something be done by your veterinary association.

If your pet exhibits the following symptoms, it's an emergency, and you should call your veterinarian at once: extreme difficulty in breathing, unconsciousness, convulsions or "fits," sudden paralysis, uncontrollable bleeding, continuous or repeated vomiting and/or diarrhea, shock. Shock may follow poisoning, severe blood loss, a fight, or being hit by a car. Signs of shock include trembling or shivering and rapid breathing and heartbeat (indicated by a fast pulse). The body temperature may be subnormal (below 101.5 degrees), and the animal may be depressed—very inactive and passive. Keep the pet warm and quiet, and seek veterinary assistance at once.

You may be able to handle other problems yourself. *Bleeding* may be temporarily stopped by applying a pressure bandage or—if bright red (arterial) blood is gushing—a tourniquet above the wound. A tourniquet should be left on for no longer than fifteen minutes, however, and then loosened for half a minute—and if necessary, reapplied for another fifteen minutes after that. If heavy bleeding continues, you should head for professional help.

Small cuts are best left open to heal naturally. When an animal licks its wounds, its saliva aids in the healing process. However, excessive licking may lead to mutilation—especially with cats, whose tongues are abrasive. If the wound seems to be receiving rough treatment from the pet itself, then it may be necessary to apply a bandage and even muzzle the animal. Sometimes it may also be advisable to bandage the animal's feet to prevent excessive scratching.

Cuts on the pads generally heal rapidly and rarely need bandaging. Another cause of sudden lameness can be a torn toenail. Unless this can be expertly bandaged, it's best to remove the nail with a strong pair of nail cutters.

Swellings can occur in the foot if a limb is bandaged too tightly. If the swelling is severe, remove the bandage at once and apply one that is not so tight. Swellings on a cat's legs that are hot to the touch and accompanied by lameness and depression are usually bite abscesses, which can develop some time after the bite itself has healed. Veterinary treatment is then needed.

Acute reactions in the eye, including tearing, redness, and swelling, may simply mean that some foreign body is in the eye. Examine the eye carefully, in good light, and use a moist piece of cotton to clean it out. If it doesn't heal soon, get to a vet before permanent damage is done to the cornea. Similarly, you may use a cotton swab, dabbed with a little mineral or baby oil, to explore an acutely *inflamed ear*—a grass seed or other foreign material may have become lodged there. If the swab comes out brown or smelly, the animal may have an ear infection, and you should waste no time in seeking veterinary advice. Acute ear problems may lead to other complications, such as a massive blood blister or hematoma on the ear itself, caused by the animal's frantic clawing and shaking of its head.

Automobile accidents are the most common emergencies. Needless to say, try to remain calm. Stay with the animal and send someone else for help—otherwise the animal may run off and hide, or struggle and cause itself further injury, or even be hit again by passing traffic. Check for signs of shock, hemorrhage, or paralysis (which could mean spinal injury). Difficulty in breathing may mean serious bleeding in the chest cavity or damage to the diaphragm.

In transporting the animal to the veterinarian or animal hospital, carry it carefully in your arms or place it in a cardboard box. A dog is less likely to struggle this way than if it's strapped to a makeshift stretcher or rolled up in a blanket. If there are signs of paralysis or of spinal or pelvic injury, keep the animal as flat as possible, placing your arms under its groin and chest, with its side against you and its legs hanging straight down.

Often if a pet is suffering from concussion, it becomes confused and frightened and may bite or struggle to escape. Talk to a hurt animal: Put a jacket or pillow between you and the animal when you are carrying it so that you will be protected if it does try to turn and bite. If possible, tie a belt or necktie or length of rope gently around its muzzle. Since a cat may claw, place it in a box or wrap it tightly in a blanket or shirt.

If your pet seems unharmed after a car accident, keep it indoors under observation for twenty-four hours. It could be bleeding internally or have a ruptured bladder or spleen or a diaphragm hernia. Watch for signs of shock, which may develop even some time after the accident. It's amazing, however, how an animal can survive an auto accident without serious injury—a fluffy coat, light body, and springy ribs act as protective buffers. But continue to be on the lookout for later complications.

Diarrhea and/or vomiting can require emergency care if they are prolonged and repeated and especially if blood is evident. If the condition is not too severe, withhold the animal's food for twelve hours, and try to give it some Kaopectate. If it accepts and holds down a small, bland meal of cottage cheese, boiled rice and a little cooked chicken or ground beef, it may not need veterinary treatment. Mild intestinal upsets often pass spontaneously.

Convulsions, especially in dogs, are common and require emergency treatment. Keep the pet quiet, and gently restrain it so that it will not injure itself. Keep a pillow or a thick blanket between you and the dog as you carry it, to protect you from being bitten. Take the dog to the veterinary hospital where a diagnosis and appropriate treatment can be given. Severe abdominal disturbances (such as a heavy load of worms), distemper, brain hemorrhage or tumor, or poisoning can cause convulsions. Some dogs develop a human-type epilepsy, with repeated seizures that sometimes respond favorably to medication.

An emergency that must be recognized early is eclampsia, or *"milking fits"* in nursing cats and dogs. Restlessness, panting, and whining are the first signs, followed by stiffness, irritability, and convulsions. Veterinary treatment, without delay, is essential.

Poisons—such as snail bait, rat poison (strychnine, thallium, warfarin), antifreeze (ethylene glycol), and organophosphorus and arsenic insecticides—may cause sudden convulsions, weakness and other symptoms. If your pet becomes ill abruptly after being outdoors, or it you suspect it has been exposed to poison, induce vomiting at once by forcing the animal to swallow a strong solution of baking soda or diluted hydrogen peroxide. Waste no time in getting the pet to the nearest veterinary hospital and, if possible, take the suspect poison container with you.

The following house and garden plants are poisonous, and may be suspect, especially for cats who often indulge in nibbling plants: monkshood, autumn crocus, English ivy, philodendron, foxglove, larkspur, daffodil, golden chain, lily of the valley, oleander, castor bean, daphne, and dieffenbachia (also called dumb cane).

Burns happen quite often to pets; many come from hot water or cooking fat in the kitchen. If the burn is small, apply ice cubes and a mild ointment afterward. Remember, a dog's skin doesn't blister like ours, and a thick coat may hide a severe burn. Because of this, it's advisable to have your pet examined by your veterinarian within twenty-four hours after a bad burn.

Electric burns, especially for a puppy chewing on electrical extension cords, can be quite serious. When an animal is caught in the act, be sure to pull the plug from the electrical socket at once to prevent further injury. Extensive burns in the mouth are the usual result. Veterinary treatment is indicated without delay if the pet is unconscious (you should immediately try artificial respiration), has difficulty in breathing or develops sloughing sores in his mouth and tongue a few days later. (Artificial respiration can be administered mouth-to-mouth in the same way as for a human being. Be sure that the pet's air passage is clear; then, holding the animal's muzzle with its mouth closed, exhale slowly and firmly with your mouth tight around its nose.)

Heat stroke is an emergency condition requiring veterinary treatment, and it must be recognized as early as possible. Symptoms are an anxious or glazed expression, together with panting, increased pulse rate, and congested, reddened eyes and gums. Vomiting, stupor, coma, and collapse may ensue. Immerse the pet in ice-cold water or hose it with cold water, massaging its extremities for ten to fifteen minutes to aid its circulation—and then get the animal to the hospital. Avoid heat stroke in the first place by never locking your pet in the car in warm weather, even if a window is down. Provide the pet with frequent drinks or ice cubes on a long journey, and if it's extremely hot in the back of the car, place a wet towel over a dog to help keep it cool.

Outdoor accidents—such as being shot by a hunter or caught in a steel trap—are rare, but could happen when your pet wanders from a vacation campsite. Rule of rules—restrain your pet at all times. Even if there isn't a myopic hunter or cruel steel trap around, there may be a porcupine or a snake in the grass! If your dog returns with only a few porcupine quills in its body, use a pair of pliers to pull the quills out, holding the pliers as close as possible to where the quill penetrated the skin. Be sure to get all the quill out, since a broken tip can carry infection deep into your animal's body. If quills cover an animal's mouth, throat, eyes and face, anesthesia may have to be administered by a doctor before the quills are removed.

Snakebite is an emergency for man and dog alike. Keep the animal quiet, provide warm blankets to combat shock, and apply a tourniquet above the bite. If you don't have a snakebite kit with you, make a single incision between the two fang holes and squeeze and

suck out the venom. Antivenin should then be given to your dog
without delay; try the ranger station or nearest human hospital if
veterinary help is too far away.

Bee and hornet stings, although not a real emergency, require
first aid. A dog or cat furiously pawing at its face or mouth may
have been stung, so examine it carefully (there might also be a
splinter or bone stuck in its mouth). Apply antihistamine cream (or
baking soda) to the sting, and use tweezers to remove the sting barb.
Swelling around the bite, hives (bumps all over the body), and
difficulty in breathing may develop later as an allergic reaction.
Veterinary treatment will then be needed.

Miscellaneous emergencies are varied and unpredictable. But a
few come up regularly, such as a cat getting its tail slammed in a
door. Keep a close eye on the tail for swelling, and later feel the end
of the tail. If it's cold, it may require amputation.

It frequently happens, too, that a puppy or kitten gets stepped on
or dropped by a child. Keep a close eye on the animal for twenty-
four hours, and if it has difficulty walking, breathing, eating or
maintaining its balance, take it to your veterinarian. Usually, however, pets sustain little injury from falling because their bodies are
light and resilient.

Blowfly strike is a problem that affects pets kept outdoors. Flies
lay their eggs in moist and matted areas on the animal's coat and the
hatched maggots may spread rapidly, causing considerable inflammation of the skin. Home-doctoring is usually adequate. Clip away
all matted fur and maggots, and apply a mild disinfectant or
antibiotic cream.

Accidental breeding is a common emergency for owners of female
cats and dogs. You have about twenty-four hours from the time of
mating to have your pet injected with a hormone which may block
or prevent pregnancy. There may be undesirable side effects to the
treatment (including death in cats), however, so consider carefully,
and before the next accident think about having your pet spayed.

Dog fights can be real emergencies requiring immediate intervention. Get a coat, broom, or trash-can lid—*not* your hands or legs—
between the combatants. A hose or bucket of water works wonders.
If you have help, try to leash one of the dogs or grab its hind legs
and, pulling it away from the other dog, swing it in an arc away
from you. Remember, though, dogs often engage in "ritualized"

fighting, emitting a lot of growls and screams but actually inflicting little injury on each other.

You might like to post these guidelines for recognizing emergencies on your bulletin board. Knowing what to do may save a pet's life—and will at least restore your animal to health that much sooner!

20

Signs of Sickness: What to Watch for, What to Do

During my early years in veterinary practice, I worked for a while in the hills of England's north country; sheep were my special interest. But no matter what I did, a sick sheep rarely survived. The reason was that I was always called too late. Even the most attentive shepherd was hard pressed to keep a close eye on every member of his flock, and by the time illness was detected it had reached a sadly advanced state. Sheep and other animals often hide the fact that they are sick, at least in the initial stages of illness—it's an important defense against being picked off by hunting animals.

If the shepherd shared his life as closely with his sheep as we do with our pets and knew their routines as well as we know each nuance of our pets' behavior, he might have saved more of them. When owners are closely tuned into the habits of their pets, they can detect the early signs of illness (unless, of course, it's an acute disease or swiftly acting poison).

Animals are creatures of habit, and they develop a particular routine in relation to your pattern of life—there is a time to get up, to eat, play, be let outdoors or taken for a walk, and so on. Any break in your routine could in turn disturb your pet. And, conversely, if your pet breaks its routine, check it out—this could be a first sign of illness, and the earlier you spot it the better.

Perhaps the legend of cats having nine lives relates to the feline's

161

incredibly sensible attitude—when sick, a cat conserves its strength and simply avoids additional stress or unnecessary activity. Like the self-preserving cougar (which lies down at once to rest so that it won't be too weak to hunt or too apparent a prey), a sick cat will seek a quiet corner and sit there, fur ruffled up to keep warm, tail tucked in. It will sleep a lot and probably refuse to eat or drink. Don't upset it further by forcing food on it or by giving it too much cuddling and indulgence. If your cat wants to be with you, it will seek you out.

On the other hand, the sicker a dog is (up to a point of fairly severe illness), the more it resents being left alone. The dog is by nature a groupie, and will respond to sickness quite differently than the less gregarious cat. This is particularly true of a dog that is overly attached to its owner. A dog may push itself to maintain normal social activities—much to its physical detriment. I particularly remember one touching case of a dog that had regularly run to greet its master with a bedroom slipper when he came home from work. It was pathetic to see the dog trying mightily to maintain this routine while he was ill. And it can be especially difficult to keep a dog down when it's recovering, particularly after surgery.

It's important to remember a dog's dependency if you are considering hospitalization. Like children, hospitalized dogs may suffer separation anxiety and trauma that could lengthen recovery time. If you can have your dog treated at home, do so.

Aside from these general behavioral and psychological changes, there are also physical signals that can help you decide whether your pet is sick and whether it needs veterinary treatment. But remember: If in doubt, never hesitate to call the vet; never wait too long for "mother nature" to work a miracle; never try home-doctoring (don't give a pet aspirin and avoid home remedies in general); never give a sick pet worming medicine to "see if that's the problem."

It is important for all cat and dog owners to be able to recognize when their pets are ill and what the problem might be. This is not so that you can treat your ailing pet yourself. Being able to recognize what may be making your pet ill means that, with an early provisional diagnosis, you will know if and when your pet needs to be taken to a veterinarian. Such knowledge is also useful when buying a kitten or puppy or when letting your pet interact with another animal (such as a stray you take in or meet in the park) which might be sick and might therefore infect your pet.

Dog and cat owners should memorize the following signs that indicate a pet is sick and in need of veterinary treatment. For cats, look out for these cardinal signs:

—becomes inactive and sits quietly, hunched up
—refuses to eat its usual food and may not respond when called
—does not groom itself and has a dull or coarse "standing-up" coat
—sneezes frequently and has a runny discharge from the eyes and/or nose
—has diarrhea for more than twenty-four hours, vomits repeatedly; has difficulty in breathing or in urinating
—bad breath, sore gums, and brown "scales" on the back teeth
—scratches behind its ears; shakes its head, and has a brown discharge in one or both ears (a sign of ear mites, which are very common in cats)

Many of the signs of sickness in dogs are similar:

—seems less active and playful and won't eat or drink
—has a dry, hot nose, red eyes, and seeks a quiet, cool place
—has a dry cough and runny discharge from eyes and nose
—has diarrhea for more than twenty-four hours
—vomits repeatedly, has difficulty in breathing
—has poor exercise tolerance and fatigues quickly
—has convulsions (runs wildly, "swims" on the floor, foams at the mouth)
—scratches or paws certain areas of its body excessively, such as ears or mouth
—yelps when touched in certain places (abdomen, ear, paw, etc.)
—drinks excessively.

The above general signs of sickness are symptomatic of a number of different disorders that can affect your pet. The most serious of pet diseases are viral in origin. There is no drug that can be used to cure a pet of a viral infection, and antibiotics are of use only in preventing secondary infections caused by bacteria which multiply once the virus has lowered the animal's resistance. The best protection against viral diseases are appropriate vaccinations with a weakened strain of virus. The immunity that such vaccinations creates does not last forever; that is why animal "booster" shots are recommended.

Common Viral Diseases

The most common and devastating virus disease, one that afflicts dogs of all ages, is *canine distemper.* Some ten days after exposure (to an infected dog, say, at the pet store, pound, or park) the dog develops a fever. Eyes may become red and runny, the throat inflamed and the nose dry. The animal may also have a dry cough and seem listless, uninterested in food or play. Over the ensuing days, secondary bacterial infections result in pussy discharges from the eyes and nose, which may become caked. The virus may affect one particular body system such as the respiratory, digestive, or nervous systems. Acute pneumonia, enteritis, or encephalitis may then develop.

The distemper virus usually attacks the brain, causing severe and often irreparable damage. Epileptic seizures, which become more and more severe, are sometimes erroneously mistaken for rabies (because the animal drools, chomps its jaws, and acts crazy). Dogs that do recover may have residual nerve damage, including blindness, paralysis, and chorea (twitching of some part of the body). Other residual signs of distemper are scars on the cornea, "hard pad" (thick, dry skin on the foot pads and nose) and brown stains and pitting of the teeth.

Clearly this is a devastating disease. Knowing something of the early symptoms can be of some help in getting veterinary treatment started at once. The best solution, because this progressive disease is only too often incurable, is to protect your dog from the disease with a vaccination.

Pups should be vaccinated when they are between six and eight weeks of age and be given "booster" shots at around twelve, twenty-four, and fifty-two weeks of age and then once a year. Veterinarians don't always prescribe the same time sequence of shots, but all adhere to the rule that one shot is not enough for a pup and that a booster is a must.

This vaccine is often given in conjunction with another vaccine against *canine viral hepatitis*. This virus disease (which has *no* connection with the human hepatitis virus) can result in serious liver and brain damage in dogs and chronic kidney disease in those that recover.

A vaccine is also available to protect dogs from a parainfluenza virus that is in part responsible for *"kennel cough"* in dogs held at the pound or kept at a boarding kennel. This is not a serious disease but can cause both pet and owner some distress.

Along with the canine distemper and hepatitis vaccine, another vaccination against a nonviral disease known as *leptospirosis* can be given. This microorganism can cause serious problems in dogs, including fever, liver damage, jaundice, and kidney failure.

Unfortunately no vaccine has yet been developed to protect dogs from *heart worm* infestation, a mosquito-transmitted disease common in many regions in the United States. Treatment of this disease, because of drug side effects, can kill dogs. Fortunately preventive medicine can be given during the warm-weather "heart worm season" and this must be given daily to the dog.

Two new virus diseases have recently been identified in dogs. As yet, protective vaccines are not available. One is *calicivirus*, which causes fever, diarrhea, heart trouble, and other problems. The other may be a mutant of the *feline panleukopenia* virus, a *parvovirus* which is highly contagious and causes acute diarrhea, fever, shock, and death in many dogs.

Cats suffer from a variety of virus diseases, the mildest of which is *feline influenza*. Kittens are particularly susceptible, older cats tending to acquire natural immunity after one or more infections. As with any virus disease, the stress and lowered resistance caused by the virus infection often results in secondary bacterial infections such as pneumonia and sinusitis.

A vaccine is available for cat "flu" and for similar virus infections called *rhinotracheitis* and *calicivirus*. It is advisable to have a kitten protected with these vaccines shortly after weaning and be given "boosters" as scheduled by the veterinarian.

At the same time, protection with a live but weakened strain of the *feline panleukopenia* (or feline distemper) virus is advisable.

This is a killer disease of cats responsible for the deaths of thousands each year. Young cats are particularly susceptible and can pick up the infection from sick animals or other healthy "carriers" infected with the virus.

The symptoms of feline panleukopenia include fever, inactivity, lack of interest in food and progressive weakness, emaciation, diarrhea, and dehydration. Secondary bacterial infections, leading to further complications, especially pneumonia, are common. Unlike the effects of canine distemper, here the nervous system is only rarely affected.

There are other serious virus diseases in cats for which no vaccines are as yet available. Most serious of all is *feline leukemia* (which has no proven connection with human leukemia). Symptoms can range from multiple tumors in various parts of the body (including the brain) to chronic diarrhea, anemia, and wasting. Sometimes this disease is instead manifested in an acute form where the cat quickly weakens and dies within a short time. This virus can also cause abortion in pregnant females, and birth defects in kittens. Kittens can be born with the disease and develop problems at a later age. A blood test is now available to check if a cat has this disease. Some are symptom-free carriers and can infect other cats. It is advisable to have two tests run with an interval of ten to twelve weeks in between. There is no need to destroy a cat that tests out positive unless it is seriously ill or likely to infect other cats.

Other serious virus infections in cats, for which there are no vaccines yet available, include infectious *feline anemia* and *peritonitis. Cystitis* (inflammation of the bladder) may also be triggered by a virus infection. A cat that becomes unhousebroken, has difficulty, strains, or cries out when it urinates, or passes a little blood in its urine should be taken at once to a veterinarian. Cystitis is a very common cat disease and can be treated with some success.

Cats, and especially dogs, begin to drink more when they are suffering from *diabetes* or from kidney failure. Older dogs often become unhousebroken because they are drinking more to compensate for *chronic kidney disease*—they should be taken out more often.

Besides preventive vaccines, what other precautions might be taken to protect a pet from developing one of the above diseases? Don't let it roam free and unsupervised. Your pet could come into contact with a sick animal, or be picked up, taken to the pound and exposed to sick animals there. Avoid contact yourself with other sick animals, too, because you could carry the virus home on your hands and clothing. Certain viruses and many bacteria live in your pet's body and only cause problems when the pet is under stress. Physical stresses—such as leaving the pet outdoors in hot or cold weather or not giving it adequate food and water—should be avoided. Emotional stresses—such as leaving the pet alone for extended periods or placing it in a boarding kennel—should also be avoided. Get a house-sitter for your pet, if you can, when you go on vacation. There is some evidence that cats and dogs may stay much healthier when two are kept instead of one. Two cats or dogs give each other company when left alone, and generally plenty of exercise and attention. The stress and possible anxiety of being left alone in a silent house all day (while the owners are out at work) would then be greatly reduced.

General Health Tips

Every new kitten or puppy should be taken to a veterinarian for a thorough checkup and given a series of shots against the common virus diseases. If you own other cats, take them and your new kitty to be checked for feline leukemia virus—one of the most serious of cat diseases. Kittens and pups are often born with roundworms, and the vet should examine their stools for this condition.

Adult dogs will often get infested with hookworms, especially if they're kept outdoors. These worms develop in the soil and then get into the dog by burrowing into its skin; from there they migrate to the dog's intestines. Regular checkups are therefore extremely important to control this parasite. Never worm any pet routinely, or give it worm medicine whenever it gets sick. All home-doctoring, unless under veterinary supervision, is to be avoided.

Adult cats and dogs should go to the vet at least once a year for a regular "physical" and to receive necessary booster shots. If your cat spends time outdoors, a rabies shot at six months or later is advisable. All dogs must be vaccinated each year for rabies.

Adult cats and dogs will often get tapeworm infestations, especially if they're allowed outdoors and eat small rodents, from whom they contract the infestation. Small, white, ricelike segments may be seen in the pet's stools. One of these tapeworms has part of its life cycle in the flea, so it's important to rid your cat or dog of fleas to prevent reinfestation.

If your cat does get fleas, use a flea powder or dip specifically for cats, since the medication used on dogs will make cats sick. You may also need to vacuum and fumigate your house, since the flea spends part of its life cycle developing as a "grub" in your carpets, and in floor cracks and crevices. Use flea collars only when they're really needed, since they can make some pets quite ill, and on large dogs and long-haired pets they are of limited use.

A few final things to look out for. Swollen and painful body areas on a cat (especially a tom who gets out) can mean abscessed cat bites. A cat who scratches its ears, has a sore spot behind either or both, and a brownish discharge inside the ear probably has ear mites. If your dog scratches a good deal and develops bald spots, chances are it has one form of mange. If it just chews one area and develops a moist "hot spot," it may be allergic to fleas. All the above problems require professional treatment by a veterinarian.

Knowing what to look out for when your pet seems to be getting sick and then taking your pet to the vet as needed are things you owe your pet.

21

Geriatric Care: Pets, Too, Deserve a Good Age

The better care a cat or dog has in infancy, the better its chances of a relatively trouble-free old age. Good nutrition, protective vaccinations, and regular health checkups from the very start all add years to an animal's life. Nonetheless, geriatric pet problems are on the increase, because the life span of pets is perhaps greater than ever before. This is the happy result of major improvements in veterinary care, disease control, and pet nutrition.

While "senility" in people is often a socially induced state of mind, both people and our pets do suffer from a variety of real aging problems that can be physically and psychologically debilitating. But there are measures that one can take to make life easier for an aging companion. The aim is *not* simply to extend an animal's life expectancy but to enhance the quality of its existence. The time will come when supportive medication and other treatment will be of little avail and the painful question of euthanasia (a humane death) will have to be faced. But let me emphasize at the outset that I am not one of those doctors who sees it as a personal challenge to maintain life regardless of its condition. Like our pets, we will all eventually die; hopefully, it will be with dignity—not strung out for months on drugs and other life supports which for an animal might be distressing if not inhumane.

Friends for life. Good geriatric care is important for both people and pets *(H.S.U.S./Paul Duckworth)*.

How Old Is Old?

I am often asked to give a dog's age in relation to a human being's. How old is old? Both cats and dogs can live to ripe old ages of twelve to fifteen years. Some exceptionally hardy pets reach the age of twenty.

Dogs reach puberty much faster than we do. A one-year-old dog (or cat) is equivalent to a fifteen-year-old person! Some other rough equivalents would be ages three, six, nine, twelve, and sixteen in a dog or cat being comparable to thirty, forty, fifty, sixty-five and eighty years, respectively, in man. An eight-year-old terrier would be middle-aged.

The onset of old age varies among breeds. Generally, larger dogs have a shorter life span than smaller varieties. Also, the more inbred varieties of cats and dogs tend to have a shorter life span than the resiliant mongrel or mixed-breed types.

PHYSICAL CHANGES

Diet

An aging pet is less active, and for that reason tends to become overweight—which is harmful to its health. Overweight can aggravate such problems as a failing heart, chronic kidney disfunction, arthritis, or vertebral disc luxations. For all these reasons, your animal should have fewer calories. It should also have exercise (unless it has heart trouble).

An oldster needs a diet of high-quality protein in order to maintain its tissues in good repair. (Proteins are the "building blocks" of the body.) Excessive protein intake is to be avoided, however, in an old pet with kidney or liver problems. In such cases, as well as for dogs with heart disorders, your veterinarian will prescribe a special diet.

One problem of old age for man and animal is a rarefying and brittling of the bones. Vitamins and mineral supplements are indicated. It's a good idea to provide a little calcium lactate or sterilized bone meal, with a sprinkling of wheat germ (vitamin E), brewer's yeast (for B vitamins), and a few drops of vitamins A and D at each meal. It is better to give a little of these supplements rather than too much.

Should your pet show a sudden increase or decrease in weight, do not start changing its diet or the amounts of its supplements. Instead, take your animal to your vet. A sudden change in weight can mean serious trouble, from congestive heart failure to a hormonal disturbance such as diabetes, or even cancer.

Eyes and Ears

Unfortunately, old dogs and cats, like old people, often suffer from a gradual deterioration of their vision and hearing. Cataracts developing over the lens of the eye are a common cause of progressive blindness. If your pet is healthy and can physically withstand the stresses of anesthesia and surgery, the cataracts can be removed. True senile cataracts in cats and dogs are less common than sclerosis of the lens, in which a gradual bluish or gray-white haze develops in the center of the lens. If it's not extensive, the old pet can compensate well for such changes in the eye. But even a totally blind cat or dog will thrive if kept indoors in a familiar environment! Some blind pets adapt so well that visitors to the house simply can't believe that they are "stone" blind. A blind pet can be allowed out only under strict supervision, in order to safeguard it from traffic and other hazards.

The deaf pet must also be protected from potential dangers outdoors. More than one old dog or cat has come to a premature end because it reacted too late and didn't hear an automobile approaching.

How will you know if your animal is beginning to lose its hearing? For one, you should observe if your pet responds as usual when called. Does it notice a knocking on the door, for instance? So far as its vision is concerned, is the animal bumping into things more often? Does it have difficulty in recognizing you from a distance? Is there a clouding of the cornea or lens?

The gradual loss of the senses of hearing and vision can make a pet more cautious and apprehensive, so it should be treated with understanding and not approached suddenly so as to startle it.

Mouth and Teeth

Common problems of old age, often associated with "bad breath," are poor teeth, infected gums, and brown scaly deposits, especially on the back teeth. Lifelong good dental care can, to a measure, retard such problems in old age. Small growths (papillomas) may also develop in your pet's mouth and interfere with eating. All these problems can be readily recognized and treated by your dentist.

Other Physical Problems

Aging will also bring with it the possibility of ovarian cysts, mammary gland cancers, and tumors and chronic infections of the uterus. These problems can generally be eliminated by spaying your cat or dog well ahead of time—that is, before it is so old that surgery is risky.

The mammary glands should be palpated every month (similar to the way a woman does a self-check for cancer). An early tumor will show up as a fairly hard lump. If detected, surgery can be performed.

Male dogs do develop chronic prostate trouble (obvious when the animal strains), and hernias. (Like master, like dog!) A hernia will show up as a soft lump in the groin or the rear end. Again, these should be checked out by your vet, and if necessary, corrected surgically.

If your pet reverts to being unhousebroken and is drinking excessive amounts of water, this may be a warning sign of kidney failure, rather than senility. The excessive drinking is an attempt to compensate for its kidney problem, so do not restrict water, and take it for walks more often. Also, take it to your vet at once.

Difficulty in urinating and defecating are common in the aging cat and dog. Constipation or a growth in the rectum may cause straining and bleeding. Straining to urinate and passing a little blood may mean that your cat or dog has a blockage of "stones" or urinary calculi. Veterinary help is needed immediately.

Exercise and Activity

With increasing age, animals do become less active. Avoid overexerting an old dog, especially on vacation or on hot days. It does upset me, seeing an obsessively compulsive jogger out on a hot day with his old dog behind him, desperately trying to keep up. Old dogs will have heart attacks and strokes when unduly stressed!

Older animals are more susceptible to cold, and it is a good idea to put a coat on the old pooch when he goes out for walks in the winter. If he lives outdoors, a well-insulated kennel is a must, and a heat pad or infrared heat lamp may be needed for very cold days.

Older pets will sleep longer, too—fifteen or more hours a day. Beyond this, any sudden decrease in activity is a signal that all is not well and that your animal is sick. Fatigue, panting after only a little exercise (even fainting), or pain and stiffness in the back, hips, or one or more limbs could mean heart problems and arthritis, respectively. Don't fill your pet up with painkilling aspirin, and avoid all home medication. Aspirin can make dogs very ill and will even kill cats!

You should regularly check over an aged pet to see that all is well, and take it to your veterinarian every four or six months for a professional examination.

Skin and Hair

As in man, the regenerative properties of a pet's skin and hair slow down with increasing age. Groom your pet daily, and if its coat is dry and brittle, adding a little polyunsaturated oil (such as safflower oil) to the diet will help. Look out for scaly skin, a "cold" feel, baldness, and darkening of the skin. This may not simply be old-age balding, but possibly, indicate a hormonal disturbance. Small wartlike skin growths are also common in the older pet, but any growths or sores that do not seem to heal or that grow quickly should be seen by a veterinarian: They may mean cancer.

Temperament Changes

An aging pet may become more "cranky" for a number of reasons. It may have pain in its hip or generally feel uncomfortable at times, and behave defensively or even avoid contact. Many prefer peace and quiet and will retire discreetly when noisy and unpredictable children are around. Their need for privacy should be respected, but you must, at the same time, be alert for symptoms; a pet that seeks seclusion may be ill.

With younger animals around, a middle-aged or older pet may suffer a loss in social status. Young upstart animals may pick on them or challenge their position in the household. If such is the case, you must step in to protect your senior citizen. Just as frequently, however, the old one is accorded a degree of respect and compassion by its younger companions—a humane lesson for us all!

If your pet is really old and grumpy, you might think twice about bringing a new animal into the home. It could cause considerable emotional upset. The old resident may be just too infirm to assert himself, to take the dominance battles that ensue with a mature animal, or even the playfulness of a pup or kitten. In fact, there have been cases where the impact was so great that it produced a heart attack in an old animal!

Since cats and dogs are creatures of habit (like us, too) it is advisable to avoid any extreme changes in routine or other aspects of an aging pet's life. A change in feeding time, for instance, or in the usual time for play, grooming, walks, and the like, can be quite disturbing and should be avoided.

Euthanasia

It is rare for a pet to die quietly, in its sleep. Often, when an animal is ready to die, it will seek seclusion and may even attempt to leave the home to die alone elsewhere.

The decision to have your pet humanely destroyed is one of the hardest but most responsible demands of pet ownership. You may have difficulty in making a decision by yourself. Discuss it with your veterinarian, who is the one to judge whether your pet's time has come. Your vet will know whether continued medication will help and to what degree your pet may be suffering. You will know yourself whether or not you are willing to continue with the time, effort, and expense of maintaining an ailing and aged pet. You will also know to what extent your pet is still enjoying life.

It is understandable how sometimes an owner can get caught in an emotional bind, doing everything to keep a distressed and sick old pet alive, unable to face the reality that it should be put to sleep. But we must not be selfish and try to keep such a pet alive regardless of its suffering, nor feel guilty when the humane decision to end its life is made.

Euthanasia can be administered by your veterinarian quietly and humanely, using a hypodermic syringe containing an overdose of a barbiturate anesthetic. There are other methods, but this is one of the most widely used and acceptable methods to date, and is endorsed by the Humane Society of the United States.

Handled with the right attitude and sensitivity, exposure to a pet's euthanasia can be a positive, if painful, learning experience for the children of the family. In this culture we have tended, until recently, to regard old age, chronic illness, and the reality of death as things to avoid talking about because of our own personal fears and ignorance.

Finally, and again with children in mind, a burial ceremony for the loved one may be befitting. Pet cemeteries, which provide a short service and a head stone over the grave for a modest fee, are available, and are not as sentimentally ludicrous as one might think. Not all people have a back garden where they can bury their pet. Even though it is just a dead body, to discard it on the city dump may not be best when children's feelings are involved. Humane euthanasia followed by the last rites at a burial or cremation service represent the final acts of a loving and responsible guardian. We can surely do no less for those pets who have given us their love, companionship, and trust.

22

Zoonoses: Diseases Your Pet Could Give You, but Hopefully Won't

I am surprised and often appalled at how ignorant doctors can be about zoonoses, those diseases that an animal can give to man. One woman was told point-blank that her puppy could give her children worms. She was given no sensible advice and, in a state of considerable anxiety, got rid of the puppy the next day. Another woman in her first pregnancy became almost hysterical when she read in a magazine that she could get a disease from her cat that might cause her to lose her baby or that might affect its nervous system so that it would be crippled for life. No one could give her a straight answer so she had her cat destroyed.

Consider the poor woman who was told that she probably had breast cancer or a form of lymphatic cancer by one physician, and after coping with this news for several days, eventually learned from another physician that all she had was cat scratch fever!

I received a sad letter from a little girl whose parents made her get rid of her beloved guinea pig because they said it caused her bronchitis, an unlikely story, considering no one ever examined the guinea pig. I also receive a lot of mail from people whose cats have leukemia or whose dogs have hepatitis, nephritis (kidney disease), or cancer of the breast. Because the names for some animal diseases are the same as for certain human diseases, some people automatically think that they might contract the disease that their veterinarian has diagnosed in their pet. No, your cat will not give you leukemia, or your dog hepatitis or breast cancer. But they can give you other diseases which may be avoided with a little knowledge and common sense.

I am apprehensive about describing some of these diseases because some people do overreact, be they hypochondriacs or protective parents! Please remember: If in doubt about the health of your pet, seek veterinary advice. Don't rush out and have it put to sleep fearing it might make you or your children ill. There are many more diseases that we get from other people, and if you really want to avoid exposure to disease, avoid crowds and keep your child home from school! The sensible way to stay healthy is not to avoid animals and people but to avoid stressing your body too much with overwork, excessive traveling, and too many commitments. A good balanced diet, clothing appropriate for the weather, sensible eating and sleeping habits, and washing hands before eating and after handling a pet are basic health rules. These are surely preferable to avoiding people and animals or stuffing yourself daily with superfluous vitamins, tonics, and medicines. Some of the more serious animal-to-man diseases listed in the tables on pages 184–187 should be explained in more detail.

First, *rabies.* This is the most terrible of the zoonoses, and in some parts of the world, such as India, it reaches epidemic proportions. This is because of the great number of free-roaming, homeless dogs that abound around villages. A dog infected with rabies may die quickly and quietly. This is the paralytic, or "dumb," form of the disease. The other form is preceded by frenzy and disorientation (the "furious" form), and an animal in this state is likely to bite people. The virus is transmitted to another animal or person in the saliva as the dog bites at anything or anyone near to it.

In the United States, rabies epidemics are prevented by vaccinating all pets, enforcement of leash laws, impoundment of free-roaming pets, and by strict quarantine regulations on all animals imported from abroad. Any animal that bites a person has to be impounded for observation and may have to be destroyed so that its brain can be examined for the presence of the rabies virus. Anyone bitten by a strange dog should report to his or her physician at once. A series of antirabies injections may have to be given.

This treatment, painful and costly as it is, may, however, be

Don't overindulge a pet—a dog should have its own separate bed. This kind of sleeping arrangement could facilitate the spread of a zoonotic disease such as mange *(H.S.U.S./Jim Atkinson).*

unnecessary in many areas. New York City has declared itself rabies-free (in terrestrial animals, but not in their bats!). So anyone bitten in the city need not be automatically subjected to antirabies therapy. The rabies virus normally keeps itself contained somehow in the wild-animal populations—raccoons, skunks, foxes, bats, etc. Though some claim that trapping wild animals prevents rabies epidemics, there is no scientific proof of such claims. It is best to avoid contact with a sick or otherwise strangely behaving wild animal. Eradicating all wildlife to prevent rabies in people is no solution! Pets should not be allowed to roam free in case they come into contact with and get bitten by a rabid wild animal.

Next on the list of zoonoses is *roundworms.* Puppies and kittens are usually born already infested, and they pass the roundworm eggs in their feces. The eggs are highly resistant to heat and desication. If contaminated feces are not burned or buried but are simply flushed down into the sewers, they can survive and could potentially contaminate the beaches, since sewage goes into the sea and most sewage treatment plants do not have a process that destroys these parasite eggs. A child playing in a backyard or park contaminated with such material runs the risk of infestation. A mild fever may develop and nothing else, or worse complications may follow, including blindness, neurological complications, and other internal problems. There are two simple remedies. Veterinary tests and treatment are needed for all pets; and owners must clean up after their pets. The latter can be done easily with a "pooper-scooper" or disposable plastic bag used like a glove which is closed after the feces have been picked up.

Toxoplasmosis is a protozoan, or one-celled, parasite that infests cats. It can cause diarrhea and general sickness and emaciation in cats, and can suddenly erupt when a cat is stressed. Cats can harbor toxoplasma without showing any symptoms, and at such times they are safe in that they are not passing the parasite in their stools. It is via the stools that humans and other cats may become infested. One should, therefore, take precautions (especially young children and pregnant women)—always wash hands well after cleaning out the litter box and especially after a sick cat has had a bout of diarrhea. A veterinary checkup will put your mind at rest.

The most common source of infection for man is via poorly cooked beef. The parasite gets into beef from cattle feed contaminated by the droppings of farm cats and mice. The mouse is a common intermediary host, and the cat gets infested when it kills and eats mice. If infested cats stay in good health, they may never develop any symptoms and therefore never become a source of infestation to other animals and people. It is only when the cat is under stress that the toxoplasma multiply and are shed in the feces. So keep your cat healthy—and cook your beef well! Also, don't let your cat go out hunting since it could easily pick up toxoplasma from any wild rodent that it may kill and eat.

Recently there has been much publicity and hysteria over two human diseases for which pets have been blamed. These are multiple sclerosis (M.S.) and leukemia/lymphatic cancer. The presence of a pet in the home has been correlated with the occurrence of multiple sclerosis in humans. The American Veterinary Medical Association has published the following news release:

MULTIPLE SCLEROSIS NO THREAT
TO OWNERS OF HEALTHY PETS

SCHAUMBURG, ILL.—Pet owners who practice good sanitation and keep their animals healthy should not be alarmed by reports suggesting a possible link between multiple sclerosis and close contact with small house pets, according to the American Veterinary Medical Association.

An article appearing in a British medical journal, *Lancet*, and a letter from a New Jersey physician published in the *Journal of the American Medical Association* have recently suggested such an association.

AVMA points out that the authors of the *Lancet* report make it clear that studies such as theirs only "show associations and not cause and effect." Their results, they warn, "require cautious interpretation." Similar associations have been found between MS and a variety of other variables including allergies, early rising, outdoor activities and eating cake.

AVMA points out that owners should have no trouble keeping pets and other members of the household free from parasites and disease if they practice good sanitary habits and see that their animals have regular checkups, routine vaccinations and other preventive medical care when needed.

Cats are known to suffer from an often fatal feline leukemia complex that is caused by a virus and may be transmitted via the saliva from one cat to another. Kittens may be born with the disease and adult cats can be symptom-free carriers. Research to date has not proven any connection between this feline oncorna virus and the human disease. Similar viruses are present in cattle and poultry (and thus in the farm produce we eat). Cooking or pasteurization treatment would inactivate any viruses that might be present. Experts warn that young children and pregnant mothers should avoid contact with sick cats. And if the cat in the home is sick, it should be tested for feline leukemia virus infection and toxoplasmosis as a safety measure.

There are probably dozens of viruses and other organisms that can live in our bodies and in our pets without causing any health problems whatsoever. There are others that we may transmit to our pets, and vice versa, like the influenzalike epidemics that will sometimes strike people and their cats in the same home at the same time.

Some epidemiologists theorize that our pets may sometimes help us resist certain diseases. After going through their bodies (a process known as "passage") an infectious agent might become weakened and this less virulent strain could, if transferred to humans, serve as a natural vaccination or protective immunization.

The key of course to preventing disease and rare cases of zoonoses, is optimal health care: clean living, sensible diet, and regular medical checkups for all the members of the family, and that, of course, includes all cats and dogs under the same roof!

The possible social and ecological ramifications of zoonoses are many. Because children can lose one or both eyes from a parasite picked up from dog feces, some people over-react, would ban all dogs from city parks and even from the cities. Laws may be passed to this effect if some pet owners continue to be irresponsible, allow their animals to roam free, and do not pick up their droppings and dispose of them appropriately. Regular veterinary examinations to check for parasites and infections such as *leptospirosis* in dogs are needed. A pet living in a crowded urban environment needs more than a rabies tag; it needs a clean bill of health as well. An annual certificate to this effect should be mandatory for all pet owners.

Although the list of zoonoses may look a bit fearful, it must be emphasized that they occur only rarely. If we are healthy, then our resistance to people-diseases and to zoonoses will be greater, and if our pets are healthy, too, they are less likely to contract animal diseases themselves.

I would be enraged and protest wildly if laws were enacted to prohibit my running my dog in the city park. What is the logical alternative to such restrictions?

Mandatory worming of all newly acquired kittens and puppies, and biannual or annual health checks by veterinarians or licensed paraveterinary aides for parasites and toxoplasmosis (together with regular rabies vaccinations) are urgently needed.

If a pet owner cannot produce a pet health certificate as evidence of compliance with state or city health regulations, then heavy penalties are warranted. One efficient procedure would be to prevent people from buying pet food in the stores if they didn't have their current pet-health card.

If a few pet owners continue to be irresponsible and flagrantly ignore local leash laws, then their right to own an animal should be denied. It would be cruel to the animal to confiscate the pet, but what else can be done when some owners will not assume the necessary responsibilities of pet ownership today? It would cost any town a fortune to enforce these regulations, but something must be done in those urban areas with a high pet and people density. The costs would be warranted, and certainly rigorous enforcement (financed by higher licensing fees for pet ownership or tax on pet food sold in the city) is a better course than an indiscriminate ban on the ownership of all dogs, as is now the case in Reykjavik, Iceland.

I would like to see some of the large pet food companies use the time they buy on national television to educate the public instead of to amuse them with cute and often inane commercials—inform the public about the behavior and needs of pets and about the social and ecological reasons why responsible pet ownership today is essential. The veterinarian and local veterinary chapters should also lend support to this consciousness-raising necessity. The poor city dog-catcher can't do it alone!

TABLE I

PARASITES AND DISEASES OF PETS THAT MAY ALSO AFFECT HUMANS

Name	Source	Complications in Man	Incidence
External Parasites			
ticks	cats & dogs	tick paralysis, Rocky Mountain spotted fever	rare
fleas	cats & dogs	sometimes severe reactions in infants—chicken-pox-like if extensive	common
mange mites	dogs (cats rare)	itching, chronic skin inflammation	occasional
ringworm	cats & dogs	itching, chronic skin disorders.	occasional
Worms			
hookworm	dogs	visceral larva migraines; creeping eruptions under skin	rare
roundworm	cats & dogs	visceral larva migraines (fever, neurological complications, blindness, especially in children)	occasional* (may be increasing)

heartworm	dogs (via mosquito)	worms in cavities of heart and in blood stream	rare
tapeworm (Echino-coccus)	dogs	hydatid disease (cysts grow in internal organs and brain)	rare (common in some countries)
Other Diseases			
rabies	dogs & cats (from bats, skunks, foxes & other wildlife)	fever, convulsions, death	rare
leptospirosis	dogs & cats	fever, muscular aches, conjunctivitis, neurological complications, kidney damage & occasional jaundice	rare* (may be increasing)
cat scratch fever	cats		occasional
toxoplasmosis	cat feces	fetal death, birth defects, jaundice, blindness, convulsions	rare* (may be increasing)
Tuberculosis	animals & man	lung & internal organ complications, chronic wasting & recurrent fever	rare (common in some countries)

*Many cases may not have been recognized in the past and accurate epidemiological figures over the years are not available.

TABLE II

PARASITES AND DISEASES OF HUMANS THAT ANIMALS MAY CARRY

Dogs and cats can be carriers of human diseases and may or may not show symptoms themselves: mumps, influenza, measles, scarlet fever and diphtheria. Keep the pet away from your children if they are sick for the pet may help spread the disease.

Name	Source	Complications in Man	Incidence
trichinosis	beef and pork (poorly cooked)	fever, muscular aches, stomach upset, lung, heart and eye complications	common (in some areas)
tapeworm	beef (poorly cooked)	gastrointestinal upset, weight loss	common (in some areas)
Asiatic flu	chinese pigs	fever, muscular aches, pneumonia, and other secondary complications	world wide epidemics
undulant fever (brucellosis)	cattle	periodic fever, arthritis, and internal organ complications	rare (common in some areas)
psittacosis	parrots, parakeets	fever, pneumonia	rare
Salmonella	turtles	fever, severe gastrointestinal upset	not uncommon

Disease	Source/Transmission	Symptoms	Frequency
encephalomyelitis	(many forms, e.g., St. Louis, equine) from animals to man via mosquito	fever, neurologic disturbances	not uncommon, occasional local epidemics
LCM (lymphocytic choriomeningitis)	hamsters	flulike signs to severe neurological complications	rare
tularemia	from handling wild game	fever, chronic sore at point of infection	rare
tuberculosis	cattle, monkeys	chronic, wasting, internal complications	rare
cryptococcosis	pigeon droppings	pneumonia, meningitis	rare
bubonic plague	rats (via rat fleas)	fever, delirum, the "black" death	rare
histoplasmosis	chicken & starling droppings	"farmer's lung," pneumonia, chronic lung problems	not uncommon
virus B	monkeys	fever, paralysis, death	rare
infectious hepatitis	apes	fever, severe debility	rare

23

Pet Problems in Summertime: Dog Days for Dogs

"Summertime, and the living is easy . . ." for cats, but not for dogs! Being desert animals, cats thrive in the heat and have no problems to speak of. But for our canine friends, summer is probably the worst time of the year. For some dogs, summer means a spell in a boarding kennel while their owners are on vacation; for others it can mean a frightening journey by plane or car, or the hazards of adapting to a new vacation home. For all too many, summer means illness and accidents.

One lady called me last summer with the sad saga of her dog's summer. It began with his being carsick and ended up with his being attacked by a skunk! After that, the poor dog was lost in the woods for a week and they had to stay on to find it, much to the annoyance of her workaholic husband!

So here are some precautions and guidelines to make life easier for your dog (and you) in the good old summertime.

First, whether you're including your dog on vacation, leaving it in a boarding kennel, or just remaining at home as usual, take your dog to the vet for a *health checkup*. Late spring/early summer is check-up time for various reasons.

First and foremost, your vet will check for *heartworm*. If your dog is infested, the immature form (filaria) of the heartworms will be present in your dog's bloodstream, and the vet will suggest a course of treatment. Summertime is mosquito time, and this biting insect can infest your dog with the filaria from an afflicted dog. (If you live in a warm climate like Florida, have your dog checked every six months.) If your dog's blood test is negative, your vet will give you liquid medicine to put in your pet's food, or a pill, to stop filaria from developing should your animal get bitten by a carrier mosquito. Every dog should be examined for heartworm!

Secondly, check on your dog's vaccination status. If you plan to travel with him or leave him in a kennel (where he may pick up a contagious disease) he will need booster shots. In fact, the better boarding kennels insist on this. He (or she!) should receive a booster for distemper, hepatitis, and leptospirosis, as well as the annual rabies shot.

A general checkup often turns up minor problems, such as toenails that need trimming, ears that need cleaning, teeth that need scaling, and so on. But more importantly, it may uncover serious problems, such as a heart abnormality or kidney dysfunction, which frequently get worse during the stresses of hot weather and/or a new vacation home. If such is the case, your vet will provide you with advice and your pet with medication and a corrective diet to help him survive the summer happily.

Some diet restrictions are also especially important if your dog is overweight. Many American dogs are overweight today and this problem, combined with summer stresses, a poor heart, weak kidneys, or other internal disorder, could mean a crisis this summer for your dog.

Since summer carries with it the threat of emergencies, you must assure yourself of veterinary help. Have the phone number and address of your vet if (a) you're leaving your pet at home with house-sitters or (b) if you're leaving your pet at a local boarding kennel. Locate a vet in the area where you're vacationing if you plan to take your pet with you, and keep the vet's phone number on hand.

If you plan to travel by car with your dog and have never done so before, give it a trial run first. Some dogs, just like some people, are prone to motion sickness. Dramamine, or a similar anti-motion-sickness drug, will help your dog immensely. Or your vet may prescribe a tranquilizer if the trip overly excites your pet. Remember, too, on a long ride your pet will need frequent toilet stops.

Don't neglect to call ahead of time to book housing. Many motels will accommodate a housebroken pet, but some won't. There's nothing worse, after a long drive, than cruising around with a tired, frustrated family and a cooped-up pooch, trying to find a motel that will take your menagerie.

For long hot drives, take along ice in a cooler. It can be melted down for water, if necessary, or used to make cool compresses, which can be very comforting to a hot animal. Dogs (and cats, too) have to pant to keep cool, and being confined in a hot crate, or in the back of a sun-heated car, can possibly cause heatstroke. To avoid this disaster, provide good ventilation for your animal (making sure it can't escape through an open window). Also provide adequate shade and plenty of water at all times. The same holds true for a dog chained or confined to the backyard. Heatstroke can be lethal, especially to large, furry, obese, and older dogs with chronic heart problems.

A common summer problem for people and pooches alike is allergy. Some dogs develop allergies to various pollens, and a weekly bath in mild shampoo (baby shampoo is ideal) will help significantly.

The most common summer allergy is "hot spot" (a moist, itchy red skin sore), which is caused by fleas. The answer, of course, is to *get the fleas!* Also, ask your vet for antiallergy pills or shots.

Fleas and ticks and chiggers are among the nastiest of summer problems in most places. Ask your vet for a suitable powder or regular dip. Flea collars are okay for small dogs, but beware—they can cause an allergic contact dermatitis, a "skin burn" around the neck. Your home may be flea-infested, too, and it may be necessary to do a thorough vacuuming, and to have a fumigation done by the health department.

We're in danger of losing the war on fleas. In many areas, fleas are becoming resistant to our insecticides. And if we were to resort to stronger chemicals we run risks of making ourselves and our pets ill, too. Many people have been getting good results using vitamin B as a flea repellent! My assistant recently used this method on her flea-ridden pooch and within a couple of days it was flea-free. But once she stopped putting yeast in her dog's food, the fleas were back.

Use the cheapest form of vitamin B—brewer's yeast—about one teaspoon a day sprinkled in food for a 30-pound dog. Using yeast, and flea collars, and dipping and/or powdering your dog with flea killer should control the pests (get a variety of preparations from your vet). Treat your dog every ten to fourteen days.

Other skin problems can be caused by chiggers, and there isn't much of a remedy for that, be they on people or their pets. Try to keep your animal out of long grass; a dusting with flower of sulfur before you all go out may help.

Some people find their living room, or even their whole house, infested with ticks—even to the point where they lay their eggs on the walls! I'm told that a heap of dry ice on the floor will attract ticks like a magnet—give it a try (also in your barn or backyard). Keep a pair of fine tweezers handy for pulling off ticks when they become profuse.

One of the most irritating problems for outdoor dogs in the summer, especially dogs with erect ears like German shepherds, are biting flies. They will attack the ear tips, and a bloody crust will soon develop. Regular insect repellent should be applied to a dog's ears morning and early evening. For those dogs that are scared of spray cans, use a cream or fluid instead.

Dogs don't get sunburns the way we do, with one exception—collie dogs are susceptible to "collie nose." This is a hypersensitivity to sunlight that affects the nose and muzzle; when exposed to sunlight they become pink, inflamed, and scaly. The condition may be temporarily alleviated by a sunscreen ointment, but veterinary therapy is usually needed.

With other dogs, sunlight acts to improve a dog's coat and general condition. Seawater also does miracles for some dog's skin and foot problems. But beware: Other dogs may develop sand or salt burns between the toes and pads.

If your pooch is long-haired and doesn't shed out to a light summer coat, it would be a good idea to take him to a groomer or "beauty parlor." This is especially important if the dog will be outdoors a great deal of the time. A damp, matted coat can cause skin infections—fungal and bacterial "hot spots." Some species of flies will lay their eggs in such mats, and the hatched maggots can cause considerable skin irritation if not spotted early.

A thick coat can insulate a dog (like a thermos flask) and help keep it cool, but many domestic dogs don't have the ideal summer coat for this kind of protection; they should have a close trim, a thinning or stripping, or a close chest and belly cut (a poodle, for instance).

I would also clip any long hair around the dog's hind quarters, ears, and feet. Humid ears, matted with fur, will erupt with infection in a hot moist summer climate; similarly, feet will develop skin problems, especially between the toes. Grass seeds or plant bristles may lodge in long hair in the feet, ears, and groin and actually burrow into your dog's skin and cause considerable irritation. A good coat trimming will help keep a long-haired dog cool and clean; ticks will be more easily picked off by yourself and by the dog, too.

If your dog comes back with bumps all over its body, or a swollen nose or mouth—yes, it may well be a wasp or bee sting that causes either a local irriation or more general hives. Try to find the sting and pull it out (if it's a bee); apply antihistamine cream (which you should have on hand for yourself anyway).

If you're away on vacation with your pet, be sure it is wearing a collar and identity tags that won't slip off, in case it gets lost. A lost animal is one of the most frequent upsets during vacation. The new, exciting, and unfamiliar place is a delight to explore but a hazard. If you're in an area with animal traps, unstable terrain, traffic, railroad tracks, shooting ranges, etc., you may want to restrain your dog.

Incidentally, one of the delights of being on vacation for a dog is to find new things—often smelly things—and to roll in them, and to chase new things—even skunks. To "freshen up" a dog who comes home "high" from a skunk or some obnoxious material, hose him down with warm water and mild detergent; then follow up with a ten- to fifteen-minute soak in tomato juice or ketchup and another soapy rinse.

There is another aspect to consider in summer. If you are one of those people who likes to adopt a pet on vacation to keep your kids happy, please reflect upon the values and state of mind you may instill in your children when you leave that pet to fend for itself after you depart from your vacation home. This abandonment of animals, as though they were used-up toys, is a widespread phenomenon today, but I don't think it's simply because people are callous.

Sometimes they are caught in an ethical and humane dilemma. The children, for example, may find a stray puppy or kitten and take care of it through the vacation. Then at summer's end, it can't be taken home. This reality can ruin a child's vacation.

Ideally, don't adopt a stray unless you *can* take it home, or unless you're prepared to explain beforehand the end situation fully to the children. Let them make every effort to find a home for the animal while you are on vacation. Instilling humane values in our children is especially important in a throwaway culture such as ours.

If you leave pets other than dogs or cats at home, don't just load them up with food and water and hope for the best. Rabbits, hamsters, gerbils, mice, turtles, fish, and cage birds, in fact, any pet and plant you may have, should be checked regularly. Arrange for a neighbor or friend to drop in daily to make sure all is in order. For example, a water bottle may become detached and all the water spill out, and the animals may die; food may get moldy and the pets starve or become ill; an animal may get sick or even have babies and need special attention. Living creatures that you leave behind need as much care and attention as those you take with you.

Summer may bring some surprises for you and your pet, but if you're prepared to meet them, you may sail through an easy, crisis-free season!

24

Cats and Dogs As Fellow Travelers: Getting Your Pet from Here to There Safely

We are a highly mobile society, and often where the family goes the pet goes, too. But a long journey by car or plane can cause an animal physical and psychological stress, and for this reason some vacation-bound pet owners decide instead to board their animal or arrange for a pet-sitter at home in their absence. However, if you simply can't think of going on a trip and leaving behind this important member of the family, here are several precautionary steps you can take to avoid unnecessary suffering and make your pet's journey a howling success.

Traveling by Car

An animal's first experience in a car can be disastrous. All too frequently an animal reacts by becoming hyperactive or car sick, trembling and salivating profusely, panicking and trying to escape, and even defecating and urinating in the acute anxiety of the experience. Needless to say, it's neither safe nor pleasant to drive down a highway with a pet in this condition. Even a calm, generally predictable animal can suddenly become a problem in an automobile. I treated one young St. Bernard that had seemed to be a fine traveler—until the moment it unexpectedly jumped out of its master's convertible at a stoplight and was hit by a truck. Even a pet peacefully behaving itself can cause trouble. Once when I was driving with my Abyssinian cat, Sam, I suddenly put my foot down on the brake and found Sam's head resting under the foot pedal! No damage was done, but it was a close call.

• The first rule then is: Keep even the calmest and the best-behaved pet restrained in the backseat on a securely hooked leash (and make sure the doors are locked—you don't want the animal tugging open any handles). Or place the pet in a cage or carrier or behind a wire screen. Even a leashed dog should be as far back in a station wagon as possible, unless it's very well-behaved and there's a youngster to keep an eye on it constantly. But whatever you do, the point is to keep the driver's area clear at all times.

• Make sure that the car windows are not open too wide, even if the pet is leashed. An animal hanging out of a moving car is a hazard for everyone, and even if the car is stationary, there could be tragedy. A pet left in a car for only a few minutes can crawl out of a partially open window—and you might return to find the poor creature half choked, hanging out of the window by its leash.

But if you must have a pet in an auto for even a short period, be sure that the windows are open enough to provide ample air. It's very important that the car be ventilated—especially on hot summer days. Dogs with thick fur and/or short muzzles, aged animals with heart problems and those that become anxious and hyperactive when left alone are susceptible to heatstroke. In fact, heatstroke is a killer of many dogs left in parked cars during the summer—so park in the shade whenever possible. Also, it's better to keep the street-side windows open for ventilation rather than the curb-side wind-ows, through which a child might try to pet or play with the dog and provoke it into biting.

• *Never* travel with your pet in the trunk of the car. It may suffocate or succumb to heatstroke or carbon-monoxide poisoning.

• In planning for a full-day's auto ride, give your pet one light meal the day before and no food during the trip, except possibly a snack or—for dogs—a rawhide chew. This advice applies as well when shipping a grown dog or cat by air for a day's trip. This way, the pet won't have the discomfort of becoming sick—and the humans involved will be spared the possibility of unpleasantness as well.

• Water is crucial, especially on hot days. Make frequent stops to allow a dog to lick and chew ice cubes or drink cold water. In very hot weather, a wet towel draped over the cage or over the animal itself will also help keep it cool. Stops along the way are also needed so a dog can have a short walk and the opportunity to attend to its natural functions. Such a rest stop isn't possible for most cats, though, since few of them are leash-trained. On a very long trip, you might have to take along a litter box.

• If your pet shows severe signs of stress in a car, tranquilizers are helpful, and your vet can prescribe them. Or try using a sedative and antinausea drug like Dramamine. But I would only tranquilize the most fearful and hyperactive animals, since drugs may leave them uncoordinated and disinterested in drinking water—thus decreasing their tolerance to other discomforts. Often an over-drugged animal injures itself, staggering around in its crate; also, sphincter control may be lost, and the poor animal will really be in distress (this is important to consider when shipping an animal by air).

Preferable to drugs is what I call "exposure habituation." Accustom a pet to car riding by putting it in the car as it stands in the garage or driveway, and rewarding it with petting and tidbits of its favorite food. Then, once it appears settled, switch on the engine, then the radio and then the air-conditioner fan. A few days later, take the pet for a short drive, and then immediately afterwards for a walk or a game of tag or whatever activity your pet really enjoys. Give it a treat of tuna fish or a bone to chew on at home. Riding in the car will then be associated with pleasant experiences, and over several days the smells, sounds, and vibrations it experiences in the car will not seem frightening. A ride in the car is frequently connected in a pet's memory with a visit to the veterinary hospital or boarding kennel, and exposure habituating will gradually overcome this negative attitude.

• Once on the road, be careful that your cat or dog doesn't roam off if unleashed at rest or gasoline stops, since animals can easily get lost in an unfamiliar place. When you arrive at your destination, keep the dog or cat confined or otherwise restrained on the property around your summer home or campsite for at least a few days. After that, if you're camping, still keep your pet close by: this could save a cat from being caught in a trap or a dog from being shot by a hunter or a farmer.

If you want to stay at a hotel or motel, phone ahead to make sure pets are acceptable. Some hotels have small kennels; some don't allow pets at all.

Shipping by Air

If you're contemplating shipping a pet, you should undertake a similar exposure-habituation procedure with the shipping crate or holding cage. Accustom the pet to being inside the crate: Make a game of retrieving a ball or chasing a string into the box. Put food inside the crate, and let your pet eat with the door open. Later, close the door and talk gently and reassuringly to the animal: then let it out, petting and praising it. Six or seven days of such preconditioning will make confinement in the shipping crate much less traumatic.

What kind of crate or cage should you select when shipping a pet by air? Many of the crates available today are quite inadequate, so take the time to shop for a safe, suitable one. Here are some guidelines:

• First, the cage or crate should be large enough for the animal to turn around and sit up in (with the obvious exception of very large dogs, such as Great Danes and Saint Bernards). Three of the four sides should be opaque to give the animal a sense of privacy and security (all-wire open cages are not advisable, except for transporting a pet in the back of the family car). There should be several air holes on each of the sides and on the top as well. Pets have been unable to get sufficient air when baggage has been piled around their crates: a liberal distribution of ventilation holes reduces the chances of such an accident.

• Don't put a lock on the cage door: two safety catches should suffice, since the door must be opened in order for personnel to attend to your pet, especially if it's necessary for the animal to stay any length of time at the airport.

• Line the floor of the crate with some absorbent material or with several layers of newspaper. A water bowl secured to the inside of the cage door is essential: so is a food bowl for long journeys. Unfortunately, most water bowls spill easily; manufacturers should design more practical containers.

• The new crates made of molded fiber glass on reinforced plastic frames are excellent if they are designed according to the specifications I mention; they are virtually crushproof and generally give the animal a sense of security. A grill door is, of course, necessary so that the animal can be checked.

Feeding and watering can be tricky, especially if the animal tries to bite or escape. Attendants may then simply pour water and food through the door bars. Ideally, the front door of the carrier should have a small door cut into the main door that offers access to the food and water bowls.

But I'm sorry to say that no matter how well-designed your crate is and how carefully you have preconditioned your pet for a journey by air, there is no guarantee that it will arrive at its destination on schedule—or even alive!

As far as I'm concerned—and my concern is shared by countless other animal lovers and breeders—the transportation of animals by air is inhumane and barbaric, and all air carriers have a public obligation to improve the situation. Although certain airlines have improved transport conditions for animals, the cold, cruel fact is that animals shipped by airfreight have *lowest* priority, even lower than baggage and other freight. Animals have died of heat exhaustion or became sick from prolonged exposure on landing docks and in cold freight warehouses. Others have been killed or injured in transit by cargo falling onto the crate in the baggage hold of the plane. Few baggage holds are temperature controlled or fully pressurized, even though some airlines claim that your pet travels in the same luxury as you do.

Unless you are flying *with* your pet and it is being checked through along with your baggage, there is no guarantee that your animal will get on any flight on any given day. If your pet is very small, it may be hand carried into the passenger cabin in a small carrier case, and whenever possible, this should be your plan. But book your pet as early as you can, since there are regulations governing the number of pets per cabin per flight.

• I don't advise any pet owner or breeder to send a puppy by air if it's under twelve weeks of age. Young animals are extremely susceptible to stress caused by such exposure and will then be more susceptible to disease. Emotional trauma may lead to permanent psychological damage.

• As things are now, if you must send your pet by air and you can't travel with it, stay with the animal until an airline agent assures you it's definitely on the plane. If it is "bumped" you can take it home or wait with it for the next flight. If possible, find a direct flight for your pet; never ship over a public holiday, and avoid weekends.

• Don't ship your pet if you learn it's being put in the same hold with dry ice (to preserve flowers, medicines, and other perishables). Dry-ice fumes can be lethal in a confined space.

• For interstate transportation, you will need a health certificate from a veterinarian and proof that your pet has had a rabies vaccination. Without these, it cannot be shipped legally. (In fact, these papers are often needed if you are driving your pet into another country: check Canadian and Mexican consulates or information bureaus before you set out over the border.)

Receiving a Shipped Animal

Make life easier for yourself and the animal that has been shipped to or with you.

1. Don't let it out of its crate at the airport, landing dock, or in the car; it might bolt and escape. Wait until you get home to release a confined pet.

2. If there are children around, keep them as quiet as possible; the pet has been traumatized enough by its trip, and its reentry into your family should be as calm as possible.

3. Offer the pet food and water, and keep a close eye on it for at least 24 hours—if by that time it's not bright and alert, eating well and otherwise acting normally, waste no time in consulting a veterinarian.

One final and important point: Whether traveling by auto or by air, your pet should have an identification tag securely fastened around its neck. Such a tag should clearly indicate your name, address and telephone number. If there's a cage or carrier, it should be tagged with this information as well.

By taking precautions, you should be able to write a happy ending to your pet's travels.

25

Family Crisis: When a Pet Is Lost and How to Find It

Losing a pet is a traumatic experience. The owner—whether a child or an adult—heartbreakingly imagines every possible disaster. What should you do if this serious emergency strikes your home? And further, what precautions might you take to prevent such a sad and disrupting calamity?

Although many of the procedures for finding a lost cat or a lost dog are similar, there are specific suggestions for handling each of these unfortunate mishaps. But whether it's your pooch or your pussycat that's missing, the first bit of advice is *don't panic*! If your pet simply slipped the leash or got out of the backyard or back door, or is otherwise lost near home, you have a good chance of recovering it.

The Lost Dog

Looking for a lost dog is somewhat like looking for a lost child. You'll get clues by knowing his character and habits. Start the search, therefore, by asking yourself, "When and where did I last see my dog around the house? Could he have followed neighborhood children home from school—or followed them *to* school?" My Welsh terrier not only tagged after the children to school, he'd sometimes go to the playground for handouts at lunchtime! Your dog may have followed your own children when they went out playing down the block; ask them when and where they last saw him.

Walk, drive, or bicycle around the neighborhood, and call or whistle for him. Don't be shy about asking any passersby if they've seen him. Is there a park nearby where you often walk him? He could be roaming around there, enjoying his freedom and all the delightful smells of other dogs.

Check out neighbors who have dogs; some dogs, just like kids, like to play together. If your neighbors have a female dog that's in heat, your male pooch could well be over there, waiting with amorous intent at their doorstep! He may also be on a doorstep five blocks down; a bitch in heat, either roaming free or out on a walk with its owner, will signal her state to male dogs every time she urinates. These signals act like a magnet for free-roaming male dogs and they will track her home.

(It's a good idea to confine a female dog when she's in heat. Having her spayed or giving her chlorophyll tablets that help block the signal in her urine will reduce these problems for the owners of the male dogs in the neighborhood. Many male dogs do get lost or even run over when tracking or chasing after a female in heat.)

If, after a thorough search of the neighborhood, you haven't found your dog, call your local police and animal pound or humane shelter and give them a detailed description of your dog. Since your pet may not be picked up by municipal animal control officers for one or more days, keep calling—twice a day, in the late morning and later afternoon, unless they advise you otherwise.

If you doubt their competence, and if they have a very large shelter with many animals, don't hesitate to go there to look for your dog on your own—especially if it's a nondescript brown mutt and, worse, has no identification tags.

Many shelters have a fast turnover rate; they destroy the animals after five or ten days to make room for more incoming strays and lost animals. Some even dispose of the animals after seventy-two hours! So you should visit more than once—I'd say every three days or so if you're not confident that they will recognize your pet. I stress this point because of an experience I once had at a very busy animal shelter. I just happened to drop by (intuitively?) two weeks after I lost my dog—and there she was! She had only just been brought in, which meant she had been on the streets for several days.

Additionally, it's a good idea to phone one or two local radio stations. Many of them have a public service slot and will gladly broadcast a description of a missing pet. And, of course, use your local newspaper. A small-town paper may even run a photo of your pet but, generally, you will have to place an ad in the lost-and-found column. (And incidentally, if you ever *find* a lost animal, don't put off notifying some authority—police, radio, pound, etc. Just put yourself in the place of the frantic owner!)

Many people have found it very effective to make a stack of small "Lost Dog" posters and stick them up on lampposts and walls in their neighborhood. The poster can be quite simple or include a photo. Offering a small reward is always helpful. Give your phone number plus a full description of the dog and its name. A team of children making house calls for you in the neighborhood can be a great help, too.

Of course, you can always hope that some kind soul has taken your dog into their house for safekeeping. One stray dog in St. Louis hit the headlines last summer by rescuing the family's small child from their blazing car. A photo of the canine hero, described as a stray they had just taken in, enabled the dog's original owners to find their animal. When they saw how devoted their dog was to the child, they decided to leave their pet with its new family, after all!

Not all lost-dog stories are so dramatic and have such a fortunate and happy ending. All too often, when people take in a lost dog they neglect to call the authorities and inform them. It's hard to believe that people play "Finders-Keepers" with a living creature.

If there's an outbreak of disappearing dogs, it could mean that a dog-napper is active in your area. Thefts of dogs have diminished considerably, however, thanks to more stringent regulations controlling the licensing of suppliers of animals for research. In the past, many a stolen pet finished up as a research subject!

Many shelters supply licensed dealers with dogs (and cats) for distribution to out-of-state research laboratories. When they impound a stray for a mandatory seventy-two hours before it is

Protect your dog: a lost dog may soon be a dead one *(H.S.U.S./M. Hegedus).*

passed over to the dealer, you don't have much time to save your pet. Within five or six days, your animal can be hundreds of miles away, so don't waste time in just hoping that your dog will somehow find his way home. If he's a stable dog, not given to panic, he may survive road traffic, but, on the other hand, if he's calm and friendly, he's more likely to be picked up fast, and then . . . ?

Take Precautions

What additional safety measures, other than making your back-yard more secure, can you take to avoid the lost-pet emergency? First, be sure your dog always wears an identity collar carrying your phone number and/or street address. But remember that collars can and do come off. Is your animal's collar adjusted so it won't slip off his head?

A number of local humane organizations have a program of pet-tattooing. In this relatively painless procedure, the dog is tattooed in the groin region or ear with a special code number or with your social security number. (I think using the social security number is much more efficient; the former method depends on who keeps the code book.) One advantage of tattooing your dog with an identifying number is that it stands a chance of being noticed by animal handlers—which could mean a short-term reprieve from euthanasia while they try to locate the owner.

Also, some humane shelters will ask for evidence to support your claim to ownership of a dog they're holding. Knowing its tattoo number is certainly proof, especially if the dog has lost—or doesn't have—collar and tags. A family photo including the dog will help, too. You may consider these proof-of-ownership requests as typical frustrating bureaucracy, but the better animal shelters are very particular about releasing lost dogs. And it's a good thing they are! It's essential to protect the impounded dog from unscrupulous people who fraudulently make claims to a particular dog just because they like the breed or type. The shelter that screens all claimants is protecting your dog. And certainly, a tattoo would make crooked claims or mistaken identities less possible.

After being free and roaming the streets for days, your dog, dirty and emaciated, may be difficult to identify even for you—especially if it's one of a very uniform breed. And its reactions toward you won't always be decisive either. Some impounded dogs are so desperate to get out, they'll jump up and greet anyone like lost friends. Others are so terrified and dazed that they don't even recognize their rightful owners.

Train your dog to come to a whistle call—it will be more effective than your voice if he ever gets lost. You could then drive around the neighborhood by car or bicycle, giving repeated signals. This method has helped me find a missing pet on more than one occasion.

Familiarize your animal with a good wide radius of terrain around where you live. If you just take him for short walks in one direction only, he won't have good bearings to find his way home, if he should stray one day. Remember, the scent marks of other dogs in the neighborhood, as well as his own, can help a dog navigate his way home.

Some dogs are inveterate roamers and will do their utmost to get out whenever they can. This becomes a problem especially when the male dog smells the urine of a female who is in heat when you take him for a walk. From then on, he'll want to get out! Regular exercise can reduce this drive in some dogs, and castration will help significantly. If you have one of these roaming escape artists, seriously consider having him surgically altered.

Do your best to train your dog from an early age to come when called (by voice and by whistle signal). You will then have control over him if he accidentally slips his leash or when he's roaming free with you on vacation in the country. Especially if your dog is a roamer by nature, you should make sure he responds to signals.

I remember a long obituary in my local small-town newspaper in England. It was for a small border terrier named Jock whom everyone knew. He belonged to a respectable family that lived in a nearby village. Jock used to regularly take the local bus to town all by himself, and then take the bus back home later in the day. He did this for years and was a well known character. Then one day Jock didn't come home on the bus, as usual—he was lost! After weeks of advertising in local and national papers, Jock was located forty miles away in a large city. He was living happily with a family in Manchester who had found the intelligent dog wandering around, obviously lost, on the busy city sidewalk. Jock had accidentally taken the wrong bus! From then on, Jock's owners kept him at home, and he lived out his years contentedly. If you have an independent animal like Jock, you'll have to use good judgment (as you would with a child) as to where to draw his boundary lines.

The Lost Cat

What to do if your feline friend is missing? Follow the exact same procedures as for a lost dog, step by step. *But remember*, that unlike most dogs, a terrified cat may not come out of hiding when you call for it. However, it may meow in response, so keep your ears well tuned. Also, look up into trees or any vertical structures your cat might climb.

A cat won't travel nearly the same distance as a lost dog— perhaps a few blocks at the most (and even that would take some time), so you shouldn't have a long search. However, you'll have to be more thorough, because of a cat's tendency to hide and/or climb up things.

A kitten may not survive long outdoors, quickly becoming disoriented, soon lost forever (H.S.U.S./Kurt W. Wildermuth).

Listen and look out for a cat's growling and screaming—it may lead you to your cat. Should your cat wander into the territory of a free-roaming tom cat or queen, it may well result in a feline ruckus and you'd better hurry to the rescue. But be careful handling your cat—it may be quite terrified, not seem to recognize you in its hysteria, and you may get clawed.

Since cats are nocturnal creatures, go out at dark, with a flashlight, to seek your pet. Call for it—it may feel more secure in the dark and come out to you or call in response to your voice. The flashlight will help you pick out its shining, light-reflecting eyes at night.

Cats can be tattooed and should wear a collar and identification tags if they are prone to slipping outdoors. As with dogs, neutering your cat will help reduce its drive to go outdoors and thus reduce the chances of its getting into trouble. Raised indoors from early kittenhood, most cats would sooner stay indoors, so it's not really inhumane to keep such cats confined. In fact, you are being a fully responsible and caring cat owner.

If your cat particularly enjoys going outdoors, you can leash-train it. You should use the leash to keep yourself attached to the cat and follow it—the reverse is usual with a dog (though some dogs do take their guardians for a walk)!

A final note to kindly, but often misguided, folk: If a stray cat is meowing at your door and it's healthy and there's no heavy traffic or other dangers nearby, don't encourage it to stay by feeding it. A hungry cat that isn't sick or terrified should soon find its way home. The rule: Let it be.

Right now, as I write, there's an announcement on my radio. "Please call Karen if you have found a young female golden retriever; she was lost last Sunday in Annadale." I hope *you* never find yourself in Karen's position. Good luck, Karen! Good luck, little retriever!

26

Euthanasia: When Pets Must Part

This is a delicate and controversial subject and one I have put off writing about for too long. Right now I'm thinking about a neighbor I see every day carrying her old, arthritic, and very blind Basenji dog. She will stop at intervals, put the dog on the ground and let it sniff around and walk a little, then she will pick it up and carry it a bit farther. It lies in her arms like a stiff rag doll. The dog is very old, but it can still enjoy life. It is not suffering. It enjoys its food and its frequent excursions outdoors. Owner and dog alike have adapted to the burden of old age, and I sense dignity and profound humanity as the woman carries her dog home.

Contrast this with a friend of mine who lives just off the highway outside of a large town. She often sees dogs, kittens, and puppies being dropped off by the side of the road or at the edge of the woods that border the highway. Thousands of unwanted pets are discarded each year this way all over the United States. Few survive. Some are picked up by the local pound. What of their original owners? Perhaps they thought it best to give the animals a chance—let nature take care of them. Nature will not take care of them. If no homes can be found for such animals, then the ultimate responsible act is not to abandon the animal to some unknown fate but to have it humanely put to sleep. "Any life is better than no life at all" is one not uncommon rationalization. Another is "all life is sacred." Others, such as myself, are concerned about the quality of life and believe that a primary obligation is to alleviate unnatural suffering (such as keeping a terminally ill pet alive on medication, or abandoning a kitten or puppy by the roadside).

There are also very practical social, public health, ecological, and economic reasons behind euthanizing unwanted pets. Until owners are more responsible and better controls are instigated to reduce pet overpopulation, the unwanted creatures must be humanely disposed of. This is the thankless task of many humane shelters. Having free-roaming cats, dogs, and their offspring in our towns and rural areas would be chaotic. Incidence of rabies and other human health risks would be increased and the impact on wildlife and farm stock by pets gone wild would be great. For obvious financial reasons, it would be impossible to provide food and regular care to keep all unwanted pets alive until they died from old age.

The time comes in the life of all pets when they must be put to sleep. While some pets expire without human assistance, from sickness or old age or a combination of both, others will linger on. And while they might be kept alive with supportive medication, the critical question arises: When is it best to decide to have a pet put to sleep? Also, what is the best, the most humane method of euthanasia? Sometimes a pet owner may be faced with having to dispose of an unwanted and unadoptable litter of kittens or puppies. Stuffing them into a sack weighted with a brick and throwing the lot into the neighborhood creek is no humane solution. Nor is taking the old dog into the yard and shooting it to put it out of its misery. In most neighborhoods, you can't shoot a firearm anyway. The pioneer days are over when our forefathers would quickly dispatch a crippled horse or worn-out dog with a six-shooter.

After years of close companionship and the countless gifts of joy, love, and acceptance that a pet can give to a person, few people would deny their pets a humane and dignified death. But there are some details you should know.

First, if you have a litter of pups or kittens and you don't bother to find homes for them but take them to the local animal shelter instead, the chances are high that most will be killed. Most animal shelters are euthanasia centers and not, as is commonly believed, adoption agencies for pets since only ten to fifteen percent of the animals ever find a new home.

Taking your aging or terminally ill pet to a municipal animal shelter to be euthanized (which means to be killed humanely) is no guarantee that it will meet death with dignity and without distress and suffering.

Many animal shelters use crude and inhumane methods to kill animals: raw and irritating exhaust fumes from a truck or gasoline engine; an injection with a drug that causes paralysis such that the animal is unable to breathe and suffocates. Various kinds of gas chambers are sometimes used, and the animals may be crowded together inside and die slowly and in great panic. One method still used widely is the decompression chamber. This device consists of a tight metal cylinder, into which the animals are placed, and a vacuum pump that sucks out all the air from the cylinder at an implosive rate, shoots the animal at explosive velocity to a high altitude. This causes unconsciousness and death. Overcrowding the chamber (cats and dogs are often stuffed in together), leaking valves that cause repressurization, and other factors make this an unsatisfactory system unless operated by well-trained and sensitive technicians. Few animal shelters have trained personnel.

Your pet, if not too far gone, could even be kept a day or so at the pound and then shipped to a medical school or research laboratory with other strays picked up by dogcatchers and pets given to the shelter for adoption or euthanasia. This is a common practice in many areas. A bill is now before the New York State senate to stop such redeployment of people's pets.

If you have any doubts about what euthanasia method your local animal shelter uses, ask them. And if you aren't too easily upset, they should allow you to see your pet being put to sleep, if you request it. If they deny you this right, chances are they are using an unsavory and possibly inhumane method of destruction.

By far the best method of euthanasia, which most veterinarians and the better animal shelters and humane societies administer, is sodium pentobarbital. This is an anesthetic that smoothly puts an animal quietly to sleep and, given as an overdose, stops it from recovering.

Those who care for their pets and wish to be certain that it will be euthanized properly will be present when their pets are euthanized. With many clients, I would have them observe and sometimes even hold their pet while I injected it. Some struggling often occurs and a little whining or twitching as the drug takes effect. If it was my pet, I would want it to die in the security of my own arms, feeling it my responsibility to ensure that it dies as humanely as possible.

Not all pet owners can take such a final step, but everyone should check in advance the credentials of the local animal shelter before taking a pet there to be put to sleep. If it is not accredited with the Humane Society of the United States (which makes sure that the euthanasia methods are humane), you should take your pet to a reputable veterinarian for euthanasia.

The next question, and indeed the hardest one, is *when* should a pet be euthanized, and for what reasons. Some people may contend that it is wrong to kill at all and that nature should be allowed to take its course; they forget that mercy killing is an act of compassion. Mahatma Gandhi once publicly violated one very strong religious law in India: not to kill a cow. Gandhi was a great religious figure and when he destroyed a calf that was terminally ill and suffering terribly, even though he knew he would be ridiculed, he did it to demonstrate responsible compassion. In other words, mercy killing, or euthanasia, has its place in society and in our ethics and moral code.

But in order for pet owners to know that their pet is terminally ill and may be suffering, a thorough veterinary examination may be needed. Suppose the animal is not suffering unduly and could be kept alive longer on supportive medication. If it is certain your pet would not suffer, that you can afford the medication, and that giving the medication (by injection or orally) wouldn't cause you, the family, or your pet undue distress, then I would support a pet's life a little longer.

Not all people would agree with me, however. An aging dog is put to sleep once its owner notices the animal is starting to lose its eyesight; another owner, whose pooch has a senility problem such that it has to be taken out to urinate more often, wants the dog put to sleep. More than once I have been asked to keep a pet alive, even though it was in obvious pain and distress from a failing heart or cancer.

These three examples are illustrative of how human sentiment, or lack of it, can cloud a person's thinking and violate the animal's right to life or to euthanasia, as the case may be.

Wanting to put a dog to sleep because it is losing its eyesight overlooks the fact that an aging dog can cope extremely well with progressive blindness. Sometimes the reason for having an animal put to sleep is sheer utility. The animal is no longer a satisfactory thing to have around; it has become a burden. But what of the debt one owes the animal after a lifetime of loyalty and companionship?

While ignorance or crass utility rather than compassion may underlie a person's decision to have his or her pet put down, esthetics is another common motive. I recall several people whose cats or dogs had to have a leg amputated. Rather than have the operation done, they chose to have their pets destroyed (and not for economic reasons either).

Not unlike the old dog going blind, a three-legged pet is just too unesthetic for some people. This reminds me of a young teenager who thought old people were ugly and weird until she got a job in a rest home for the elderly. She learned that the blind, the crippled, and the bedridden can still enjoy life—and give love, too.

In my experience in veterinary practice, I have also encountered some owners who would have their three-legged or blind pet destroyed because they consider it inhumane to keep a physically incapacitated, and therefore unnatural, animal alive, even though it wouldn't be in pain. (Ironically though, they would never dream of euthanizing a person, such as a war veteran, who lost one or more limbs.) While I can fully appreciate the point of view that an animal has a right to be whole and natural, this is way off the mark. First, it is amazing how pets can adapt to a wide range of handicaps. I have seen very healthy and happy two-legged dogs living a full if not very active life. Wild animals are able to survive after they have lost a foot in one of those barbaric steel-jaw traps that provide the fur industry with cruel profits. There are even cases of blind birds being tended and fed by their companions.

It may be argued that a cat cannot be a cat without four legs and should be destroyed if it loses one. How much does selfish esthetics influence such an opinion? The real question surely is the amount of physical and psychological suffering the animal might experience once it is incapacitated. In my experience working at a large humane society clinic in St. Louis, I found that many owners can't bear the thought of their pets suffering at all. Yet some suffering is part of life. We wouldn't dream of euthanizing an aging relative who has arthritis or a failing heart or kidneys. Why, then, is a pet with similar ailments often considered a fair candidate for euthanasia? So *how much* suffering is acceptable before the decision to have the pet humanely put to sleep is made?

Some veterinarians, like some doctors, and some pet owners, like some relatives of the terminally ill, would keep a patient alive at all costs. The fight against death becomes an all-consuming challenge, and to lose is a personal failure. Death with dignity may then be denied and the patient subjected to unnecessary and prolonged suffering for the purely selfish motives of the owner, parent, or doctor in charge, as the case may be.

There are no simple answers here. Each case must be weighed on its own merits. Animals, like people, can cope with many handicaps and considerable suffering and it is often as hard for those who are caring for them to cope with the burdens of responsibility and empathy. Let us not get carried away with fellow feeling and become mercy killers at the drop of a hat. Nor, by the same token, should those who care deny a merciful death when the time comes.

We don't really know what death is. If we did, ethical decisions and the burden of responsibility might be quite different. We do know what death isn't. We have legally defined criteria, such as the cessation of brain activity. The trouble is, all our definitions are based upon body mechanics—physiology—but mind (and soul) are not mechanical things.

Because of our limited understanding of death, and because of our fear of it ourselves, and lack of contact with it in our everyday lives, our children may be short-changed when the family pet has to be put to sleep. In the old days, we grew up with death: Relatives died at home; we killed animals for food. Today, relatives die in a hospital and few of us ever see the animals that we eat.

Parents who do not take time out to explain to a child what euthanasia is and why the pet has to be put to sleep may feel the child's hurt as anger and resentment directed toward them. Parents who hide their emotions may seem callous and indifferent. The death of a pet in the family should involve the entire family in open exchange and sharing of feelings. A child who learns that life does not go on forever and that each moment of relationship is special will have a deeper insight about life, and perhaps a glimpse of something even greater when the good times spent with the pet are remembered. Such reflection can add a heightened appreciation to future relationships with animals and people alike.

So often, though, I have heard the remark, after I have euthanized someone's pet, that they will never get another animal again.

Such denial I interpret as a wish to avoid further hurt and loss. Understandable though it is, to attempt to avoid further hurt and loss is to turn one's back on life and is a poor example to set for one's children. As the Buddha taught, all of life entails some suffering, and the "cure" is not to avoid it but to embrace it with compassion, empathy, and understanding.

The loss of life is a loss of relationship to those who live on, and a time of mourning is both natural and appropriate. I have known parents to immediately give their child a replacement pet. This, like "never getting another one," is also to be avoided since it may prevent the child from learning to cope with the finality of death.

Death is not suffering. It can be a liberation from suffering, and euthanasia can be the ultimate act of responsible compassion.

V

Friends and Neighbors:
Pet Owners– and Pets–
As Responsible Citizens

27

The Pet Population Problem and You

Owning a pet today is no longer an unqualified right—it's a privilege and a responsibility. What would you do with the neighbor who lets his cats roam free over your property, spraying on your front door and killing the birds by your feeder? How would you feel as a father, seeing your six year-old son torn to pieces by a pack of dogs in the street? Can you empathize with the insomniac next door who has one bad night after another because your watchdog barks at every shadow and overdoes its job? And what about the pregnant woman who is told by her doctor to get rid of her cats because they might infect her and deform her unborn child, or the dog breeder whose child is now partially blind from a puppy worm infestation? Then also there is the breeder who thinks his stud male is naturally "spirited" when it attacks him and is selling puppies that are virtual psychopaths. There are the commercial enterprises—wholesale puppy farms and attack training schools—that all too often ship animals with as much care as they would potatoes and use inhumane methods to brutalize them into becoming aggressive. And the fun sport of dog baiting is on the increase; in many areas people enjoy watching and gambling on two trained dogs that are being spurred on by their owners to kill each other. This rural plague is oddly complemented by free-roaming packs of dogs killing livestock. You might not like the sheep rancher shooting your dog, but being

Homeless cats being fed by a concerned woman. But simply feeding the strays and doing nothing about their growing numbers is misguided altruism *(H.S.U.S./Vincent Grimaldi).*

in his boots for a week, especially at lambing time, would soon change your mind. In many areas, dog- and cat-napping is not uncommon, purebred animals being sold for a good price and others ending up in research laboratories that pay a fair price for a clean and healthy animal. City dog and cat shelters kill thousands of unclaimed pets annually.

These are but a few of the crises that involve pets in society today, and we may all wonder why things have gone so awry and what may happen next. It is not really the pet's problem, but a people problem: our lack of care, indifference, ignorance, and irresponsibility toward their pets. What is needed is a radical change in attitude in most members of society towards animals.

Mayors, aldermen, and city health officials would like to see an end to the urban pet problem. So, too, would the dogcatchers. Those that I know don't like dog-catching because they know that most of the strays they pick up will be killed.

How can the pet problem be ended to the benefit of pets and people alike? Put an end to pets or at least ban dogs from cities— this would solve the problem. These are not unfamiliar statements from concerned and frustrated city officials and animal control personnel. I personally prefer education to legislation, but in many areas the pet problem in society has reached such proportions that legislation may be the only effective answer. How would you react if a stray dog bit your child or infected one of your children with one of a number of diseases? What's your reaction when you see a dead pet on the highway every other day on the way to work?

The media are not guilty, nor am I, of overdramatizing the problems. Actually they need more publicity because basically it seems that irresponsible pet owners generally have a very narrow world view. By this I mean they do not realize that allowing their pet cat or dog to roam free over a few blocks is simply adding to the pet problem, which extends not just to the next street corner but across the United States and Canada. Dogs are more of a problem than cats and indeed under certain circumstances such as on farms and rundown city areas the cat may be man's ally as a ratcatcher. Dogs form packs, in the city often temporarily, but in suburban and rural areas they will often pack together for the day, or for longer periods. The dog pack is a danger to people, traffic, livestock, and wildlife. Free-roaming pets are also potential carriers of rabies from infected wildlife to man.

So what is the answer to these many problems? Imposing heavy fines on pet owners for allowing their pets to roam free doesn't work as well as one might think. If the pet is impounded the owner may not come and pick it up if the fine is too steep. With a higher fine for second offenders, the owner return rate drops off even more.

So rather than destroy such pets, many animal shelters get extra revenue, which they sorely need, by selling the animals to medical and other research institutions. Although one may rationalize that it would be wasteful just to destroy and incinerate the pets and better to put them to some use, surely on humane grounds a pet should not be used in any long-term experimentation. They are simply not preadapted like laboratory-raised cats or dogs to a strictly confined life in a laboratory animal facility.

The pet-napping that I mentioned earlier is one problem with a concrete solution. Some dogs have been rescued at the last moment not because they are wearing a collar and identification tags—such can be easily removed—but because they had been tattooed with an identification code on the groin or ear. Just as cars carry license plates and their owners are taxed annually to defray associated city and state expenditures, pets, too, might carry license plates in the form of an identifying tattoo. This would not only help protect the pet, it may well force owners to be more responsible. Tattooing can be done quickly and painlessly by an expert, and although it would be an enormous undertaking, it may be one major inroad into the problem of pets in contemporary society.

There are other additional procedures that could also be instigated at the local level by responsible pet owners, breeders, kennel clubs, veterinarians, and town and city officials as the case may be. I recently attended an international meeting on pets and society in Toronto, and some of the following possible solutions are recommendations from this meeting. Interestingly there was a small demonstration on the streets while the three-day conference was being held, the sentiment being "don't take away our pets or legislate them out of our cities and our lives." This could happen but the meeting was essentially pro-pet, since it was the consensus that the pets are not primarily to blame but rather their irresponsible owners and a minority of unethical exploiters of animals.

First, consider how suitable the home environment is for the pet, provided it is kept indoors or in a yard. High-density, high-rise

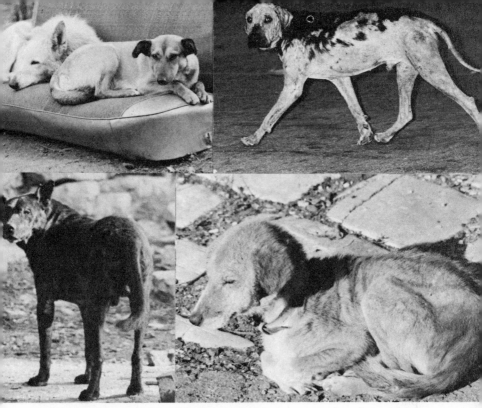

Abandoned, lost, sick, and homeless dogs in St. Louis. Few survive more than a few weeks *(M. W. Fox)*.

Collecting and destroying stray dogs is a sad and costly job for municipal Humane Societies and would not be needed if pet owners were more responsible *(H.S.U.S./Charles L. Franck)*.

apartments may be inhumane for many large and active breeds of dog. It should not be legal to keep wild animals as pets. Officials in one city recently had to remove a lion from an apartment. Keeping large reptiles, birds of prey, monkeys and carnivorous mammals such as mountain lions, ocelots, and wolves as "pets" should be discouraged since they can rarely be cared for properly and given the right environment in the cities.

Public education programs on local radio and TV would be an asset. Some pet food companies could contribute excellent "awareness" training in one or two minutes of advertising without, as they might fear, offending or otherwise turning off the viewer. Especially in grade and high schools, educational programs would be extremely beneficial, covering such topics as proper care, feeding and grooming of pets, their health requirements and public health aspects of pet diseases communicable to man.

Some towns mail out educational pamphlets with tax or gas and electricity bills, explaining the need for rabies vaccinations, adherence to leash laws and preventing the pet from roaming free.

On-the-spot fines for allowing a dog to defecate on the sidewalk, or checking up on whether or not the owner has paid for the annual license and has a valid rabies vaccination certificate, both would cost more than the potential revenue from fines levied. A partial solution here may be an added local sales tax on all pet foods which would help pay for "pet-control" officers.

One very strict method of pet control, forcing the owners to be more responsible, has been adopted in Czechoslovakia. A license fee for a dog costs seventy-five dollars annually but this fee is waived once the owner produces a certificate to the effect that both he or she and the dog have attended an approved obedience school. We expect a driver of an automobile to have a valid license; similarly, at least any person with a large guard dog or one that has been attack trained should have a handler's license.

Consider the man in Illinois, for example, who knew nothing about dogs, bought a shepherd, had it attack-trained, and came home one day to find his wife in pieces throughout the house.

I also feel strongly that cooperative veterinary hospitals should be set up to provide facilities for neutering pets—an essential remedy for the pet overpopulation problem, though not a total solution in itself. (The best canine contraception is the leash!) As it is now, many townships are building pet-neutering clinics where local vets contribute their time, much as they do for the rabies vaccination clinics. A less costly arrangement would be to use the existing veterinary facilities of those veterinarians who are willing to cooperate in such a socially and ecologically important pet-control program.

Another problem that needs straightening out fast is the purebred dog breeder. Are you one of those who, having a purebred pooch, wants to breed it? Few breeders make any money on such ventures, and as a hobby I have nothing against it, except that, today, everyone should think twice before breeding *any* dog. There are just too many purebred dogs around. The market is saturated. With breeders anxious to find *any* home for them, they may well finish up with irresponsible owners who are not prepared to put in the time and effort needed to raise a puppy. A visit to any city animal shelter will convince you of this problem—lots of purebred dogs and first generation mutts from indiscriminate matings. Open your Sunday newspaper and check out the ads for pets and see what I mean. The dog breeder is a major contributor to the pet crisis in society today.

This problem could be solved in two ways. Locally, dog licenses should be much higher, say, twenty to thirty dollars for an unneutered dog, and five to ten dollars for one that is neutered. This extra revenue might be used to fund neuter clinics or pay for more pet control personnel.

The second solution involves the purebred dog clubs and state and national breed associations. Only approved licensed dogs of top quality should be permitted to breed. This would help each breed, for the more popular ones are suffering from degeneration due to overbreeding. It would also make a great dent in the pet overpopulation problem and help control the mass production of low-quality pups from the puppy factories. Cats and dogs and other animals (except perhaps cage birds, small rodents, and tropical fish) should no longer be sold in pet stores. These should be pet supply shops only.

Perhaps, because of vested interest in the four- to six-billion-dollar-a-year pet business, many influential parties would be against some of the above recommendations. It is in their interest, however, since some municipalities may soon come down very hard, imposing very strict regulation on pet ownership and drastically reducing the pet population—not to mention pet industry profits.

Pet ownership is not a constitutional right: It is a privilege and a responsibility and I hope that some of the tentative solutions to problems that I have discussed will make life better for both pets and people. Life without the former, for me at least, would be unthinkable, but the problems facing us today are serious and must be solved soon.

28

Is Neutering Necessary?

Recently, I received the following letter from a pet owner: "Dear Dr. Fox, Neutering dogs and cats is inhumane, and so are you for proposing it. What right does any human being have to mutilate another living creature? Someone should castrate you!"

This certainly is an overly emotional response to the matter of neutering, but, believe me, this pet owner has many followers in his camp, each with his or her own "logic" as to why a pet's sex life should remain unaltered. And yet the scientific fact is that in today's world a neutered pet is a happier and healthier pet. Besides, we have reached the point of no return; neutering is no longer a question of choice but one of absolute necessity.

At least fourteen million unwanted cats and dogs are destroyed annually by humane shelters and pounds in the United States alone. It is a costly and tragic business. Millions of other animals die alone in fields, side streets, and abandoned houses; it's a sad reminder that human love for these pets is short-lived, and often ends when a kitten or puppy stops being cute and starts needing care, discipline and responsible ownership. If neutering were to help improve this problem even slightly, that alone would make it worthwhile. But animals don't walk into clinics or vets' offices on their own, and the humans who *should* bring them are often opposed to neutering for reasons that turn out to make little sense.

Here are a few of the frequently expressed arguments: "Since most pets are forced to live an unnatural life, unable to roam freely and to hunt as they wish, we should at least allow them the one natural function of sex." Another view is that "animals have rights, and to neuter them is to violate their most fundamental right."

But my research with wild canids—wolves, coyotes, foxes, and other cousins of the domesticated dog—has clearly shown that domestication and selective breeding over thousands of years has served to *intensify* the animal's natural sexuality. This increased sexuality has been useful to man when he wished to breed animals as often and as early in life as possible. What this means, however, is that the domesticated male dog today is constantly fertile, while a wild dog is only seasonally potent. Domesticated male and female dogs attain maturity a year earlier than wolves, and domesticated bitches are twice as fertile as she-wolves and tend to be more sexually promiscuous. Similarly, domesticated male cats are constantly fertile; they have an intensified sex drive that is relatively abnormal in the wild-cat kingdom. Indeed, evidence points to the fact that a pet cat or dog is *closer* to its normal or natural state if it's sterilized.

There is sometimes a deeper, and generally unexpressed, reason why some people abhor the thought of spaying or castrating their pet dog or cat: Neutering is a threat to their own sexuality. A pet is often a mirror of its owner's needs and aspirations. Consequently, a pet's potency and uninhibited sexuality is a vicarious source of pleasure and fulfillment for some owners. In fact, some people regard a castrated dog as abnormal or inferior and, as such, an unworthy companion.

It is interesting to observe that the dog-owning public displays the same double standard toward sterilizing male and female animals as society displays toward men and women in general. Hardly a second thought is given to spaying a female dog, but a castrated male often is thought of as "less of a dog." Similarly, the human female must assume the responsibilities for contraception; few men would disrupt their bodies with hormone pills, but a woman must. It is the lot of the female, both human and animal, to be forced to bear the brunt of birth control.

And have you heard this one? "We decided to let our dog get pregnant and have her pups because it's educational for the chil-

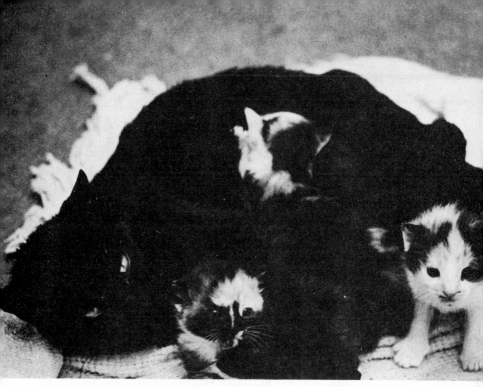

Don't *litter—NEUTER!* (H.S.U.S.)

Neutering stops this problem—unwanted puppies that must be destroyed (H.S.U.S./Paul Bauer).

dren." Well, my answer to that is to show children an intelligent film or picture book on the subject instead. Then explain to them that allowing their pet to have pups or kittens will only make more problems for other pets and other people. If the children are involved in the decision to have their pet spayed, they will learn a real lesson in responsibility. If they want puppies or kittens badly, there are hundreds waiting to be adopted at the humane society or the pound.

A neutered pet makes a better pet on many counts. It is less aggressive, less likely to roam and get into fights, and easier to handle. Above all, a male will not become so intensely frustrated when it does smell or meet a female in full heat. Neutered male cats are also less likely to spray in the house. Neutered females don't develop uterine or ovarian problems, and neutered males are less susceptible to prostate diseases. These changes help the average pet adapt to the confines and sexual privations of life in a suburban home or high-rise apartment.

Regarding the neutering operation itself, there is no more "mutilation" than in any other surgical procedure. It is performed under general anesthesia, and it is painless. Furthermore, an animal suffers no psychological problem over its sexual identity as a result.

What does spaying actually mean? It means removing the ovaries and uterus of the female. There is no point in merely tying off the tubes, because the animal will continue to go into heat and continue to be a nuisance even though it cannot become pregnant.

Castration of the male involves removing both testicles—also a relatively painless operation performed under general anesthesia. Vasectomy is possible but not advisable for male dogs—unless the animals are needed specifically for attack or guard work, and it is feared that castration might reduce their aggressive instincts. A vasectomy will not decrease an animal's sex drive, nor is it likely to improve a dog's behavior in any way; although the animal will be infertile, it will still want to breed whenever and wherever possible.

Neutering operations are usually performed in the morning in the vet's office, and the pet goes home in the evening. Stitches are removed about ten days later. The animal appears to suffer no aftereffects and is usually active immediately thereafter. Ask your vet about preparations he may want you to make, such as the feeding of your animal the day before, and so on.

For best results, females should be neutered at about five to six months of age, and males (they mature more slowly) at ten to twelve months. Some vets suggest waiting until after the first heat to spay to avoid later complications that might occur if genitals are too small. (This is debatable, but it's best to follow your vet's advice in the matter.) Spaying an animal that is actually in heat is out of the question, however, because both cats and dogs are much more likely to hemorrhage internally after surgery at such a time.

The major complication to look for in neutered animals is obesity; they may be less active or simply more prone to put on weight. But this is easily remedied by careful regulation of diet content and caloric intake. Occasionally, altered female cats and dogs become irritable or hyperactive or develop skin problems. Hormone treatment can rectify such minor problems.

Apart from surgical operations, there are other methods of neutering that have not been well developed to date. Research is being done using hormone injections that will sterilize an animal permanently. And a birth-control pill called Ovaban, which was developed in England for bitches, is now available. I personally don't favor the use of hormones for any extended period of time to inhibit pregnancy in human or animal. However, the pill I mention can be used when necessary to postpone an animal's time in heat. This can be convenient when an owner is traveling with an unaltered pet, for instance, or when the animal is being shown in competition.

There is also an intravaginal plug, which, like the IUD, can be removed from a bitch at any time the owner wishes to breed her. This may be of value to breeders who must cage animals of the opposite sex together, but I wouldn't recommend it to the general public. It would be too easy a temptation to let the bitch roam free when she's in heat and wants to get out. She wouldn't become pregnant, but she *would* be the focus of a pack of amorous dog followers. Such packs of dogs can become a very serious hazard to traffic and to passersby, especially if any of the frustrated and competitive male dogs should become aggressive.

Incidentally, chlorophyll tablets, given orally, do block out the odor signal in a bitch's urine when she's in heat. It may keep canine callers from your door, but don't let your dog out. She can still conceive!

If your pet is accidentally bred, there is an injection that can be given her to prevent pregnancy, provided you get her to the vet within twenty-four to thirty-six hours after the event. However, this injection, which may have to be repeated after ten to fourteen days, can kill cats who receive it, so think twice about resorting to such tactics. Abortions, per se, cannot be given to a cat or dog: The viable alternative is to have its ovaries and uterus, with fetuses, removed as early in pregnancy as possible.

Your vet, of course, if perfectly capable of neutering your animal. And, to encourage pet owners, humane organizations have set up clinics that sometimes neuter for a reduced fee.

If we revere life, both human and animal, we must begin to control it; improving quality of life by regulating quantity is a most urgent social and ecological issue today. We may not want to do things to animals that we would never dream of doing to people, but so far as the pet-population problem is concerned, we must.

29

Good Neighbor or Nuisance: Remember That Your Pet Is Also the Pet Next Door

Public nuisance number one in many places is the dog. Although it's not always the dog's fault, it gets the blame anyway. Although hard to believe, it is true that one of the most common complaints by the public to local municipal authorities is about their neighbors' dogs. Cats do not escape negative public comments either. From my own syndicated newspaper column, a significant percentage of my mail is from non-pet owners who are having a problem with their neighbors' pet. I will detail the major problems so that pet owners can check to see if they are being good neighbors—which means being responsible pet owners. I will also give some suggestions as to what you can do if and when you have a problem pet, or a pet-owning neighbor to cope with.

Pet owners beware. I know of several instances where neighbors have taken the law into their own hands. Nuisance dogs have been poisoned and shot, dog droppings shoved into pet owners' mail boxes, and cats trapped, killed or cat-napped and dumped at the local pound for destruction.

Pet owners should remember that neighbors are generally reticent about face-to-face confrontations, and if they are having a problem with your pet, they are not always likely to tell you straight out what's bugging them. As happened once with me, the first time you hear about a neighbor's complaint is via a letter from the local

231

municipal animal-control department. Or worse, your pet might simply disappear, angry neighbors having called up the animal pound to pick up your pet, which they have cornered in their yard or garage after it has trespassed onto their property. Some pounds are too busy or indifferent to tell you that they have your pet, and it could be put to sleep within 48 hours. Sometimes a dogcatcher is sent out and if your dog plays hard to get, a dart gun may be used to tranquilize him. Often nicotine compounds are used, and these drugs could easily kill your pet. Then, too, you may have a fine to pay and even have to appear in court. Pets don't have to be public enemy number one, but the following problems, which are a frequent cause for public complaint and outrage, speak not against the pet but against bad pet-owning neighbors.

By curious coincidence, I was thinking about writing this article while endeavoring to put together one of those assemble-it-yourself sets of garden furniture (which always seem to have half the screws missing). What made my job much harder was the incessant barking of two Yorkshire terriers, two yards away. Much as I like dogs, continuous barking is something that really gets to me. After an hour or more of their racket, I visited politely with the owner, who was a very deaf old pensioner. Ironically, other neighbors were complaining amongst themselves, but no one went to ask the old man civilly to take his dogs inside and shut them up.

Pet owners whose pets are a neighborhood nuisance should bear this idiosyncrasy of human social behavior in mind. Neighbors may not tell you directly that your pet is a nuisance to them, and the local animal-control authorities usually will not let you know which neighbor is lodging the complaint. People generally like to be anonymous when the possibility of a confrontation arises, which doesn't help foster a sense of neighborliness or community spirit. I remember once having a note in the mailbox stating that my dogs must be kept in the house at night because they would freeze outside in their pen without a wood kennel. It was winter and my animals were fine, with well-insulated metal kennels in a sheltered, windproof enclosure. I called the local humane society, which had left the note, but they would not give me the name of the well-intentioned neighbor who had called them. Fortunately, they later explained to the neighbor that my animals were in good hands. Earlier that week I had appeared on a local TV news piece advising people about proper pet care for the cold winter!

Back to the barking Yorkies and my assembling the garden furniture: Soon after the dogs had been taken indoors and silenced, a distraught lady came running into the yard, anxious for me to look at her cat. She was convinced that a medical student who lived nearby and whom she had seen chasing the cat out of his yard, had declawed her cat! I examined the free-roaming tom, and sure enough, he had all his claws and was suffering from a cat bite on one front paw.

The moral of this story is that some pet owners do often jump to conclusions about neighbors whom they think "have it in" for their pets. I have treated several sick cats and dogs whose owners were convinced that some neighbor had poisoned them. None had been poisoned, though such instances are on record. There is a small segment of the populace that is zoophobic—they can't stand animals. Some of these "zoopaths" will poison, shoot, or otherwise injure or kill someone's pet. "Son of Sam" and other psychopaths have histories of torturing and killing animals. Pet owners should be on the alert for such possibilities but shouldn't become paranoid like the lady with the injured tom cat!

But when pet-owning neighbors continue to be bad neighbors by allowing their dogs to bark excessively or allowing their cat or dog to roam free and be a neighborhood nuisance, aggrieved neighbors may well take the law into their own hands. This is more likely in rural areas, not only because people have easier access to strychnine and other rat poisons for use on the farm but also because there may not be a local animal-control authority for them to contact with their problem.

Now to spell out some of the more common problems. The barking, yapping, or howling dog is the most common public nuisance of all. Number two, based on the letters I receive from readers of my syndicated column, is the free-roaming cat who sprays on people's doors and shrubs and also uses their gardens as a toilet. Other neighborhood complaints include: the dog using the sidewalk in front of someone's property as a toilet, or worse, their shrubs or front lawn; the dog who stays around his home but chases cars, joggers, cyclists, and other passersby; the cat who goes a-huntin' and who waits in ambush near a neighbor's bird feeder; the dog owner who has an aggressive animal and never keeps it on a leash when out for a walk, which cam make life miserable for other dog owners who are afraid that their pets might get hurt.

To balance the score, there are some anti-pet complaints that are unwarranted. A common one is a neighbor's too-hasty complaint about a dog's excessive barking. "Excessive barking" is *sometimes* excusable, as when a dog is barking at the garbage truck that invades his territory twice a week, or at a work crew who are repairing the road or house next door for a few days.

Another one concerns the "attractive nuisance," where a dog is kept in a fenced yard and barks at children who run by or who tease him. Some clemency should be given here, especially if the dog nips one of the children through the fence because he is overexcited, is defending his territory, or has been teased before.

There is *no* excuse for pet owners who have complaints filed against them because their pets are roaming free, fouling others' property, killing birds in neighbors' yards or chasing cars and passersby.

I recall one bizarre neighborly spat between a friend of mine, who is a very responsible pet owner, and one of her zoophobic (and coprophobic) neighbors. She was out walking her dog, who was on the leash, when the dog decided to go to the toilet by the side of the road—a perfectly acceptable place in that neighborhood. This place, however, was in front of a neighbor's townhouse and plot of green, and the resident turned a garden hose on my friend and her dog. Shocked and without other recourse, my friend picked up what her dog had just passed and threw it at the man. She later filed a complaint for assault, won her case, but dropped all charges! It is generally advisable not to take the law (or anything else!) into one's own hands. The sad fact remains, however, that constructive exchange to resolve a neighborhood problem involving a pet doesn't always take place. Very often, the pet gets the short end of the stick. Much unnecessary tension and polarization into pro- and anti-pet factions could be negated by people being more open and taking the risk of sharing their grievances with each other.

I recall an amusing incident a few years ago when a neighbor complained about the "eyesore" created by a small dog-cage run I had put up in my backyard. He could see it (only just) from his kitchen window. Really he didn't like me having two animals there because they would smell and bite his children if they reached through the cage. As it turned out, I kept the cage clean, so there was never any odor, and eventually his children were playing regularly with my gentle animals. Still the neighbor kept his distance and generally ignored me. Then, after a few months, he decided to get a German shepherd for his wife's need of security and to cap it all, he came over, since we were moving, and bought the terrible "eyesore" cage from me!

Pet owners should do their best to talk to their neighbors and establish friendly understanding. They should realize that for every right of pet ownership there is a corresponding responsibility toward neighbors and toward their communities. Pets don't have any sense of civic responsibility, but their owners should have. Early training of the pet can help a great deal in preventing the occurrence of neighbor problems. Cats can be leash-trained and should be kept indoors and only allowed out under supervision. The same holds true for dogs. No one wants a neighborhood child falling off a bike because an unsupervised dog has scared or chased him. No gardener wants a dog digging holes in the lawn, raking up the flower beds, or cats using the garden as a giant litter tray. A free-roaming dog will make other dogs bark at it from their yards, not only creating more noise but also getting other dogs into trouble.

All dogs should be leash-trained and should be quiet and easy to handle when out for a walk. Since most dogs prefer to evacuate outdoors, train it to use a part of the backyard. If you don't have a backyard, train your dog to use the curb of the road. In heavily populated areas, you should pick up after your dog. Don't let your dog urinate on a neighbor's shrubs or lawn: Dog urine kills green things.

Neutering cats and dogs (both males and females) will make them much more adaptable and less of a neighborhood problem. Neutered early in life (around five to six months), cats and dogs won't want to roam the neighborhood so much, and consequently they will be easier to restrain and more adaptable to being confined indoors or in a yard and more accepting of supervision when outdoors.

Since the most common neighborhood pet problem is the barking dog, this subject requires special consideration. The following details are recommendations made by the Environmental Protection Agency (Noise Office) in collaboration with the Humane Society of the United States. (Individual brochures may be obtained from either organization.)

Good Dog or Nuisance?

Determine for yourself whether your dog is a good companion or a neighborhood nuisance, by answering the following:
> *Does your dog bark excessively*
> - *when he is left alone and lonesome?*
> - *when another dog barks?*
> - *when the kids next door come out to play?*
> - *when he's outside and wants to get in the house?*
> - *when the neighbors leave or return home?*
> - *when you come home?*
> - *at garbage collectors, passing cars?*
> - *when he hears a siren?*

If your answer is "yes" to any one of these, your dog could be a neighborhood noise nuisance.

Dogs bark for many reasons, such as when other dogs bark, when they are generally excited or frustrated, when a stranger intrudes on their territory.

Excessive barking can be extremely annoying to neighbors as well as to those who have to live with a noisy dog. A constant barker is more likely to be ignored if there is an intruder, since he seems to "cry wolf" all the time.

One of the most common public complaints is about neighbors' barking dogs. Is your dog an excessive barker and a potential public nuisance? EPA's Office of Noise Abatement and Control, together with the Humane Society of the United States, would like to pass on an effective training method *to responsible owners.*

Water Training Method

The water training method works *for almost all dogs.*

If possible, consider going to a reputable local obedience training school. An obedience-trained dog will stop barking on command, and knowing obedience signals will help you control your dog in other situations and make life happier for all.

Consider the times when your dog's barking is a nuisance. If it's when he's left alone all day, help relieve his loneliness by leaving the radio on. If your dog is an outside pet, allowing it more freedom of movement in a fenced yard or pen may quiet its barking. If practical, you might consider a companion pet. Be sure you have plenty of toys available for amusement.

Don't be overly effusive on leaving or returning. Overexcited dogs are more likely to bark and yelp.

- *The first training rule is to* be consistent *and* persistent. *You can't expect a dog to learn if barking for the wrong reason is corrected one time and not the next.*
  - *Second, be ready for an* immediate response. *Have a plant mister filled with water.*
  - *Say "Quiet, dog" (or whatever its name is) and give one or two squirts of water at the dog* while it is barking. *He will stop at once. If you wait until he stops barking, it may confuse him.*
  - *If the dog moves away,* repeat *saying "Quiet" as you go to him and give one more squirt of water at him. Repeat each time he barks needlessly.*
  - *Usually a day or two of training is enough if you are consistent (five to ten water treatments).*
  - *Remember to reassure the dog that you are still friends by petting him later when he's quiet.*
  - *With this conditioning procedure your dog will soon learn to expect a squirt of water when you shout "Quiet," for once he has made the association, you won't need to squirt him again—only rarely should he forget.*

Definition

Do you know what a nuisance barker is? The following definition is contained in the new law passed by the city and county of Honolulu in cooperation with the Hawaiian Humane Society and Citizens Against Noise. It is given as an example of the way one community is adopting a barking-dog ordinance.

> *(d) "Barking Dog" shall mean* a dog that barks, bays, cries, howls *or makes any other noise continuously and/or incessantly for a period* of ten minutes *or barks intermittently for ½ hour or more to the disturbance of any person at any time*

of day or night regardless of whether the dog is physically situated in or upon private property; provided, however, that a dog shall not be deemed a "barking dog" for purposes of this Article, if, at the time the dog is barking or making any other noise, a person is trespassing or threatening to trespass upon private property in or upon which the dog is situated or for any other legitimate cause which teased or provoked the dog."*

Honolulu also has a penalty for owners keeping or permitting a barking dog within the limits of the city and/or county. After receiving a warning citation, the owner is required to follow specific instructions for the dog's training by the Humane Society.

TIPS FOR DOG OWNERS

- *Always find out why your dog barks. Unless it has a watchdog reason, you must correct it at that time.*
- *Do not turn a garden hose on a dog or throw rocks or tin cans at him.*
- *Spanking/hitting is an ineffective substitute for water treatment (and angers people).*
- *Whenever your dog barks for a trained watchdog reason, praise it or pat it.*
- *Remember, dogs are companion animals and should be kept in the house during the normal night hours whenever possible.*

IS YOUR DOG TRAINABLE?

A dog that is chained up or left alone and tied indoors and is allowed to bark hour after hour may no longer be trainable. Such a dog may have become too neurotic for an inexperienced trainer. If this is the case with your dog, consult your veterinarian or a qualified dog trainer.

---

*Definition given for informational purposes only, not endorsed by the U.S. Environmental Protection Agency or the Humane Society of the United States.

Dogs will pack and sometimes gang up on a single animal—or a child—and the play can lead to more serious consequences. This pooch sought the security of its owner when the pack became too rough. *(M. W. Fox)*.

REWARDS

Correcting unnecessary barking is more convenient during the day, but getting up a few times at night will prove worthwhile. After that, you and your neighbors will know that when your dog barks there's a real reason. If your neighbors are home and you're not, they will check to see if police should be notified.

The security of knowing you have a real watchdog, and the resumption of peaceful and quiet nights for you and your neighbors, make it all worth the effort.

Being a good pet-owning neighbor also means being good to one's pet, since much of what is good for your neighbors is either directly or indirectly good for your pet, too. Unsupervised pets roaming the neighborhood can and do get injured or killed by cars and by fighting with each other. They have many natural drives which, if allowed free reign, could bring them to harm as well as causing neighborhood problems. The urban and suburban environs are not natural places for pets to be free in any way and any pet owner who believes that his or her pet should live a free and natural life is a bad pet-owning neighbor and shouldn't have a pet in the first place. Much as I empathize with this naturalistic attitude, I feel it is unrealistic. Responsible pet owners are good neighbors, since they appreciate the fact that they and their pets are a part of the world. Those who believe that the whole world centers upon them and their pets are very wrong. They make life even harder for more responsible people and their pets by setting up negative attitudes in their communities toward pet owners and animals in general.

Pet owners who don't care about their neighbors don't really care, in the fullest sense of the word, for their pets either. While we are not responsible for each other, we are, as social beings, responsible *to* each other, and a measure of such is surely reflected in the responsible love that we have for our pets.

30

A Dog's Life? Pets, Apartments, and High-density Housing

I have come down hard on students and other people for abandoning their pets or putting them up for adoption at the drop of a hat, but there is one overriding circumstance for which they are not to blame. Many condominium and apartment buildings allow no pets. No pets, period, is often the letter of the lease and eviction soon follows if a tenant tries to sneak in the loved one. Someone, if not the landlord himself, sooner or later will notice they have a pet and complain. Quite often a landlord will suddenly do a turnabout and when the annual lease comes up puts in a no-pet clause, much to the dismay and indignation of pet-owning tenants, who are then faced with an ultimatum: Either get rid of your pet or move out!

Some landlords are more discriminating and will allow some pets but not others. Dogs and sometimes even cats are banned, but gerbils, hamsters, and parakeets may be allowed to remain. Or an older resident with a well-behaved little dog is sometimes given a special sanction, much to the annoyance of other dog owners who feel discriminated against. "If so-and-so can keep her pet, then why can't we?" Then again, some landlords will add on an extra ten or twenty dollars per month to the rent bill for pet owners, or restrict pets to one particular floor.

There are good reasons for all of these actions. Property owners are weary of irresponsible pet owners. It is unfortunate that an irresponsible and indifferent few can make it impossible in some urban areas for more responsible pet owners to find rental accommodations. Some landlords also have a misinformed view of pets, believing that cats attract vermin and any dog will destroy an apartment. The indiscriminate banning of any and all pets is neither fair nor rational, but pet owners should realize also that keeping a pet is more of a responsibility than an unqualified right per se.

With the cost of single-house property escalating beyond the means of young families, more and more are obliged to live for some time in urban high-rise developments. Life for children without any contact with pets under such sterile, crowded, artificial circumstances may not be conducive to normal development. This lack of nature contact is certainly compensated to some degree by turning one or more rooms into green jungles, and the sale of indoor plants and related literature have reached unprecedented proportions. But the lack of social contacts, of close relationships with other people, is often compensated for by the keeping of pets. The less society offers in terms of community, the more important the pet becomes as a substitute for many. Soon, however, we may reach that critical point where whole segments of urban high-rise development are off limits for any animal species other than people (and persistent roaches and rats whom no landlord can control or evict for long).

There are six interrelated factors to consider in attacking the problem of how pets might adapt to high-rise apartment living: the needs of the pet; the needs of the pet owner; the needs of the property owner; the needs of non-pet-owning residents; the lifestyle of the pet owner; the suitability of the urban high-rise environment for pets.

The needs of the pet vary greatly according to its species: Gerbils, hamsters, parakeets and canaries, and of course, tropical fish do just as well in a mansion as in a one-room efficiency apartment. Their requirements are contained simply within the confines of their cages or aquarium tanks. Our concern here is specifically for our traditionally uncaged pets, the cat and dog.

First, the dog. Breeds, and individuals of the same breed, vary a great deal in the amount of space they need in which to exercise. Small breeds, such as Yorkshire terriers, toy poodles, pugs, and the like, do well in apartments. Larger, active breeds, such as Afghan

Apartment pets? Not all breeds are compatible with a particular life style (H.S.U.S./Frickey's Studio).

hounds, shepherds, sheepdogs, retrievers, and setters, don't always adapt well to confinement. Consider the size of the apartment and the size and activity requirements of the dog. Is there a suitable and convenient area where it can be exercised outdoors—an apartment-complex enclosure specifically for dogs or a nearby park (where, hopefully, dogs are allowed)? Are you prepared to walk your dog regularly early every morning and evening? Are you going to respect leash laws (also for your pet's safety near busy streets) and are you prepared to clean up after your dog has defecated? This latter point is one of the main reasons why dogs (or, more exactly, dog owners) are becoming less and less popular in urban areas—not only because of the inconvenience to others but also because of very real public health concerns.

And, if you are prepared to clean up after your dog, can you "contain it" until you get out of the apartment, down the stairs (or elevator) and out of the lobby? Many dogs use the elevator on the

Dogs need space outdoors for toilet and exercise, a fact not sufficiently recognized in the design of urban communities (H.S.U.S./R. J. Ruff).

way down and the owner pushes the top floor button as they step out. It's left for the janitor, and the landlord soon gets the backlash of such indifference! Some people have suggested setting up doggie toilets, designated areas where they can "go." While this might work for their urination, especially for male dogs, it won't do for their number twos. A dog usually defecates whenever he's ready to when he's out of his home base—and that means anywhere.

Another need for the dog is to defend his territory by barking. Although the dog's protective instinct might be desirable from the owner's point of view, a dog that barks when anyone comes up or down the stairs or past the apartment door on their way to another apartment will often be an irritant to other residents. If he is very vocal, especially when left alone for extended periods, you might expect an eviction notice pretty soon.

Some dogs will respond to inhibitory training, but others will not. A muzzle may help (but this is hardly humane) or debarking—a surgical operation that more or less eliminates the bark. How far are you prepared to go to make your dog adapt to such a life?

Admittedly, many dogs adapt well to apartment life, but the important point is you can't know until you try it out. Then what happens if the pup doesn't adapt? I therefore strongly urge apartment dwellers who do not have a dog not to get one. Even if there is a 75 percent chance of the dog adapting well, that means that twenty-five out of every hundred dogs will be destroyed, discarded, or, if lucky, adopted.

It is even harder for a mature dog that has grown up in the country or in a suburban backyard to adapt to high-rise living. Knowing this, people who for one reason or another are obliged to move into an apartment or condominium will either have their pet adopted or humanely destroyed, rather than forcing it to adapt to such a radical change in life-style. Since they already have a dog, though, I wouldn't advise them to give up without first giving the pooch a chance: He *may* settle down even better than they, provided he gets outdoors regularly.

There is a viable alternative to a dog, and that is a cat. It is 99 percent more convenient and adaptable than a dog. First, it will use a litter tray and doesn't need to be let out to attend to its toilet. Nor does it need open spaces to run in like a dog. Though problems may arise, just as with a dog, if the cat has earlier lived a free and unconfined existence, cats adapt well to apartment life (more so when there are two of them), and when they are raised the right way they will be as companionable and rewarding in their own way as any dog. Of course they don't give people the sense of security and protection that a dog might, an important factor today in most crime-ridden cities. A dog, however, is no substitute for maximal security, and a well-designed and run apartment complex should be quite safe from most would-be intruders. A burglar alarm system is more efficient and less costly than a dog and won't give a dozen or more false alarms each day, to the annoyance of neighbors!

Because of its convenience and self-reliance, the cat is rapidly becoming established as the most adaptable apartment pet. It *is* undoubtedly the pet of the future. It is advisable to have the cat neutered. It is less likely then to spray and smell up the whole apartment floor (even worse with recycled central heat and air-conditioning). It will also be less prone to howl and to go out when it is in heat. Some cats, especially Siamese, have such a loud voice that neighbors might think you are abusing a human infant, and that would certainly bring in a shower of complaints!

On human grounds alone, many breeds of dog should not be confined all day in an apartment, especially when both husband and wife are out working most of the day. The more independent cat can more safely be left alone.

The cage and aquarium animals mentioned earlier are highly suitable apartment pets but certainly less satisfying for most people than a couple of cats or a small, well-adapted Yorkshire terrier or toy poodle. Some cage pets should not be kept in apartment complexes, though. Snakes escape easily and can get lost and starve to death, not to mention terrifying residents. Birds—notably of the parrot variety—are not only very noisy, they could transmit infectious diseases to people, especially via a central air or heating system where the air is recycled and fed to all apartments. A clean bill of health would be essential.

What of people who are allergic to animals, especially to cat fur? This point brings up an important general issue, namely, the *design* of apartment complexes compatible with human health and psychological well-being. Such considerations are usually secondary to the profits of the investors. Recycled air-conditioning and heating is obviously contraindicated since it would increase the spread of human disease. Apartment design should cater more to the needs of residents and to the plants and pets many would like to keep: Balconies, sun porches, and a small enclosed yard with grass and bushes (for dogs) are not only conducive to the well-being of pets, they create a more diverse and less sterile habitat for the residents themselves.

The needs of other non-pet-owning residents must be carefully considered if you plan to bring a pet into your apartment. Some people are really terrified of dogs and it would be extremely stressful for them to meet a large dog on the landing or walking into the elevator. Even on the leash, a big dog is a big dog, and bigger still to those who are afraid of them.

Special consideration should be given to allow elderly people to keep their cat or parakeet with them when they move into an apartment complex or subsidized housing development. Few realize how much a little animal can mean to such folk; without their companion they may feel little purpose in life and have little to live for.

A neighborly service in an apartment complex that permits pets would be helping older residents exercise their dogs and feed their cats and other pets when they are away on vacation or are sick in hospital. Only too often, pets are neglected when someone has to leave them suddenly, and worse, like the student who "dumps" his pet at the end of the semester, some owners will leave their apartment pets for several days without anyone attending to them. Such irresponsibility, as unbelievable as it may seem is unfortunately all too common. However leaving a cat alone for the weekend isn't too bad, especially when it has another cat for company and is actually provided an ample supply of dry chow and water. Another mark in favor of cats—you certainly couldn't do that with a dog (although many apartment dwellers do).

Landlords do have a problem with irresponsible pet owners, especially those with dogs. Complaints come from other residents over barking; dog droppings in the halls, stairs, elevators, and around the apartment grounds; damage to property, especially floors and carpets permanently stained with urine and feces (the latter made worse with color dye additives to dog foods!) and scratched-up and chewed doors, furniture, and other fixtures.

But why ban *all* pets in the lease? This is going overboard and is a frequent cause of unnecessary heartbreak for families, children, and elderly people who are forced to get rid of their pets or get out. Property owners, especially those concerned materialists who put money before people, should not castigate all pet owners on the basis of a few bad experiences with irresponsible pet owners. Such are in the minority as a rule. Why not make up a *conditional lease* giving owners and pets a trial period, and if there are justifiable complaints, then out they go. Some tenants will buy a pet in order to purposefully violate the lease so they can "get out of it"! Some landlords will insist upon a little extra rent and a thorough inspection for possible damage when the leasees eventually move out. This is surely more equitable than banning all pets. Dogs are generally more of a menace (or at least their irresponsible owners are) than other kinds of pets so it's a good idea to specify in the lease what animals and how many a person may keep. Some landlords have a wholly unhealthy and even unrealistic attitude toward animals. I was once evicted because the property owner believed that any cat "encouraged vermin." Actually my cat kept the vermin down in her dilapidated building!

There was once an Italian gentleman who bought a calf and took it home to his apartment in Toronto. Eventually the people living in the apartment below noticed some foul brown liquid coming through their ceiling. The authorities found the source of the problem—the calf was now a fully fattened steer, almost ready for slaughter! People of other cultures will bring chickens, goats, and lambs home to slaughter, especially on religious festivals, and I empathize with landlords who want to protect their property, the interests of other residents, and at the same time wish to avoid any racial or religious conflicts!

These are hardly pets, though. Pets, however, do belong in our hearts and lives (as distinct from our stomachs), and I have touched on a number of social issues that I hope will make the lives of pets and all concerned a little easier in the ever expanding environment of high-density, high-rise apartment life.

31

Attack Dogs and Those That Bite (or Might)

Something is going on in dogdom that sounds ominous. More and more people are getting bitten each year to a tune of $100 million or so per annum for medical care. Estimates range from one million to three million cases. Many are children who are bitten on the face, hands, and arms, often by dogs in their own homes or by neighborhood dogs roaming free. Free-roaming packs of homeless, feral dogs aren't to blame—the sensationalists have it wrong. It's the self-confident pooch at home who bites. Many of these dogs aren't entirely to blame either, for three basic reasons.

First, a lot of purebred dogs are emotionally unstable—timid, defensive fear-biters or really psychotic animals, so volatile that when they reach maturity they don't think twice about biting anyone—stranger or master, man or child. Some of these breeds, notably the Saint Bernard, may well be suffering from excessive overbreeding. Commercial breeders don't (and won't for dollars' sake) follow the responsible practice of destroying or not breeding from emotionally unstable dogs, or halting the breeding of parents who have produced unstable offspring. This is why one of the safest kinds of dog to buy today is the All-American Mutt.

The nation-wide epidemic of dog bites may also be due to people failing to relate in the right way toward their dogs from puppyhood onwards. Failure to give dogs obedience training to establish the owner as dominant leader—which leads the dog to respect all people—is partly to blame. Associated with this is the tendency of many people to overindulge and to be overly permissive with their dogs. Consequently, when such a dog is frustrated or disciplined by a person, it may lose all social inhibitions (if it had any to start with) and bite. If not properly raised, a dog will regard a child of the family as a sibling rival—a littermate if you wish—and may have no inhibitions about biting such a child.

These two factors—heredity and early experience—may interact and aggravate the problem, increasing the likelihood of the dog's becoming a socially maladjusted psychopath and biting and even killing someone.

So what to do? Prevention is easier than a cure, so those who haven't a dog but intend to get one soon should go to a reputable home breeder if a purebred dog is wanted, or to the dog pound for a good mutt puppy. Don't buy a purebred pup if you can't see one or both parents and the rest of the litter. Then socialize it right from the start—my book *Understanding Your Dog* spells out the steps. Castration at six to nine months will reduce some aggression and make your male dog less likely to want to roam. At this age, too, you can start obedience school, especially if you have a large dog. People with horses learn to ride and to control them and it is no less important if you have a dog. A dog you can't control will get into fights, may chase cars and joggers, get run over, or get you a lawsuit for injuring someone.

I receive a call almost every month now from a lawyer or distraught owner on this last point. It's hard to defend yourself when you have an uncontrollable dog that has bitten someone or killed a child. It could be your own child, for that matter.

If you have a biter, what's the cure? First, a muzzle and strict control and confinement. Obedience-school training may help, and so may castration in some cases. If your vet or trainer thinks it's more of a genetic, overbreeding problem, resign yourself to having your dog destroyed. I have had several cases where the owner of such a dog insisted on trying everything and ended up with a lawsuit or mutilated wife, child, or neighbor.

Basically there's nothing wrong with dogs—it's people who don't breed them and raise them right. I also blame people for not relating properly to dogs. Some, expecting all dogs to be friendly, take

Knowing about a dog's body language and territorial instincts can help you to respect a dog's wishes—and avoid being attacked and bitten too *(H.S.U.S./V. Scruby).*

liberties, often violating canine etiquette. To suddenly approach and pet a strange dog may put it on the defensive; it may bite defensively. Talk to it first, let it sniff you and understand that your intentions are friendly. Remember, a dog is more likely to be aggressive when it is with its owner on the leash, in the owner's yard or car, when it is eating, has some favorite toy, or has puppies.

Many people have dogs that are overly protective of their property and they should be alert to the fact that their dogs may bite not only an intruding burglar but a delivery person or a child retrieving a ball from their yard.

Instruct your child that dogs sometimes bite when they are afraid or are trained to do so. Don't tell them to keep clear of dogs because all dogs bite. This could get them into trouble. Instruct your child to be cautious and quiet around a strange dog and not to pet it unless he or she has been introduced by the owner, or unless you are 100 percent confident that the dog is friendly. Be sure to tell your child not to try to pet even a familiar and friendly dog who is barking in defense of his yard or inside the owner's automobile. More than one child has been bitten by reaching a hand through the fence to pet a dog with whom, on other occasions, the child has played in the park.

If a dog does threaten your child, don't pick your child up. The dog may misinterpret this as you attacking the child and leap up and join in. Also, with the child in your arms you would be defenseless. Keep yourself between the dog and your child and stare the dog down and shout "No, boy; go home." Keep a jacket or sweater rolled up around one arm as a padded shield, just in case.

Attack and Guard Dogs

Undoubtedly the worst thing for dogs (other than dog shows!) is the upsurge of attack-training schools. Paranoid people are being taken in by unethical trainers who promise to create an attack-trained dog out of their pooch. They are more likely, after psychologically and physically brutalizing the dog, to create a sick and potentially psychopathic killer. A well-trained dog has to have a well-trained and emotionally stable owner. Few owners are trained handlers, and many who feel they need an attack-trained dog are emotionally unstable. Add to this the high probability that their dog has not been well trained for attack work, and a potentially disastrous combination is created: an unpredictable killer dog and an unstable owner. Anyone who has an attack-trained dog should have a state license of competence as a handler. Ownership ideally should be restricted to the police and the military.

Unethical dog trainers have pulled a fast one on the gullible public—a good dog doesn't need to be attack-trained. In my mind these people have violated fourteen thousand years of careful stewardship of dogs for a few bucks, not only abusing dogs in the training process but also creating a hazard to both the owner and the general public. Attack-trained dogs have gone berserk and attacked their masters, killed family members, and killed children and innocent passersby in guarding stores, construction sites, and the like, especially when they escape. I know of some of these dogs who are just dumped off at night in a junkyard or construction site to do their work—with neither food, water, or shelter, no matter what the weather.

All this naturally should be outlawed. If someone wishes to feel safe, electronic security devices are cheaper, safer, and far more effective. A prepared intruder can easily poison a dog, or kill it, especially when it wears a collar or choke chain.

I repeat, a good dog doesn't need attack training, especially the more protective breeds like the Doberman and shepherd. For home and public safety, such fine breeds should be obedience-trained, and that's all that is needed. More apprehensive and fearful people are apt, by their temperament, to make a dog more protective toward them. If such a dog is not obedience-trained and therefore not under the owner's control, the consequences could be disastrous. A child running by could be mauled, or an innocent stranger who happens to startle the owner, which in turn may trigger the dog to attack.

Unfortunately certain breeds—thanks to sensationalistic movies and pulp paperback stories—are made out to be killers. A large segment of the general public comes to believe that all big dogs, black dogs, dogs with cropped ears, or Dobes or shepherds, are killers. The way in which they behave around such animals and the fear they transmit could easily spook the most docile dog and make him more likely to threaten or attack.

Statistics show an increase in recent years in ownership of larger dogs. Larger dogs of course, do more damage when they bite than small ones. Over the past decade there has been an 11-fold increase in the Saint Bernard population and an estimated 200-fold increase in cases of people being bitten by these dogs. Great Danes and Doberman Pinschers have increased 6-fold in population. Shepherds make up 10 percent of the dog population and they (probably including a number of shepherd cross breeds and shepherd-like mongrels) account for 40 percent of all reported bites to humans. I reiterate: It's not the dog's fault. It's primarily bad ownership (poor socialization and obedience training) and overbreeding.

Experts estimate that three out of four bites are unprovoked, as when a child runs past a dog to catch a ball. The dog misinterprets the benign human action as threatening. Any dog who attacks without provocation should be examined by a veterinarian or animal psychologist and most likely should be destroyed.

If you are bitten by a dog, or your dog bites someone, the name and address of the dog's owner should be reported to the police and to the attending physician. Even a small puncture wound should be treated immediately since it may heal over prematurely and cause a

Attack-trained dogs should only be in the hands of well-trained and experienced persons—police, military and security officers (H.S.U.S.).

serious infection. Antibiotics are indicated for all bites, and tetanus shots as well. Rabies vaccinations are not needed if the dog is quarantined for ten days of observation and proves disease-free, or if the dog is a local resident and the region is rabies-free.

Many dogs develop specific likes and dislikes for certain people. This makes it imperative that all dogs large enough to inflict physical injury should not be allowed to roam free and should be obedience-trained. If all dogs had to be tattooed (painlessly) in the flank skin with their owner's social security number, locating the owner of a tagless dog that has been impounded for biting someone would be easy. Laws and fines could also be more surely enforced.

Prejudiced Dogs

A distraught owner of an all All-American Mutt consulted me the other day. She had a tough problem that deeply concerned her.

Her dog seemed to be prejudiced! A black couple had moved into the house opposite and whenever the dog saw them, he would bark furiously, and this embarrassed the lady. Whether the dog was in the yard, in the car, or out on the leash for a walk, it would turn into a barking menace if it saw the new neighbors. The lady assured me that she wasn't prejudiced herself and this ruled out the possibility that the dog's reactions were being cued in some subtle ways by her.

My first question was whether her neighborhood, or at least the area to which the dog was accustomed, was all white. It was. So what makes a dog prejudiced and how can its behavior be changed?

Actually dogs aren't prejudiced in the racist sense we ascribe to some misguided persons. But they do show very clear likes and dislikes toward certain people, an understanding of which may help you recognize and correct this problem. Prejudice can be triggered by a number of factors that cause dogs to be aggressive or fearful toward blacks, children, handicapped people, delivery people, individuals in uniform, and even friendly toward women and not to men or vice versa.

Sometimes a dog's prejudice is unconsciously encouraged by the owner, who is suspicious, fearful, or angry toward a certain individual. The dog may generalize from this and react in the same way toward all individuals of the same category. A women who doesn't like men or someone who doesn't like blacks does so sometimes because of some prior unpleasant experience perhaps with one particular individual. This is called generalization, and it also occurs in the dog. I knew of one dog who was viciously attacked as a puppy by an Afghan hound. As an adult, this dog was aggressive to any and all Afghan hounds that he ever met—be they friendly or unfriendly, male or female!

Childen may scare a nervous dog, especially with their noise and quick, unpredictable movements. Black people may be perceived to have a more penetrating and intimidating stare than whites, the whites of the eyes being set off more in contrast by a dark than a light face. Handicapped people—the blind, or crippled—may make some dogs uneasy because of their unusual behavior. Delivery people who "invade" the dog's territory are especially likely to trigger an attack. This may be associated with some dogs' aversion for people in uniforms. A dog socialized just with women may be more wary and sometimes aggressive toward men (and vice versa) if not given social experience with the opposite sex of the owner early in life.

Sometimes you may find yourself in a tight spot with a dog. Here are some pointers that will help you avoid an attack and even get on friendly terms with dogs you may meet in the park or on the street and around people's homes. Joggers, cyclists, delivery and service people, strollers and dog walkers take note!

There's no one simple answer or set formula to avoid a dog's attack, and if you do stick to one, you could end up in trouble. Each dog is different, but all dogs tend to conform to certain predictable rules of behavior, and knowing them can help you avoid trouble. First, some general rules for you:

1. If you meet an obnoxious dog regularly when you are out, find where it lives and call up the owners and ask them to control it. If they don't, you have every right to lodge a formal complaint with the police.

2. Never stare at a dog. Staring is a threat and a dog may read it as a challenge and attack you. Never run past a strange dog or run or walk quickly away from it. Your flight may release its chase response and you may get bitten. Always walk slowly, even backward, facing the dog, if you feel he may chase you when you leave his territory (which is his house, yard, front lawn or part of the block).

3. Try to hide your fear—a dog can read fear in your eyes and body movements. Play it cool; whistle, walk slowly, and pretend he's not there.

4. Remember that even friendly dogs will bark at you. It's their job to defend their territory and you may be a regular intruder, even when you walk past the front of his house. He may look forward to your coming so that he can do his thing and feel important. Talk to the dog and smile and if he wags his tail and doesn't snarl or put the hair up on his back, stand still and call him to you. He may want to make friends. If he approaches in a friendly way, stand still so he can sniff you. That's good manners. Then bend or squat down and let him sniff your hand. If he doesn't back off, pet him on the head between the ears. If you have a cookie or dog biscuit, he may become one of your regular canine buddies on your route if your job entails home deliveries or other services.

5. As you are walking slowly toward a strange dog, observe how

he reacts to you as you draw closer. If he is on his own territory, he will probably bark at you. As you get closer, he may bark more and when you enter his territory, if he stays put or backs off, he probably regards you as dominant and will be too scared to attack. If he walks or runs toward you with his tail wagging in the low position, even if he is barking, he is probably friendly and not likely to bite. But if he stiffens up, hold his tail high, snarls and stares at you, doesn't relax when you say "Hi, old boy," and stays put or approaches as you get nearer, be on guard. If he lowers his head as though ready to charge, or is snarling and showing his teeth and has his hackles and tail up, it may be safest to go no closer. But if his tail is tucked between his legs, you may be able to bluff him by shouting and pretending to throw or hit him with a rolled up newspaper. As you leave the dog's territory, remember the golden rule of cool—don't turn and run; back away slowly, keeping the dog in your sights all the time.

6. Don't forget, most delivery people and passersby get bitten as they are *leaving* or moving away from the dog's territory. Turning your back and walking away may be read as weakness or submission by the dog and so he may then chase and bite you. With a dog who seems like he's after you—snarling, staring at you, walking stiffly or in a slinky way with the hair up along his back—stand your ground. Call out to the owners. Stare back at him. Hold up a clenched fist like a club, swipe at him, and shout in a powerful, angry voice, "No, boy; down. Go home." This may be sufficient bluff to scare him. Never lean back. Any backward movement will disclose your fear. Keep your weight forward so if he jumps at you, you will be ready. An upward thrust with your knee into the dog's chest and a faceful of your jacket sleeve will deter many dogs.

7. Dogs rarely attack, so don't start worrying and acting scared around any dog you meet. Most are like you and me. They are scared about getting into a fight but they like to act tough sometimes, especially around their own block. Don't ignore dogs you may meet—they may be suspicious of you then. Say "Hi, dog. How are you today?" If you act friendly and confident, he won't be scared and will have less reason to challenge you. Many dogs will respond to your greeting by wagging their tails and sometimes even grinning at you. Others will play it cool and ignore you, so don't be pushy and overfriendly.

8. Remember, dogs can tell if you like them, and a doggie biscuit

in your pocket is a better insurance than a stick or a can of Mace or other dog repellent. Don't feel bad if you like dogs and they all seem to bark at you and hate you: They are just doing their job.

In conclusion, the old truism that a dog's bark is worse than his bite deserves some qualification. A silent dog is often more likely to bite than one who makes a lot of noise defending his territory.

32

Is Man Dog's (and Cat's) Best Friend? What Overbreeding Is Doing to the Breeds

As a child I used to wonder if dogs and cats thanked people for their being born, since, after all, we humans were responsible for allowing them to have babies in the first place. My first rude awakening came when I was playing around in one of my favorite spots: the local pond. There I could observe and collect all kinds of fascinating creatures—waterbugs, newts, frog spawn, tubifex worms, and a host of other amazing things. On that particular day, though, I found a floating sack—treasure perhaps, or loot from a burglar? I dragged it to the bank and tore it open and there, only a few hours dead, was a litter of kittens: five or six unwanted creatures each of which I could have found a home for among my playmates. But their fate had been decided upon already. They would never thank anyone for being born.

Only many years later did I come to realize that this seemingly inhumane act could have been one of responsible compassion. It is kinder perhaps to destroy unwanted and homeless creatures than to turn them loose or to give them to indifferent owners. Yet why let them breed in the first place?

Besides spending hours playing in the neighborhood fields and around the bullrush pond, my other hobby was identifying every animal I saw. Dogs soon ceased to be just dogs as I began, with a suitable guide book, to learn all the various breeds. Like some

259

children enjoyed naming the various makes of cars, I got a charge out of naming the various breeds I might see on the street or at the local dog shows. How incredible it seemed that people could actually create such a diversity of dogs, and cats, too, I learned later: muscular mastiffs and svelte Salukis, tiny Chihuahuas and gigantic wolfhounds; luxurious Persians and inscrutable Siamese.

At the shows most people were happy to tell me all about their animals and I soon learned much about the distinctive qualities of the various breeds.

That was thirty years ago. Going to a dog show now is a bit like opening up that sack of dead kittens I found in the pond. It's a shock. Something seems to be very different. Is it the dogs or the businesslike professional handlers? The modern show seems less of a gathering of dog-devoted hobbyists and more of a highly commercial and competitive enterprise; top show dogs may go from one show to another and be on the road with their handlers for weeks or months. Many of these dogs are not homebodies at all. They don't seem quite real and some seem as lifeless as those kittens in the sack.

Two more unforgettable childhood experiences are coming to mind now. One was the time when I peeked through the backyard fence of the veterinarian's on my walk home from school. I was six or seven years old then and I had difficulty understanding what I saw: Two trash cans spilling over with dead cats and dogs and a heap of fly-buzzed dogs between them. I don't know what I had expected to see—but so much death. Only later did I learn that these pets were just a minute fraction of the millions that are destroyed every year. Is man the cat or dog's best friend? They all must have suffered, I thought; how good it would be if I were to become a veterinarian and help them. Ironically, as a veterinarian years later, I would be asked to kill perfectly normal and healthy pets whose owners had abandoned them, lost interest in them, or found them too much trouble.

The other more joyous memory was Bruce, the old Irish setter who lived at the small bakery store opposite the vet's. Bruce often accompanied me home and on weekends he would visit and we would go exploring together. He was a wise and affectionate dog, patient and understanding. He taught me many things about dogs and about the countryside in general which, without his senses to help me, lizards, birds' nests and many other things would never have been found.

Bruce was a significant "person" in my life; he had a "magnetic" personality. Years later, when I visited a kennel of "Bruces"—pureblood Irish setters—I was appalled. These animals were zombies, thin-boned and overrefined, narrow-skulled and mindless. Some were hyperactive, others just plain soft, sweet nothings. All were priced at three hundred dollars and up, and for what? I pitied this fine breed for what man had done to them. The same is true for many of the more popular varieties of purebred dogs today.

During my training at veterinary school in England and subsequent research at the Jackson laboratory in Bar Harbor, Maine, I began to learn what can happen to our dogs and cats when people start to breed them "pure" and don't follow certain rules of good breeding. So many physically and psychologically deformed and otherwise impaired pedigree animals are being created today that I wonder again if cats and dogs thank people for being born. For many, death—even by being drowned in a sack in the local pond—would be a kindness. More of this and the reasons why in a moment.

I have had two more shocks in recent years, worse, I think, than that experience with the kittens in a sack. One was a weekend meeting of dog breeders and show people to whom I gave a lecture on dog behavior and development. At their afternoon workshop they placed a little terrier onto a grooming table and three experts got hold of it and pulled its hind legs backward and proclaimed, "It should look and stand like this." What they were doing was streamlining the little box of a dog to look like a slinky, low-hipped shepherd. For what purpose? None, except for esthetic reasons. They were going about changing the standards of this terrier breed, which was hundreds of years old and which had been developed for good reason. The end result of what they were suggesting would be a breed of cripples with deformed hips and weak, almost functionless, hind legs.

The other shock was an international cat show in Canada that I visited a couple of years ago. One prize-winning Siamese was the most pathetic and unhealthy-looking feline I had ever seen. It had been bred to look "refined," such that its limbs were thin, its head stupidly narrow and wedge-shaped, and its back permanently arched. The top winning Abyssinian was going the same way, too—compared to my lithe and chunky Abby at home, this one looked positively emaciated and lifeless.

Faddism seems to be destroying our purebred cats and dogs and many are doomed to a sickly life of chronic debility, recurrent illnesses, and a number of other problems that I will describe shortly. The physical characteristics of certain breeds of dog and cat, especially if exaggerated by overbreeding, can lead to a lifetime of constant suffering or serious limitations in their general activity. These problems are inherited but are so much a part of the breed that to eliminate them would essentially mean to stop breeding altogether. But some of these problems can be partially overcome with special attention by the owner.

Here are some of the more common genetic anomalies to look out for.

Cats

The long-haired Persian can be a problem if you aren't prepared to groom it every day. Some of these cats will give up grooming themselves—and I can't blame them—and they will then develop great knots and balls in their coats and get quite smelly. Skin infections may follow. Others get so neurotic about their fur that they groom excessively and half choke each day on furballs that they have swallowed.

By far the most pathetic man-made feline freak is the cross-eyed Siamese. Some have such impaired vision that they walk into things, knock things over, and are even too scared to jump or to ever venture outdoors for a walk. This eye abnormality is so common in Siamese cats that some people think that it's quite normal for a Siamese to have a squint. Believe me, it is not, and to continue breeding them is inhumane.

Dogs

In contrast to the problems that dogs have, cats have it easy. The most tragic consequences of monstrous breeding is undoubtedly the English bulldog. Their pushed-in faces and overlong soft palate can lead to chronic breathing problems, just as though the dog were being suffocated for its entire life. In hot weather, they can get into serious trouble. Their efforts to breathe can become so strenuous that the windpipe collapses. Why do fanciers still breed them? I wonder. Why don't they at least selectively breed to elongate the face more to ease the problem?

Other breeds have serious man-inflicted problems, too. The heavy, pendulous ears of cocker spaniels require constant attention otherwise they will smell and become chronically infected due to the lack of ventilation and build-up of moisture. Poodles, with their abnormal fluffy coat, often have ears blocked with fur, another man-made problem. If the ear canals aren't cleaned out and defluffed regularly, chronic ear troubles are inevitable.

It especially annoys me to see a heavy-coated dog like an Old English sheepdog or a malemute living in hot, moist climates like Florida and Louisiana. In other states, such dogs are dependent on air-conditioning in the summer to prevent heatstroke or moist-skin fungal and "hot spot" diseases. These are examples of geographic

Working breeds such as this Malemute are becoming increasingly popular as sedentary, nonworking companions—often to the detriment of both dog and owner *(H.S.U.S./Mike Kellogg).*

"misfits," and this is especially serious now since Arctic breeds—malemutes and huskies—are becoming increasingly popular as pets. Many, for various reasons, have abnormal coat-shedding patterns and suffer miserably in the summer with a full coat. A ride in the car could mean an emergency case of heatstroke.

Giant breeds—Great Danes and Irish wolfhounds in particular—often have acute growing pains, and the slightest upset in health or nutrition can lead to impaired skeletal development. Such giant breeds were once bred for specific purposes—for hunting and some even for war. If we still want to breed them just for fun (and profit), we should be prepared to feed them right and to expect many problems and frequent visits to the veterinarian.

This brings us to another problem. Many varieties of dog are strictly working breeds—malemutes and huskies are sled or draught animals; terriers are ratters and small vermin catchers; others, like the bull terrier, are bred to be fighters. Some breeds are protectors; the shepherds and sheepdogs have been bred to hunt; pointers and retrievers, like the bloodhound, are born to track. Yet today, few are worked, few are given an opportunity to develop and exercise their specific attributes and instincts. For many of these dogs, confinement in the home as an untrained and unworked pet is inhumane and a source of stress and frustration.

Some working breeds are being altered now, their basic skills and specific attributes eliminated so that they will be better as pets or easier to handle in the show ring. This is all very well to a degree. They look like the real thing, but they tend to be bigger and lighter boned facsimiles of the original breeds, like that kennel of Irish setters that only faintly resembled old Bruce. Some breeds seem to be in transition between being working dogs with stamina and intelligence and becoming weak, inbred "sweet nothings." If this is what people want—though I find it hard to believe—then it's probably better than keeping a good breed of dog indoors, bored, unworked, and frustrated.

Some breeds have gone through this transition already—Weimaraners, English and Irish setters, certain lines of Doberman pinschers, Border collies, Old English sheepdogs, Saint Bernards and countless others. Some of these dogs are sweet and affectionate perpetual puppies in many instances. Other are unpredictable because they have been bred for looks and not for stable temperament, trainability, and intelligence to do certain kinds of work.

Man has created these zombies, and they may be happy in their perpetual puppyness and infantilized innocence, but many suffer worse consequences of bad breeding: The congenital and inherited abnormalities would now fill a book. A book of pathology, of gross abnormalities in body structure and conformation, notably hip dysplasia, cryptorehidism (having only one testicle), increased disease susceptibility, hemophilia, glaucoma, epilepsy, progressive blindness due to retinal atrophy, autoimmune disease complexes, arthritis, certain forms of cancer, digestive disorders such as acute bloat and ulcerative colitis, endocrine disorders such as hypothyroidism and diabetes, and unstable temperaments that lead to chronic anxiety states, hyperactivity, fear-biting and unpredictable aggression.

Many of these genetically related problems are now well recognized, and laboratories use affected animals as "models" to study similar abnormalities in man. It seems ironic that as we unwittingly create these problems in our dogs, they are helping us to solve such problems as they affect humans. Perhaps in the final analysis, the dog is man's best friend, but the reverse is surely questionable. The ethics of keeping sick animals alive and breeding them to create more generations of suffering in order to understand comparable human disease is questionable. We must also question some breeders' claims that they are "saving the breed" (from extinction!) by keeping alive genetic deviants and faddishly created monstrosities.

The moral of this account is that if you plan to buy a purebred dog, be forewarned that yours may be an expensive pet, requiring more trips to the vet for one genetically related problem or another than you would have with a mongrel dog. Many of these genetic problems are due to excessive inbreeding and overbreeding. Producing many offspring from a narrow base of interrelated stock leads to inbreeding, and when there are no records of how the progeny develop and no culling or sterilizing of defective offspring, then you have overbreeding. This combination of inbreeding and overbreeding is taking its toll on our good breeds of dog, and as cats become more popular and varieties well established, they too will go the way of the dogs.

We can change these things at various levels. Dog shows should cease to be for people and their whims and focus more on dogs. They should stop being beauty shows with standards set by people with little knowledge of a dog's structure, genetics, and behavior.

Breeders must become more ethically responsible and not cover up or turn a blind eye to breeding defects. They should keep detailed records on all offspring and start out afresh by producing fewer animals and focusing on quality. People who breed dogs just for show, and large commerical puppy-mill breeders who are motivated by profit only, are aggravating these problems. The public "consumer" should not decide on the basis of a dog's good looks alone. Very often the breed you like to look at isn't for you. Your life-style, your temperament, or even the climate may not be optimal for the breed of your choice.

In the final analysis, man will become cat's and dog's best friend when he stops imposing unsound standards and faddish values. Breeding for narrow-skulled collies is now blamed for collie eye blindness (retinal detachment), which may affect 95 percent of the breed. Breeding for racy, low-slung hips leads to crippling hip dysplasia in thousands of shepherds and many other breeds. We are learning that mother nature—natural selection—works best. When we breed for style or particularly unique traits, there can be serious repercussions, especially when a defective dog becomes a show winner and is bred with many dogs. His defective genes will spread rapidly throughout the breed and it will then be too late to correct the problem. We work against sensible selection for soundness by keeping alive with drugs and protective environment various breeds of dog and cat that could otherwise not survive. Some, like bulldogs, Boston terriers, Pekes, and Persian cats, can't even give birth normally because their offspring have such large heads. Many have to be delivered by caesarean section. This may be good for veterinary profits, but veterinarians, humanitarians, and good dog and cat breeders are unanimous in their agreement that we must put an end to all of this. Raising animals that require surgery, drugs, and other supportive treatments is a sickness in itself that creates more unnecessary sickness and suffering in the animals that we bring into this world. Let us stop this game of sick pets and become responsible stewards of our four-legged friends. They deserve more than what we have given them so far.

I am repeatedly asked which is my favorite breed of dog. Many breeders of purebred (pedigree) dogs would urge me to say "poodle," "schnauzer," "Great Dane" or "Sheltie"—or whatever particular breed they happen to propagate. Some breeders feel that I should start a placement service, running psychological profiles on prospective owners to match them with the most appropriate kind of dog! Other breeders would ask me to be silent and not voice any preference, knowing full well that, so often, once a breed becomes popular, overbreeding will cause incidence of psychological and physical defects to soar.

The alternative to a purebred dog—and an alternative I whole-heartedly approve—is a mongrel—the mutt, or mixed breed of dog. The renaissance man of dogdom, the mongrel is generally looked down upon by the racists or purists of the dog world. National obedience trials no longer allow well-trained dogs to compete if they are not purebred, and, to cap it all, even some local obedience classes (a *must* for any conscientious dog owner and a great experience for young children) are closed to all mongrels! I am not going to plead for equal rights for all dogs, but I think that some of the underlying values and public attitudes concerning the breeds need airing in order to help would-be dog owners make the right choice.

The first myth to be dispelled is that a mongrel dog is inferior to a purebred one. It isn't. But many owners and would-be owners place value on having a dog that has its "papers"—a pedigree record as long as your arm (or as big as their egos). At one time a pedigree was of value, and it still is to a knowledgeable breeder in tracing lineage and programming future matings. But today it has become a meaningless thing, flouted and toted like a warranty on a new car that is no guarantee of soundness and of no intrinsic value to the nonbreeder pet owner except for status or snob appeal. Possessing papers gives some owners a vicarious sense of history, ancestry, even aristocracy. Rather like a human pedigree of aristocratic lineage, though there may be repeated patterns of inbreeding (incest?!)—brother x sister and father x daughter marriages, and, more frequently, crosses between first and second cousins (all in the "royal" family). And just as in many of the medieval human lineages, inbreeding has produced degenerates, both physical and psychological.

The blame for this widespread degeneration is to be directed at the dog breeder and breed clubs, who, until only the last decade or so, have done little to control such problems, being more concerned with how a dog should look (in relation to breed standards of size, body proportions, coat type and color) than how it functions and behaves. The tide is slowly changing; many breed clubs hold intensive seminars on such problems and study genetics and sound breeding practices. Much veterinary research is being conducted, often supported directly from contributions by some breed clubs.

These are the concerned, ethical breeders of purebred dogs; unfortunately there are many who aren't or who are not hard-nosed enough to kill off defective animals or at least never to breed from a physically or psychologically unsound animal. Worse, a defective or slightly below-par "pet-quality" pup is often sold to an "amateur" who breeds the animal when it matures, much to the detriment of the breed in question. "Professional" breeders can get no guarantee that the owner of a below-par purebred dog will never breed it. Remember, such a dog will have a pedigree, and you could be taken

Pure-bred or mongrel? Note the cropped ears on the Great Dane, as unnecessary and inhumane mutilation, outlawed in Britain, yet still accepted by judges and show people in the U.S. *(H.S.U.S./ Kathy Garvey).*

in by someone flaunting its papers in your face. Many pet stores, especially the large "puppy-mill" establishments, sell such pet-quality animals at prices you would pay for a show-quality one.

Only show-winning dogs should be allowed to breed—and then, only after a rigorous veterinary and psychological evaluation. Simply allowing only registered breeders of superior dogs to produce puppies would help. Today, anyone with a purebred dog with papers feels justified in breeding it, and this not only increases the percentage of unsound animals in a particular breed, it adds significantly to the pet overpopulation problem. Fourteen million unwanted cats and dogs are destroyed by animal shelters each year. Many of these are purebred dogs, spawned by unethical or unknowledgeable breeders, often just to make a quick buck.

So what's the advantage in having a mongrel over a purebred dog? The former manifests what is termed hybrid vigor, combining the best qualities of its parents, and often is an improvement upon both. Some first-generation hybrids, crosses between two pure breeds, are gaining popularity because of this superior "mongrelizing" effect. Cocker spaniel x poodle ("cockerpoo"), terrier x poodle ("terripoo"), puli x poodle ("pulipoo") and shih-Tzu x poodle (no, I won't combine that one!) are some of the popular breed combinations. The advantage of such known cross breedings, as with a purebred puppy, is that you know what it will be like when it matures. With a mongrel pup of unknown parentage almost anything could happen. It's often hard to tell what a little mongrel pup will look like—huge tail, big head, odd ears, strange coat, long body, short legs, or an unexpectedly large size—when it is fully grown. Some people, especially experienced personnel at pet adoption centers, can give prospective owners a fairly accurate assessment of what a six- or eight-week-old mongrel pup will turn out to look like—but one can often be in for a surprise later!

I'm also pro-mongrel because I have had them as pets and studied them in my research and can find nothing against them functionally or psychologically. Of course, some may have timidity, defensive-aggressiveness, or hyperactivity problems just as purebred dogs do, but generally they are sound in limb and brain. So, too, are purebred dogs from *good* kennels, so if you do opt for the latter, you must sleuth around and find a reputable breeder.

A major feature of purebred dogs is that they have special traits and qualities specific for the breed in question; for the prospective owner it is important to know if these are really what is wanted. In the average mongrel dog, such traits are generally less exaggerated, which is sometimes to one's advantage. Do you really want a purebred dog that will weight 200 pounds when it is fully grown (like a Saint Bernard), that has a coat that needs daily attention (like an Old English sheepdog), that has a hyperactive "working" temperament (like a sheepdog), or a superprotective guard dog (like a Doberman), a feisty scrapper of a dog (like most terriers), a racing type that needs lots of exercise (like a Saluki or Afghan hound) or a "superspecialist" bred not as a pet but to perform specific tasks (like a pointer, coonhound, retriever, or bloodhound)? I wonder why most people who want a general-purpose pet dog buy one of these "specialists," never to employ them for these functions.

Some breeds are developing both working and show varieties. Contrast a field retriever with a show Labrador; the latter looks superficially like its working counterpart but is finer boned, more even-tempered, and has little or no inclination for field work.

Should breeders in fact change temperament—once an important standard of the breed? I think two things have to be done. Temperament can be improved by instigating tests in the show ring to eliminate unstable, fearful, and hyperaggressive types. Temperament can also be modified (in fact it *must* be in some breeds) to make pure bred animals more adaptable as contemporary housepets. Selectively breeding terriers to be less feisty, working breeds to have a lower activity requirement, and so on can help considerably. It does seem a tragic waste, however, when an owner has a supertrainable working dog like a Border collie or a shepherd whose selectively bred potential is never developed. A general-purpose mongrel might have filled the bill nicely.

In many ways, our dogs mirror the problems that modern man is encountering in his own evolution. Civilization and domesticity—the world of man and tame animal—both adapt to change. There is no one to help us or them except ourselves. We are as much responsible for their future as we are for our own. Some would say that the human race has already "gone to the dogs," and we do seem to learn slowly from our mistakes, but when I come home and am greeted by my ex-dog-pound mongrel dog, my faith is restored in nature—both animal and human.

33

Pets: Contemporary Problems and Future Shocks

There's something uncanny about many science fiction stories such as the great tales of H. G. Wells. They give us a glimpse of the future, and a generation or so later often turn out to be true. George Orwell's *1984* and Huxley's *Brave New World* are particularly ominous novels that seem to be accurate predictions of where we are going. Where are we going with our pets? What does the future hold for them and our relationships with them? A good science fiction writer develops his theme on the basis of logical probabilities, gleaning his insights from bits and pieces of information, of new creations and trends that are here with us today. Suddenly time seems to twist back on itself and the future is now. Talking dogs, psychosurgery for pets, hearing and "feeling" dog aids and therapists, genetic and psychological counseling, bionic pets, summer camp, regular day or night school (with diplomas for graduates), special burial services, and pet health insurance—these and other "far-out" aspects of "petishism," of the growing subculture of pets and their owners and of exploitative or innovative entrepreneurs (both ethical and unethical), are not future speculations. They are here today—and here to stay. This is a kind of "future shock," the shock being in the realization that what seems to be future fantasy is a *now* reality.

Recent advances in veterinary medicine and animal behavior,

new "uses" of the pet, changing relationships between pet and owner, and the innovations of pet-trade commercialists give us many glimpses of the future. These contemporary pet-related phenomena must be seen and appreciated in a worldwide perspective where increasing costs, decreasing resources, and changes in economy and life-styles will influence the future of people and pets alike.

New and Future Veterinary Innovations

One of the few positive benefits to our pets in using animals in medical research is that some of the advances tested for future human application can also be applied to pets. Dogs used in eye research, for example, have given us the know-how to treat glaucoma, retinal detachment, and to surgically graft new corneas in humans. Some veterinarians are now able to perform such surgical procedures on pets, including the use of laser beams to reattach a detached retina. Cryosurgery, and, in many university veterinary hospitals, radiation treatment and chemotherapy for cancer are routinely performed on people's pets. Radioactive isotopes and sonar scanning techniques are used to aid in the diagnosis of endocrine gland, brain, and heart disorders. New biochemical tests are being used to identify allergies, enzyme deficiences, and complex autoimmune disorders. Some pets are walking around today with prosthetic joints—artificial hips and rebuilt knees and elbows—and others even have artificial teeth. It will not be long before pets wear cardiac pacemakers on their collars, and other bionic devices.

Many pets are now being maintained on daily drugs, just like humans, to control epilepsy, diabetes, hyperactivity, thyroid dysfunction. The birth control pill is commonplace. Some pets undergo heart surgery, brain surgery for tumors, and psychosurgery (frontal lobotomies) for various emotional disorders. Soon, kidney grafts may be performed to prolong the life of a pampered protein-overloaded pet; plastic surgery (to correct a floppy ear, an abnormal eyelid or to add one testicle if one is missing) has been performed on many pets and show animals for several years now. We may well see more corrective dental surgery (and orthodontics) in pets, especially in toy breeds who are prone to all kinds of dental problems at an early age. Owners are advised to brush such a pet's teeth every day. New pet toothpastes will be marketed, along with more hair conditioners, deodorizers, and the like.

There is now an American veterinary association of acupuncture, and this departure from traditional Western medicine heralds a new frontier for both human and nonhuman medicine. Dogs and cats are being treated for a variety of disorders with acupuncture needles and electrical stimulation. Some veterinarians are exploring homeopathic techniques, herbal remedies, and megavitamin therapy, as are the less insecure or conservative MD's. A departure from mere treatment of symptoms with drugs (often causing further drug-induced or iatrogenic complications) is evident. Future emphasis will be on preventive medicine and sensible diets and life habits, to the benefit of people and pet patients alike. While this may not be in the best interests of the drug industry, it will certainly be of benefit to the sick. Western medicine still regards health as the absence of disease, which, to say the least, is not a healthy view of normality!

Genetic counseling to breeders of purebred animals, like that given to parents in whose lineage some inherited abnormality has been identified, is another future-shock concept that is being practiced today. Such counseling is essential in order to save some breeds and to improve most so as to eliminate such debilitating inherited disorders as glaucoma, hip dysplasia, epilepsy, aggression, paranoia, and a number of other problems. If pure breeds become even more popular, the future will bring more and more genetic problems to the surface as a consequence of inbreeding and overbreeding.

Related to this future-oriented genetic improvement is the practice of artificial insemination. Dog semen can be frozen and stored for future use. This means that a very fine dog could still provide his "seed" years after he has expired. Similarly, sperm and egg "banks" may be developed for further research into inherited and developmental anomalies.

As preventive medicine becomes more effective (bringing about better diets, a wider range of vaccines, more sensible and responsible owners), pets will live longer. This will mean that geriatric pet problems will increase, and one of the new frontiers in veterinary medicine will be pet geriatrics.

On the basis of present trends it would seem that in the future both pets and people will depend more heavily upon supportive medical aid. This will be greatly reduced, however, if inherited problems are mitigated by genetic counseling and if the diets and life-styles of pets are more conducive to good health. The adaptability of pets to owners' changing life-styles may be critical here, and those pets that do not adapt well will either be aided by therapy (medical or psychological) or will be discarded. "Misfits" that do not respond to therapy will be destroyed or at least not bred. A high proportion of the fourteen million cats and dogs that are destroyed each year are such "misfits." Presumably the surviving "fittest," the most adaptable, will be bred and thus transmit such attributes to their offspring. In this way, which is a form of accelerated evolution, pets may change very rapidly in the short period of only a few generations. This is possible because there are so many animals to choose from and, unlike people, all are early-maturing, prolific breeders.

Clinical/Counseling Psychology

Over the past decade there has been an increasing interest in pet behavior problems. Veterinarians in practice are now counseling pet owners on how to remedy certain emotional and behavioral troubles in their pets. It's no longer a question of disobedient pets that need a whack with a rolled-up newspaper or a course of disciplinary training. That Victorian approach to raising both pets and children is out. People are now beginning to recognize that pets are like children in that they can develop emotional problems and psychosomatic disorders. Some vets now refer problem cases to a good dog trainer (who often has a background in psychology). Also several clinical psychologists with PhD's and licenses to work with people are now working on pet problems. They are filling an important role since many pet problems involve the owner's attitudes or some complex problem in the family as a whole. The future will most likely entail more of this pet and family counseling and therapy.

Twenty years ago, most people would have ridiculed this and certainly would not have envisioned the area of pet psychology becoming an established practice. Such ridicule, based upon the attitude that "the family can take care of its own problems," has changed considerably today. Families seek out counsel for problem children, marital difficulties, and the like. Possibly because the old extended-family structure and sense of community have all but disappeared, especially in urban and suburban "nuclear" families, outside help is a necessity.

Other psychotherapeutic tools that are used on people are now being applied, for better or for worse, on pets. Drugs—stimulants, depressants, tranquilizers, behavior modification (desensitization and conditioning) and even psychosurgery (frontal lobotomies)—are being administered to pets. I personally have some misgivings about these futuristic pet therapies. Good breeding, proper rearing, and balanced relationships within the family are the keys to a healthy and happy pet. Such "preventive" medicine is surely better than drugging a pet or performing brain surgery, although the former, as in humans, may help alleviate certain acute problems.

Super Pets and New Roles

With special breeding and rearing programs, pets of super intelligence and high emotional stability and adaptability will be developed in the future. Some breeders and pet owners are already using programs that I have developed (and which the army's veterinary corps has used effectively in their "superdog" program).

New roles for pets in society are emerging. Dogs are now being trained as "hearing aids" for deaf people, an invaluable asset for those for whom an electronic hearing aid is ineffectual. In another growing role, pets are used as "feeling aids," or cotherapists. Working with a therapist, a pet can break down the barriers of a withdrawn and emotionally disturbed patient and act as a bridge for the therapist.

Pet Products

Innovations drawing upon advances in technology and animal psychology may herald an era of creative playthings for pets, especially for those pets that are left alone for extended periods while their owners are out at work. Electronic gadgets in the form of toys (substitute mice and other prey) to keep the pet occupied, and videotape programs with interesting sounds and visual displays, may soon be marketed. Pets are responsive to animal sounds and some to TV pictures: special pet-time programs during the day may be developed.

These devices for keeping pets peacefully occupied are certainly preferable to products that are marketed today. One brand of shock collar to stop dogs from barking has been recently recalled by the FDA. This is because the collar may deliver ten times the amount of shock stated by the manufacturers and will burn the dog's neck. It may also be triggered by other dogs barking close by.

Radio-activated training collars are now available, and one could imagine the next development: electronic control of one's pet either via brain electrodes or special signals given via a radio attached to the collar. One could then adjust one's pet from a distance as one might adjust one's TV with a remote-control hand unit. Hopefully such technological gimmicry will not come to be. Ominously echoing *A Clockwork Orange*, impersonal methods of behavior control for animals or people can only destroy intimacy, compassion, and our natural abilities to communicate with one another.

Other "Futuristic" Developments

In many areas, special pet training schools are flourishing. Here dogs can work for higher degrees in obedience trials that are held all over the country. Day-care centers for pets are also increasing in popularity. Instead of being left alone all day, they can enjoy the company of other dogs and go out for walks with their caretakers. Other pet services include pet-sitters for evenings and vacations, and country summer "camps" for city pooches have even been developed. Multipurpose pet centers franchised nationwide, where one can get not only a full range of pet supplies and beauty treatment for coats, nails, and teeth but also super hotellike accommodations for boarding, day care, pooch pick-up and delivery services, and veterinary and psychological consultations, are not beyond the bounds of probability.

In some areas, medical health insurance for pets can now be obtained and, of course, burial plots, a variety of headstones, silk-lined coffins or urns for the loved-one's ashes, and full funeral facilities with various forms of services.

While Saint Francis in his infinite wisdom regarded animals as our little brothers and sisters, one may well wonder just how far we may go into treating our pets like little people—if not like overindulged children. Perhaps the two most positive future eventualities will be the following. First, improved *two-way* communication between human and nonhuman animals, based, as in my books, upon empathy and a sound scientific knowledge of animal patterns of communication.

Second, in a more enlightened society, animals will fall within the scope of our moral concern. Rather than being regarded as utilitarian objects, as mere property, they will be accorded rights and have more legal rights than they have today. Such rights will not be exclusive to pets, but to wild animals and those that are used in research and are raised on farms for food. Before such a golden era of harmony between animal and man, as I emphasized in my book, *Between Animal and Man*, the immediate future has some ominous possibilities. Unless the human population is constrained, many wild species and their habitats will be destroyed forever.

Increasingly our meat-eating cats and dogs whose diets are now better than that of many third-world children, may have to eat exclusively vegetable protein and cereals. Even such foods may become so costly that few will be able to afford to keep a large dog. One could almost foresee people hiding their pets if the consensus were to hold that it is immoral and illegal to feed them. An acute world food shortage with two-thirds or more of the human population starving could make pet ownership a privilege for the indifferent rich, or an illegal occupation.

Because of the increasing problems associated with free-roaming pets and irresponsible ownership, vigilante groups may clean out neighborhoods to protect their children and livestock, or city ordinances could simply outlaw the ownership of dogs, or of dogs above a particular size. Already many communities have polarized pro- and anti-pet factions. Socially, ecologically, politically, and economically, this issue is a potential powder keg and the fuse has already been lit!

The future of pets and other domestic animals, and of those in the wild, is inseparable from our own. I believe that the ultimate "use" or transcending value of a pet is to help us become more human—that is, humane, compassionate, and responsible. To be wholly preoccupied with the interests of one's pet is as unbalanced as to be wholly immersed in human-centered values and needs. The key to the peaceable kingdom of the future encompassing animal and man is a worldwide reverence for all life, human and nonhuman. Such an eventuality will come provided we can change those human values and attitudes that cause the demeaning and exploitation of others (including animals) for purely selfish ends. This is why I am now working with the Humane Society of the United States. The Humane movement is a directing force toward a future golden age of world peace: of harmony between humans and the rest of creation. It will not come without active involvement and support from those who have faith and hope in the future. In many ways, our pets are our mirrors, they are sensitive and accurate indicators of our attitudes and values. We may mature in the future and accord them deserved rights. But we can never make them, nor should we, into little people or substitute children. They are animals, not humans, and always will be, though they are no less worthy of our respect and affection. Surely a healthy relationship between animal and man will foster a healthy relationship between man and man and nation and nation. If we demean and exploit nature and animals, where do we draw the line with people? A reverence for all life is nonjudging and nondiscriminating. Hopefully in the future, our species will indeed be more human and people of all nations will share a reverence for all life. Is this not the only key to world peace and harmony between animal and man?

34

Values –Animals and People

In the previous chapters, I have rated (and berated) pet owners on how responsible they are toward their pets, pointing out a number of serious urban and environmental problems that can arise from irresponsibility. Some public authorities would urge legislation to regulate pet ownership more stringently today, while others press for educational programs in schools and college extension programs. What seems to be at the root of the pet problem—and the related problems of wildlife exploitation (which is leading to the rapid extinction of species and destruction of their natural habitats)—are the attitudes of people.

Consider a student who has enjoyed the company of a fine old springer spaniel for several years. When he graduates, he dumps it on a student acquaintance who knows little about dogs. The result is a depressed dog that is pining away for its master. College students are notorious for abandoning their pets when the semester is over and parents won't allow them to bring their animals home. With little foresight, kittens and puppies are obtained in the springtime, only to be discarded when, unexpectedly, they are too much of a problem in a dormitory or apartment, or when the semester ends. Fortunately not all students treat their pets like throwaway plates. Some work in liaison with animal shelters in trying to get such unwanted pets adopted. In fact, on more than one campus, local townsfolk drop off their own unwanted pets, hoping some student might adopt them.

Being responsible for a pet's life is only half the picture; one is also responsible for its death, for when its time comes, it is entitled to a quick and painless end. For a person saddled with a pet that cannot be adopted or that doesn't fit into the home or life-style of the owners, the ultimate responsibility is to assure its humane destruction. Some people will not take their unwanted pet to the shelter to be destroyed because they fear that it might finish up in the hands of some biomedical researcher and be treated inhumanely. Those that do, and who are concerned about this very real possibility, insist upon seeing the dog put to sleep just to make sure. This is not always possible, however, since not all animal shelters use the most humane method of euthanasia—intravenous injection of an anesthetic—and consequently, don't allow witnesses!

Thousands of pets are scraped up from the roads in the United States every year—some are free-roaming, uncontrolled pets, others discarded misfits or unwanted toys. Fourteen to sixteen million unwanted pets pass through animal shelters each year in the United States, and only a few are adopted. Most are destroyed. Humane societies have become slaughterhouses, a hideous necessity brought on by just one major factor: the public attitude toward animals.

Pets, like everything else, are "consumed," and if they are not acceptable or no longer of interest they are simply and unceremoniously discarded. I have personally, at the local humane society, tried to reason with owners who insist upon having a young dog killed because it isn't what they want (it won't protect the house, won't come when called, chews up things in the house, etc.)—but to no avail. Not realizing that a pup is more than a potted plant, that it needs lots of attention and training and not just food and water, they believe they have a misfit. Only too often they go off and get another pup: easy come, easy go. I hesitate to think what brutalizing consequences such an attitude may have upon their children.

Of course some people have healthier attitudes toward pets; for them, pets provide real companionship and emotional support. But simply appreciating the pet for its own sake, rather than as a source of selfish gratification, is perhaps the most healthy and desirable attitude. It is certainly better than regarding the pet as a mere object (for status or as a toy for the children) or a utilitarian "thing" (for guarding the yard or for show and breeding purposes only).

What is your attitude toward pets? Perhaps you do not regard a dog as a pet—as an emotional support or companion—but rather believe that it should earn its keep. Working dogs on a ranch, farm, or for security work and for hunting and the like do work better when they are closely bonded emotionally to their masters. But often the master does not reciprocate. His often-dominionistic attitude toward the livestock or wildlife he manages or kills for pleasure and profit, may also extend to his dog. Reverence for life is too often lacking and I wish such "masters" would show more of the compassion and concern that their dogs display!

Not all men have this dominionistic and utilitarian attitude toward their dogs, though: while for some, their dogs are an extension of their egos (say one word to demean their dogs and they take it as a personal offense), others have a deep respect and appreciation for their animals. I wish there were more people of this caliber voicing their concern over the general abuse of pets and wildlife today. One I met recently at a symposium on pets and society in Toronto. He was a sheep rancher who felt that fewer and fewer people today had that deep respect for the earth and reverence for animals, wild and tame: Too many exploit and few are as close to the land as some of their fathers were.

Yet why should we care at all for animals? some ask; surely we should focus our concern upon the ills of society and human suffering. The point is, however, that animal and human suffering are intimately interrelated, and once a person sees the connection, it doesn't matter where he decides to focus his concern. Indifference to animal suffering is related to general indifference toward all others. Racism and "speciesism" (demeaning nonhuman animals) stem from the same attitudes of mind. Today the equal rights movement for discriminated minorities is paving the way for establishing natural rights for all living beings—including wild and domestic animals and their natural habitats as well.

Perhaps you are one of a growing number of people who feel more for animals than for fellow human beings. Much as I can empathize with this point of view I can only think it's rather like dropping out and giving up on life. If you really care for animals there are many good societies and associations to support so that you can join the fight to protect and conserve animals and what little natural habitat there is left for them in this world. Disenchanted as I am with the attitudes of people toward both human and nonhu-

Dog fighting, a popular, illegal and inhumane rural sport in the U.S. *(H.S.U.S.)*.

man animals, I am as much concerned about those who devote their lives to animals and have nothing more to do with people as I am about those who are wholly indifferent toward animals and would have nothing to do with their protection and conservation. The well-being and future of animals and people are so intimately related that we must concern ourselves with both and not one at the exclusion of the other. The humane movement, with its concern for educational awareness and the fostering of ethical responsibility and reverence for all life, is a growing, positive influence in society today. And we must not only educate, we must also fight in the courts for legislation to ensure humane treatment of pets, animals in research, in zoos, and in rodeos, and for the protection and steward-ship (rather than management and harvesting) of wild animals. The fact that more people are showing concern for animals today is a positive sign of our "humanization" and that animals are making us more human. I hope that soon there will be a dog in every classroom for underprivileged children, and that the deprivation of our essential link with the natural will soon be rectified. Animals can indeed make us more fully human; in nature is our ultimate fulfillment. In assuring the well-being of our animal kin we may well find our own salvation.

35

Animal and Human Types and Archetypes

"Me, I'm a cat-person," says one of my friends. "Can't stand them myself, too aloof and untrainable. Give me a dog anyday," says another, who adds, "A dog's more intelligent and friendly, anyway."

There's another kind of person, too, who sees nothing of intrinsic value in any animal: "If you can't eat it or wear it why bother with it!"

Why do some people have such aversion to cats (or other animals, for that matter) and likes and dislikes that seem to follow no logical pattern? Two friends, for example, who really get along well with each other, may almost come to blows over the relative merits or superiority of one kind of animal over another. This gets even worse in discussions of breeds of dog, where some proclaim the superiority or unique qualities, say, of Afghan hounds or malemutes over other breeds. Echoes of racism, or ego identification with the products of one's careful selective breeding!.

Some prefer dogs over cats because they prefer a pet that is open and effusive in its affection or is easily controlled. One who prefers cats may instead wish to have a companion animal that is graceful and sophisticated, and even mysterious and inscrutable.

These preferences and aversions are indicators of inner needs, prejudices, and expectations. The more clear-cut one's preferences or aversions, the more of a problem one may have, I believe, in relationships with others, be they animals or people. A tendency to dislike cats because they are supposedly distant and aloof or to abhor dogs because they are so subservient and dependent may indicate a basic flaw in human nature, one which is the root of human conflict, prejudice, and destructiveness.

We tend to see others (animals and people) principally in terms of how well they satisfy our needs and expectations. How much better it would be to be free from such biased and self-centered perceptions and simply to accept dogs, cats, or whomever for what they are as distinct from what one wants or expects from them. We also tend to reject those qualities in others that we do not care for in ourselves or would not like to have, such as fatness, shyness, weakness, and other so-called negative qualities. "I don't like this and I prefer that" is the kind of black/white judgment that limits our experiencing and ultimate capacity to love and be loved by all.

Someone who identifies closely with cats may be what I refer to as an "inner-directed" person—one who is independent in thought and action. But some cat people tend to be swayed by others and are dependent conformists and enjoy the cat as a symbol of what they would like to be—free and independent. In contrast to the cat archetype, the dog archetype is the "other-directed" person—one who thinks and acts in conformity with the wishes and expectations of others. Ideally, we should be part cat and part dog—with a strong inner sense of self combined with a sensitive regard for others. Understanding animals clearly does give us a deeper understanding of the more polymorphous and complex nature of man.

Our language is rich in animal analogies, euphemisms and the like that reflect a deep collective awareness in our culture, an affinity, though not necessarily a kinship, with animals. Descriptive terms—graceful as a swan; proud as a lion; wise as an owl; cute as a kitten—allude to essentially human qualities that we see or imagine in our animal kin.

Then there are more derogatory phrases which reflect an ignorant and often judgmental attitude toward animals: crazy as a coot (or loon); filthy as a pig; dumb as an ox; sly as a fox; stubborn as a mule. Such statements imply a limited anthropocentric view, and reveal our prejudices and biases. Owls aren't particularly wise, nor are lions proud or loons crazy.

I regret having to write articles and books showing the wolf, for example, as a highly intelligent, affectionate, and sociable animal as if I had to *prove* that the animal, maligned by myth, is worth saving. All creatures by virtue of their very existence have a right, equal to ours, to live. One should not have to prove that anything in nature, be it a whale (because of its large and complex brain) or a tree and marsh (because it is ecologically important for our survival) is of special worth or value. Everything is a precious, unique product of the incredible phenomenon of creative evolution. This awareness replaces the narrow anthropocentric world view with a deep and meaningful reverence for all life.

This kind of labeling and thinking, where animals are endowed with good or bad human qualities, is a serious misconception adding to man's ignorant brutalization and exploitation of animals. Few would think twice about killing an "ugly"-looking shark or crocodile or would have little empathy or regard for a "stubborn" mule, "filthy" pig or "dumb" ox. But a "cuddly" baby rabbit or kitten, a graceful fawn, or magnificent eagle have a more positive appeal and would more likely evoke empathy and care if injured or endangered. It seems unfortunate that those creatures whose qualities we most like or admire have a better chance of survival than others that are ugly, ungainly, or potentially dangerous. We also have a utilitarian attitude toward animals—those that are potentially dangerous or venomous are often destroyed rather than being respected and avoided. Others, useful to man for food, fur, or sport hunting or fishing, are selectively protected and propagated.

What a fantastic leap in consciousness it would be if we could clean up our animal vocabulary and our minds alike to change our anthropocentric world view so that we might simply see and accept all animals (and people) for what they are and value them in their own right! The trouble is, when we see an animal—or any object, for that matter—it evokes feelings and thoughts—"It could hurt me," "I would like to cuddle it," "I wouldn't like to look like that," or "I would like to have one," and so on. I often listen in on comments between people and particularly between parents and children looking at animals in the zoo. The simple and pure sense of wonder and curiosity of the child is often warped and contaminated by the values and judgments of the parents. Ideally they could give the child a deeper sense of appreciation and understanding, but

The inscrutable feline archetype—aloof, distant, reflective, mystical *(H.S.U.S./James A. Marshall).*

instead, they often play to potential emotions of fear, disgust, and amusement and convey false information as to the nature of the animal in question—vicious, dangerous, shy, stupid, silly looking, etc.—ad nauseam!

With my surname of Fox, I was teased and ridiculed at grade school by my peers and branded as sly, cunning, crafty, and not to be trusted. So often we label people with animal qualities, our language is full of such zoomorphisms. "You cow," he growled, "you're always bitching at me and getting my goat!" "And why not?" she whined. "A rat-fink like you, always horsing around, is there no end to your monkey business and bird-brained ideas?" . . . and so on.

A judge recently admonished a criminal by dubbing his offense as "beastly." Even the most educated scholars of today fall easily into this trap. Our language and thought degrade animals, and in so talking and thinking we degrade ourselves also. The more we study animals, the more we appreciate their real nature and the natural laws that govern their relationships, which superficially seem cruel. What is regarded as "beastly" in man is not really a product of his animal nature, which Freud mistakenly thought was the source of many of man's ills. What is wrong with man is not the animal within him (his "nature") but rather his nurture—the values, priorities, pressures, and conflicts that stem from his culture.

American Indians have a tradition of giving their children additional animal names like Running Horse, Coyote, Fools Crow, and Sitting Bull. Such names reveal their close spiritual ties with all things of earth and are related to a pantheistic religion which holds that all creatures great and small are of one essence. In some Indian tongues, there is no separate word to distinguish man from animal: *All* are brothers and sisters. This religion, in the light of modern scientific knowledge of the interrelatedness of all things via evolution (time) and ecology (space), is something to respect. It is unfortunate that the Judaeo-Christian teaching that man was given dominion over all creatures has been so misrepresented in thought and action. Dominion should mean stewardship rather than control and exploitation of natural "resources" (God given!) for man's selfish indulgence.

Because man is a product of the evolutionary process, his very cells, body structure, and nervous system contain elements that we can trace back not only to apes but to reptiles, fish, slime molds, and even grasses and bacteria. Man is, I believe, a polymorphous creature—incorporating in mind and body many of the diverse qualities present in other living creatures. At the psychological level of character or personality structure, we do manifest certain animal archetypes that are worth exploring so we can understand ourselves a little better. So and so is a shrew, or bullish, or wolfish, or she's a cat, or mousy, or he's leonine or hawkish. An effective and often revealing party game is to form a circle and have each person write down two animal names on a piece of paper that must fit each person in the group. It is amazing how often a person will be given the same two or very similar animal names by different people.

Another game is a fantasy trip that can lead to significant self-disclosure. It is best done before the aforementioned game and one only discloses one's fantasy after the above game is completed. Try it!

Sit back and relax, listen to your breathing and to the sounds around you, then slowly imagine that you have a movie camera in your head with which you are going to make a film. The film will be about animals. Now choose an animal that you really like, and start the film rolling. Record what it is doing, how it feels and follow it closely for a while . . .

Now choose a second, very different animal in a new setting and continue recording its activities and feelings.

Finally, place the two animals together in the same scenario and film how they respond to each other, how they feel, and any other impressions you are able to record.

After completing the first game, each person, if he or she chooses, can describe his or her inner filmed fantasy. Very often the animals that they have chosen are archetypal projections of their own character or personality: a quiet, shy and docile chipmunk; a free-spirited eagle; a powerful, clumsy bear; a happy dolphin, a timid fawn, and so on. Sometimes the two animals in the fantasy get along well when placed together, or instead get into some kind of conflict. A person may then suddenly recognize his or her inner conflict between a quiet and shy nature (chipmunk) or fearful disposition (fawn) and a desire to be free (eagle) or happy (dolphin).

This is something like the projective test of evaluating what you see/imagine in a series of Rorschach inkblots. I prefer the animal fantasies because they can capture one's feelings, self-image, and relationships with others with a clarity that requires little "depth" analysis or intimidating overtones of being "shrunk" or "exposed."

For children, especially after an early-morning visit to the zoo (when hopefully most of the animals weren't inactive or asleep), a more active fantasy game can be great fun. Have each child choose an animal, and then *be* it in mind and body. They have to behave and if possible look and think like the animal they have chosen while the others try to guess what it is. With my children, since the age of four, this has been a favorite game for the entire family.

In more intensive adult encounter and psychodrama groups this children's game has been used. Quite often, under the "permission" granted to assume a particular animal role, a lot of blocked energy and emotions can be released and sudden insights made into a person's inner needs and conflicts. To think of a reserved and inhibited man acting like a crazy chimpanzee or two women with some unresolved conflict between them hissing and back arching and mock-fighting like two cats may appear ridiculous and immature. But many who have tried such an intensive exercise attest to its value. But please, if you try it, mind your claws and don't take playing werewolf too literally!

36

From "Petism" to Animal Rights: In Defense of Companion Animals

History of "Petism"

Once each year in India there is a nationwide festival in honor of the dog. Food is put out and the countless stray *pariahs* eat their fill. The few people who keep dogs as pets in that country are those who have perhaps acquired the custom from the British, and, furthermore, they are usually among the few who can afford to feed an extra noncontributor in the home. Yet a visit to any small village will reveal dozens of dogs lying in the shade or waiting patiently by a baker's or butcher's store. No one owns them; they are part of the village. They are an accepted and integral part of everyday life. Many are, like their human counterparts, in various states of emaciation, diseased, or nursing scrawny pups, few of which are likely to survive to maturity.

Similarly, in Africa and Australia we find native settlements with a raggedy assortment of dogs, and again, they often belong to no one. But they are more than just a part of the scenery. They are commensals and symbiotes, not pets. They share the same environs, if not the same rooms, with people, and they do them a good service by keeping down pests and warning them of intruders—strange humans or potentially dangerous wild animals. In return, they receive what shelter they can find under the eaves of huts and canopies over shop stalls. Their staple diet is garbage and human excrement and rarely a wild animal, which they may kill and eat if the villagers don't get there before they can consume it. One or two villagers may even use some of the dogs occasionally to go hunting or poaching, though the dogs are not trained. They are just used as beaters to flush out the quarry as the Maharajas would employ the villagers themselves in the old days to bag a tiger.

Although appalled at the poverty of the people and the pathetic condition of many of the dogs in these Indian villages, I learned two important lessons. First, that these people are generally accepting and nonabusive to these pariah dogs because of the Hindu belief in the sacredness of all life and because of the Buddhist-Ghandi teachings of *Ahimsa* concerning non-violence toward life. Second, people accept the animals because they were born and raised with them. They traditionally share the same ecosystem, both physically and psychologically. But there is no love, and resources are insufficient to indulge them with good food and medication when needed. The dogs, like the people, have to fend for themselves, peaceably and usually democratically.

This kind of relationship was perhaps the first social relationship that early man had with an animal. Archaeological evidence indicates that the dog was the first animal to become part of the family of man. But as in India the dog has not crossed the threshold to become an integral member of the family. Historically, such a transition occurred slowly, first among the aristocracy, who selected smaller village pups as cuddly companions. These were the first pets, and there is some evidence that, in Europe at least, a person was not allowed to wear clothes or to possess a dog "above his station." So irrespective of whether a person could now afford to feed a nonworking pet or "lap" dog, there were certain restraints related to social status.

But the commoners were not without their dogs. They created many fine working breeds. The tenant farmer had his sheepdog, the lord's gamekeeper his kennels of hounds and bird dogs. Many had their own socially acceptable working and sporting dogs like the terrier and whippet, and fighting dogs like the bull terrier.

The dog was valued among these people on the basis of its performance, and the owner's self-esteem rose and fell accordingly. From this *utilitarian* relationship with the dog, and derived social status by association, it was a natural transition for the dog to become an integral part of the family. The dog earned its right to lie by the hearth at its master's feet.

No less the cat. Imported to Europe from the Middle East, the cat earned its place in the home as a significant contributor, keeping down vermin which abounded in the towns and villages of our ancestors.

Pet Ownership Today—and Its Critics

Six thousand miles away from India, or an evolutionary distance in time of ten thousand years, we find that a very different relationship has evolved in the United States between people and their cats and dogs. In some areas we may still see free-roaming cats and dogs not unlike those of the Indian villages, and we also find some people who still keep cats and dogs to perform specific tasks much like their ancestors did in the Middle Ages. But the most striking contrast is in the number of people who, like the aristocrats of old, keep animals simply as nonworking pets. We find veterinarians specializing in dermatology, cardiology, ophthalmology, and the like, geneticists counseling breeders, and nutritionists formulating scientifically balanced diets for pets. Pets have training schools, beauty parlors, psychological counselors, and in toto represent an estimated $4 billion to $6 billion animal industry.

Such indulgence which reflects the affluence of our society is dubbed as misguided and wasteful *"petism"* by many critics. These critics suffer from *"specism"* themselves, failing to see the many values of pets above and beyond their monetary worth and the expenses that are lavished upon them. Admittedly some people do overindulge their pets, but it is neither fair nor accurate to rubricize all pet lovers as misguided zoophiles.

There are many subtle advantages to pet ownership which a crude utilitarian evaluation overlooks. Pets provide companionship for lonely people in our alienated and dehumanized society, giving a sense of family and community to countless elderly retired people and also to young couples who are thinking twice about bringing children into this overcrowded world. They are always accepting, and with the unconditional love that they offer, they are conducive to a person's emotional well-being.

Providing elderly people in retirement homes with pets has significantly eliminated frequent episodes of depression. People need to be needed and to have someone to love, a desire which many pets—cats, dogs, and parakeets—will reciprocate. The loyalty and devotion of a dog can help an insecure child or adult maintain a sense of belonging. A pet can be a nonthreatening subordinate "other" to a child, and as such can give the child a sense of unconditional acceptance and foster responsibility and compassionate understand.

The one greatest "value" of pets (the ultimate nonutilitarian "use" of an animal) is to help people regain their "animal/nature connection": to become more fully human via a transpersonal relationship which breaks down egocentric and humanocentric perceptions and valuations.

I have received "sick" mail from some of the more extreme anti-pet people. Some are crazed with paranoia over the possibility of their contracting some disease from an animal. Others extend this paranoia to the point that *no* animal should be in the house or be touched by their children. No less sick is the utilitarian view that argues that since pets today rarely perform any specific function, they should be done away with. One lady wrote chastising me for wasting research funds in my studies of dog behavior and brain development "when people are sick and starving and children need help and research on their problems." This I see as a confused utilitarian with good intentions. Like those who fail to see the many values of having a pet, so others see no value in research with animals. While admittedly there is much needless research done on animals (often entailing unnecessary suffering), animal studies can and do give valuable insights into both animal and human problems.

The Ultimate Values of Pet Companionship

Contact with nature and with animals can help breakdown the artificial, culturally created, specist barrier between animals and nonempathetic humans. Once the animal/nature connection is reestablished, the human species may indeed survive its current biocidal activities, realizing that a whole and healthy earth is essential for a whole and healthy humanity. When we demean an animal or defile nature, we do no less to ourselves, for in ecological space, and through evolutionary time, all of life is one. Those people who enjoy nature and the companionship of tame animals for unselfish reasons find it hard to explain their pleasure. There is something ineffable in the transpersonal relationship with a fellow nonhuman creation but it is nonetheless compelling.

Choosing to share one's life and family with one or more animals, being concerned over the humane treatment of animals and the conservation of wild species and their habitats—these are expressions of this transpersonal kinship. It is based upon a nondiscriminatory reverence for all life and responsible compassion: in sum, *humane stewardship*.

Maturing of the Pet Relationship

To demean all pet ownership is to reveal an immature and limited, if not ignorant and insensitive, mind. While admittedly some pet owners are irresponsible and need to mature, nonconstructive criticism and anti-pet talk will not help them or the pet problems that they create.

Some owners have developed a positive, but incomplete and ultimately irresponsible ethical attitude toward pet ownership: they allow their animals to roam freely and to breed indiscriminately, adding to the problem of pet overpopulation, believing that their cat or dog is entitled to live as free and natural a life as possible. This is misguided, but is a step in the right direction.

Other pet owners, ironically, are still hung-up, like their utilitarian anti-pet critics, on valuing their animals for selfish reasons. The pet's intrinsic worth is not appreciated; the animal is only valued to the extent that it satisfies its owner's needs. In essence, the pet is exploited and is only loved conditionally, that is when it satisfies whatever demands its owner places on it. Indeed, many human relationships are like this—demanding, conditional, and exploitive. "See me for what or who I am and not as you might use me" is the silent cry of nature, of animals and of human rights movements such as women's liberation. As relationships with others, pets included, improve, so our level of consciousness will be raised. People often have illusory and unreal *expectations* about pets, knowing and caring little about their basic needs and natural behavioral tendencies. Dogs like to bark, to roam, they don't like to be left alone in an apartment for extended periods; cats like to claw furniture, sometimes to spray the house and to go out acourtin' and acaterwaulin'.

Life gains greater depth and significance when we have animals in our lives *(H.S.U.S./Frantz Dantzler; Kellner's Photo Service)*.

Human expectations can get in the way of appreciation of the animal for itself, but in keeping and getting to know a pet one can break through this barrier, gain respect for and understanding of a unique animal companion.

Animal Rights and Human Liberation

Pet owners are frequently chastised for treating their animals like little people, buying them nonessential accoutrements, and being wholly anthropomorphic in their perceptions of their pet. I find nothing wrong with this, provided the indulged pet does not suffer physically (with obesity or other dietary problems) or psychologically (by becoming neurotically overdependent). Many pets, bred and raised for this role, thrive on it; for many owners they are necessary child substitutes and of inestimable value for the owners' mental health. The unconditional love of a pet is now being used as a therapeutic "tool" for bringing emotionally disturbed children and schizophrenic adults out of their withdrawal. These pets are cotherapists. However they are not emotional slaves for people who need an animal to dominate and control, nor do these animals serve to alleviate their owners' sense of inferiority or insecurity as might a show dog or attack-trained dog.

There is not much wrong in being anthropomorphic to a degree. There is good scientific evidence to support the contention of many pet owners that cats and dogs share emotions and sensations similar, if not identical, to our own—fear, pain, anxiety, jealousy, guilt, joy, depression, anger—and the brain centers mediating such states are virtually identical in man and other mammals. We are close, then, to being morally obliged to consider the rights of animals. The right to "own" a pet may be questioned, but the intrinsic rights of animals cannot.

It is unfortunate this "rights" issue has been neglected for so long. But as the liberation of slaves and of women did much to elevate the consciousness of slave owners and chauvinist husbands, so the liberation of animals (and of nature) may elevate us all to a higher level still: that of humane stewardship. This is why, for educational reasons in the most general yet most total and perfect sense, I favor the keeping of animals as "pets," as companions, cotherapists, and, indeed, as teachers. Animals can make us more human, more compassionate, patient, understanding, and responsible humane stewards. They can take us out of unhealthy humanocentric preoccupations and pseudopriorities. They, like the very earth, can keep us grounded in the larger reality that is life. Through this animal connection, we may discover our own animality and at the same time fulfill our godlike obligations: for between animal and god is mankind.

We have yet to learn to become humane stewards, cocreators, working in harmony with the forces of nature. We have assumed dominion over the rest of creation without having first gained dominion over ourselves. The mistakes that we have made with our pets—the abuses, excesses, neglects, exploitations, and genetic anomalies—are all lessons to us at their expense. They are our mirrors, and as we learn from them and from our mistakes, so may we gain insight and grow. Many pet owners are already "there" with their pets and with the world, but countless others have yet to mature. When we all give due accord to animal rights, there will be human liberation. And our pets, undoubtedly, are essential to our reaching that goal.